INDIA
MOVING

Dear Amit, Shobha,
Mira and Maya,
of the great Indian
diaspora !

– Chinmay

Vumbe

11th Oct' 2018

CHINMAY TUMBE

INDIA
MOVING

A HISTORY OF
MIGRATION

FOREWORD BY ARVIND SUBRAMANIAN,
CHIEF ECONOMIC ADVISER

PENGUIN
VIKING
An imprint of Penguin Random House

VIKING

USA | Canada | UK | Ireland | Australia
New Zealand | India | South Africa | China

Viking is part of the Penguin Random House group of companies
whose addresses can be found at global.penguinrandomhouse.com

Published by Penguin Random House India Pvt. Ltd
7th Floor, Infinity Tower C, DLF Cyber City,
Gurgaon 122 002, Haryana, India

Penguin
Random House
India

First published in Viking by Penguin Random House India 2018

Copyright © Chinmay Tumbe 2018
Foreword copyright © Arvind Subramanian 2018

10 9 8 7 6 5 4 3 2

The views and opinions expressed in this book are the author's own and
the facts are as reported by him which have been verified to the extent possible,
and the publishers are not in any way liable for the same.

ISBN 9780670089833

Typeset in Bembo Std by Manipal Digital Systems, Manipal
Printed at Replika Press Pvt. Ltd, India

www.penguin.co.in

Contents

Foreword

I am delighted to be writing this foreword for one of India's brightest and rising young economic scholars, Professor Chinmay Tumbe of the Indian Institute of Management Ahmedabad. *India Moving* is terrific in many ways. It is the kind of book that I would want to write and read, and dip into and refer to from time to time. But those are not the only reasons for me writing this foreword. Nor are my motives sullied by the obligation of reciprocity: Chinmay, who I got to know serendipitously, contributed wonderfully to a chapter in the *Economic Survey of 2016–17*. The reasons for my enthusiasm are different.

There is a certain kind of scholarship that young Indian academics, especially in economics, have shied away from. A major reason is the suffocating straitjacket of the discipline as it is currently practised in prestigious universities of the United States. Increasingly, the rewards are confined to, and conferred upon those, practising a certain narrow conception of scholarship. This privileges the asking and answering of small questions because only these can be answered through methods that the high priests of the Academy certify as rigorously kosher. As a consequence, Dismal Science risks becoming Small, Lesser, Wannabe Science.

Against this background, it takes a certain confidence—chutzpah even—to escape the choke of a throttling Academy, especially for someone as professionally young as Chinmay Tumbe, and for someone who practises his vocation in India, far away from the academic centres of gravity. But make no mistake, *India Moving: A History of Migration* is a Big Book, taking on nothing less than the history of national and international migration from, to and within India over the last several centuries. Just the daring of, and defiance implied in, the attempted project deserves resounding praise and wide readership.

But Chinmay does much more. He skilfully combines economics, history, vignette, anecdote and the odd literary reference to lay out when, why and how Indians have moved over the millennia. The book is backed up by years of serious scholarship but avoids both narrowness and dreary denseness. It is animated by curiosity, wonder and a sense of joyful exploration. Chinmay has clearly had fun writing *India Moving*, and it shows.

The erudition is worn lightly and Chinmay's wide reading leavens the exposition. One learns a lot from the book. How big is the Indian diaspora? What are the hotspots of emigration in India? How did Indians settle in the French territory of Réunion or find their way to the distant Pacific island of Fiji? What is the background behind Sikhs settling in Latin America? How did Indians first go to the Middle East? What were the associations between movements of particular communities and the building of economic capital? What are the two constants of the Indian diaspora? (Spoiler answer: the use of water, not toilet paper, to perform ablutions, and the pressure cooker as the ubiquitously reliable kitchen aid, and more recently, how has migration changed within India and how have remittances affected development within the country?)

The comprehensiveness of coverage is impressive: it seems that no internal displacement, no migration-related conflict and no significant international migration over the last century has escaped the author's attention. A not insignificant contribution of the book might therefore be to serve as a treasure trove for others who wish to explore in greater detail one or more of the numerous instances of migration catalogued in the book. *India Moving* may well be the starting point and provocation for numerous PhDs.

India Moving should be read, savoured and applauded. I hope it will encourage and embolden other Indian economists to emulate this example of undertaking rigorous but accessible and interesting scholarship. I cannot recommend this first effort from Professor Chinmay Tumbe highly enough.

Arvind Subramanian
Chief Economic Adviser
Government of India

Author's Note

Everyone has a migration story. I can vividly remember the day I had first landed in a new place for schooling, for higher studies, for work, and even for love. Divya, my wife, and I have now lived in five different cities across three continents, and when we look back at old photographs, we recollect how we pulled it off through beautiful landscapes, unending winters, strange furniture designs and restrictive visa laws. Memory, nostalgia and selective amnesia are powerful ingredients used to pepper personal and family migration narratives. These migration stories collectively form a system of internal and international migrations, of voluntary and involuntary migrations and many other such typologies. This book is about one regional migration system—India—which has witnessed some of the largest voluntary and involuntary mass migrations in history. It is also the first book on the history of both internal and international migration and voluntary and involuntary migration related to India.

The book describes the origins of the incredible human diversity found within India and covers the migrations of artisans, merchants, slaves, students, warriors, workers, women, and many others. It reveals the persistence of labour migration since the late 19th century, and provides a new perspective on the migration of business communities both within and outside India. It shows how 25 million people who traced their roots to India in the past three centuries were dispersed across the world from Japan to Jamaica, and why internal diasporas matter as much as international diasporas. It documents the mass migrations caused by multiple partitions, refugee crises and other displacements in Indian history and their disproportionate impact on particular communities. And finally, it provides a perspective on migration and development, in history and in 21st century India.

In writing this book, I offer four core arguments. First, that migration or spatial mobility is not a recent phenomenon in India in scale or variety and that the country currently sustains the world's largest and longest voluntary migration episode in migration history, what I call the Great Indian Migration Wave. Second, the history of migration in India has often been closely bound with the idea of 'circulation'. Third, migration and circulation have not influenced all sub-groups evenly and, in particular, the lack of substantive spatial mobility continues to disempower the lowest-ranking castes of India. Finally, I argue that greater spatial mobility is a prerequisite for maintaining the pluralistic traditions of the country.

Writing a book of this nature, wide in scope and reasonably concise, requires certain maxims and justifications for the regions and time periods chosen. In general, I cover those topics that have been well-researched and have some body of evidence. This is important to state because virtually every Indian community has an origin myth that is fascinating to hear and is plausibly true but extremely hard to verify. I also lay more emphasis on regions that appear to have a larger demographic weightage in Indian migration history. I use the old and new names of places interchangeably, usually denoting the names as they were used in the time period being discussed. The printing of maps on the Indian subcontinent has been constrained due to recently revised publication guidelines.

This book is the culmination of an exciting decade-long academic and personal adventure that began with my doctoral research on migration history at the Indian Institute of Management Bangalore (IIMB). A year at the Migration Policy Centre of the European University Institute in Florence, Italy, and another year on a parental break spent in reading books at St Louis, USA, helped me appreciate the contemporary and historical migration challenges faced in Europe, Africa and the Americas. The experience of teaching urban studies at the Tata Institute of Social Sciences (TISS) Hyderabad and the 'HitchHiker's Guide to Business and Economies across Five Centuries' at IIM Ahmedabad opened new angles on migration history (and the writings of Douglas Adams) that I had not explored previously. As a member of a ministry-appointed working group on (internal) migration and research projects, with bodies affiliated to the ministry of overseas Indian affairs, I was privy to important contemporary debates on internal and international migration. Working with the office of the chief economic adviser led to innovations in methodologies in estimating migration stocks and flows.

My research has therefore benefited from interactions with scholars across the world: Rupa Chanda, Arvind Subramanian, Irudaya Rajan, R. Bhagat, Carol Upadhya, Vegard Iversen, Philippe Fargues, Anna Triandafyllidou, Geoffrey Jones, Youssef Cassis, Jorge Flores, Meenakshi Thapan, Kathryn Lum, Tirthankar Roy, Douglas Haynes, Bishnupriya Gupta, Dwijendra Tripathi, Nilanjana Ray, Aseem Prakash, Amit Upadhyay, Hema Swaminathan, Errol D'Souza, Rakesh Basant, Anindya Chakrabarti, Imran Khan, Valatheeswaran C., Rajiv Khandelwal, Umi Daniel, Varsha Malwade, Kalyani Vartak, Priya Deshingkar, Divya Ravindranath, Deepak Malghan, Alakh

Sharma, S. Chandrasekhar, Partho Mukhopadhyay, and many more. Michel Danino and Himanshu Prabha Ray were kind enough to point out the literature on migration in ancient India, which has attracted little scholarly attention till date outside the Aryan migration debate.

I would like to thank the editors and reviewers of the *Indian Economic and Social History Review*, *Business History Review*, *Migration and Development*, *Indian Journal of Labour Economics*, *India Migration Reports*, *Ideas for India*, *International Growth Centre Working Paper Series* and the *Journal for Interdisciplinary Economics* for providing an outlet for my research, some of which is reflected in this book. I would also like to thank the organizers of over forty migration seminars and conferences that I participated in, and the staff at the following libraries and institutions—IIMA, IIMB, CDS (Thiruvananthapuram), IIPS (Mumbai), CSS (Surat), ISID (Delhi), LSE (London), EUI (Florence), National Archives (New Delhi), Vrunda Pathare and Sanghamitra Sen at the Godrej Archives (Mumbai), Census Office (New Delhi and Bangalore), Gubbi Labs (Bangalore), Exim Bank and Aajeevika Bureau (Ahmedabad). Anil Kumar and the IIMA library staff, in particular, went out of their way to make me comfortable for several months as I plodded along typing in the library. The delightful students of TISS Hyderabad provided valuable assistance in collecting a hundred precious migration histories in Ratnagiri district. The students and 'history interns' of IIMA provided a great source of intellectual stimulation by asking seemingly naïve but intensely thought-provoking questions. They include Devika Kerkar, Anusha Rajan, Harini Alladi, Shobhit Shubhankar, Shashank Krishnakumar, Amish Sarpotdar, Deepti Raj, Shayoni Mukherjee, Kirthika Ashokkumar and Sandeep Badole. Above all, I would like to thank the numerous migrant workers I have interacted with, across India and abroad, in buses, boats and general compartments of trains, on railway platforms, at airports and worksites and homes, for sharing their life histories with me.

I am grateful to my schoolteacher, Jayant Tengshe (JT) for inculcating the spirit of inquiry; Rupa Chanda for nurturing my doctoral research on migration; Tirthankar Roy for inspiring my foray into history; and Arvind Subramanian for kindly agreeing to write the foreword of this book. My friends and family members—Nandini Huzurbazar, Raajasi Huzurbazar, Varad Huzurbazar, Sailaja Ravindranath, C.R. Ravindranath, Mohan Tumbe, Anuradha Tumbe, Krishnaraj Tumbe, Lalitha Surabhi—and colleagues at various institutions have been extremely supportive of my research, egging me on to write a book that they can read. To meet this challenge, I owe a great debt to the wonderful team at Penguin Random House India and Swati Chopra's incredible enthusiasm for carefully attending to my queries and believing in me to write this book.

Divya has seen this book 'move' at varying speeds and, true to her name, was the shining light of inspiration behind it. My son, Siddhartha, began to read and write at the same time that I started working on this book. Strangely, I now empathize with his experience of being a first-time writer. I learnt almost everything in life from my parents—Sudha Huzurbazar and Vasudev Tumbe—whose love story began in an iconic symbol of Indian migration: the train. They are both light sleepers with a good sense of humour and hence I dedicate this book to them, and their sleep.

1

Indian Diversity and Global Migrations

'India is a geographical and economic entity, a cultural unity amidst diversity, a bundle of contradictions held together by strong but invisible threads.'

—Jawaharlal Nehru[1]

Why is India such a diverse country? Why do Indians speak so many languages, celebrate a number of festivals, devour assorted pickles and buy a variety of fairness creams?

Is it because of successive waves of migration which, for example, explain the stunning human diversity seen in a New York subway train? Or is it a diametrically opposite reason: one of group isolation preserved over a long time and forced into unification only in recent times? After all, Papua New Guinea, a small country of less than 10 million people in the Pacific Ocean, hosts more languages than India, a country of over a billion people, as human traits evolved separately with minimal contact between the islanders.[2]

It is important to recognize these two separate routes to diversity observed in any region: one through migration and the other through isolation and the *lack* of migration. In this context,

1

a popular and enduring view of India is that it was, and is, a land of low spatial mobility, that it was essentially a land of around half a million self-sufficient villages lying undisturbed until the recent big bang of modernity. In this view, people eventually died in their villages of birth. According to one historian in the 1960s, a village looked outside 'for little more than its salt, its spices, the fine cloth for its holiday clothes, and the coin in which it pays its revenue'.[3] The idea of spatial mobility in Indian history was confined to the occasional pilgrim, merchant or warrior on a particular mission and little else.

This view of low spatial mobility in Indian history is seriously questionable. Not only has India witnessed some of the world's largest episodes of voluntary and involuntary migration, but it is also unique in currently sustaining considerable immigration, internal migration and emigration—all three at the same time. A reading of Indian history, as shall be seen in this chapter, reveals that migrations, internal and external, and events before the late 19th century had already created a unique amalgamation of cultures that can be observed in India today. The past century and a half, however, was critical in reshaping existing diversities within, and more importantly, exporting these diversities outside the subcontinent, a fascinating phenomenon that informs the rest of this book. But we must begin by asking a more fundamental question: Who exactly are the Indians?

Brownian Motion

To depict an Indian as a brown-skinned human being with black eyes and black hair, like Apu in the animated American sitcom *The Simpsons*, would be accurate only as a crude average with large variations around the mean. Human beings are a colourful bunch of primates with interesting variations in the colour of skin, hair and eyes. Skin colour, for instance, has been found to be positively correlated with latitude and ultraviolet radiation levels, and has adapted over time to new environments.[4] Until we started decking up our bodies with clothes, human skin faced the full onslaught of penetrating solar rays and was a ripe candidate to undergo evolutionary change consistent with the Darwinian notion of natural selection. Some ultraviolet radiation, UV-B rays to be more precise, is good as it aids the production of Vitamin D that helps strengthen the immune system and other functions in the human body, but too much of it can be destructive. Skin pigmentation plays the role of a regulator of UV-B rays. In tropical Africa, where as per current knowledge the origins of Homo sapiens are said to be, the high intensity of UV-B rays led to more production of a compound called melanin to serve as a natural sunscreen and, consequently, darker skin. Closer to the poles, or at higher latitudes, the annual average UV radiation on the earth's surface is far less than in the tropics. Also, the UV-B rays are more scattered by the atmosphere due to the Earth's tilted rotational axis. As human beings moved outside the tropics, they were moving to areas that received less intense UV-B rays. The evolutionary response was a change in pigmentation or less production of melanin to absorb UV rays more efficiently. Consequently, this led to lighter skin colours.

The empirical support for this elegant theory on the evolution of skin colouration is of recent vintage. Charles Darwin (1809-82) was a keen observer of traits, even commenting on the people of India as we shall see later, but he had famously rejected this theory.[5] Among other grounds, he pointed out that Dutch families did not undergo the 'the least change of colour after residing for three centuries in South Africa'. But evolution, as we now know, is a very gradual process taking place over thousands of years. This is why, in the modern world of substantial cross-latitudinal migration, people stand to face health risks when they

live in latitudes with different UV-B ray intensities from what
had dictated their skin colour from an evolutionary perspective.[6]
Advances in the sciences, which in the past also led to spurious
claims of racial superiority on the basis of skin colour, have now
made more people aware about the follies of racism and the solar
links with skin pigmentation. When Indians go to places in the
northern hemisphere with less exposure to the sun, the big D
associated with their skin may no longer be Discrimination but
deficiency of Vitamin D.[7]

Back home though, many Indians are less concerned with
vitamins and more with fairness creams. Whether such an
obsession about looking whiter than the rest emerged from the
colonial era or much earlier is difficult to trace, but the natural
colour gradient from lighter skins in the extreme north to darker
skins in the extreme south is fairly evident. This would be in
line with the theory of the evolution of skin colour, especially
if there was some evidence of humans originating in the Indian
subcontinent, some sort of a *swayambhu* moment of self-creation
that is routinely attributed to the emergence of unexplained
divine shrines in India. For the moment, however, the 'out of
Africa' hypothesis and the subsequent migrations, some 80,000
years ago, to Europe and Asia and from there to Australia
and the Americas, is a more compelling narrative backed by
archaeological and genetic evidence.[8] These migrations have
inevitably been attributed to climatic changes, little ice ages and
shallower or frozen seas enabling crossings between seemingly
unconnected lands.

It is such genetic evidence in India that now clearly points
to two divergent populations ancestral to the majority of the
present-day population, providing clues to the colour gradient
and much more.[9] As one landmark 2009 study in the scientific
journal *Nature* argued, 'the "Ancestral North Indians (ANI)",
are genetically close to Middle Easterners, Central Asians, and

Europeans, whereas the other, the "Ancestral South Indians" (ASI)', are as distinct from ANI and East Asians as they are from each other.' The study also shows the mixture between the ANI and ASI groups, such that 'groups with only ASI ancestry may no longer exist in mainland India'. Two small groups consisting of tribes in the Andaman Islands in the Bay of Bengal—the Onge and Great Andamanese—were found to be genetically related to the ASI group but had no traces of ANI ancestry.

The difference between ANI and ASI is by definition, couched in genetic terms, but on the surface it reveals a broad north–south divide in Indian culture and language, running roughly through central India, with the word 'Indo-European' used for the north and 'Dravidian' used for the south. The big question for the Indians then is on the origins of the ANI and ASI groups. This has partly been framed in competing terms on the question of the Aryan migration in the north, linked as it is to the question of the origins of the culture revolving around the Vedas, a collection of hymns and religious texts dated between 1500 BCE (Before the Common Era) to 500 BCE and sacred to the Hindus who comprise around 80 per cent of the Indian population today.[10] Did the Aryans mentioned in the Vedas arrive from the north-west or were they indigenous to India, to the extent that they trace their roots from some other source? The genetic evidence from the 2009 *Nature* study suggests strong similarities between north Indians and their western neighbours, but could the migrations have taken place *from* India to the west and not vice-versa? And what about the origins of the ASI (not to be confused with the Archaeological Survey of India) and the tribes of the Andaman and Nicobar Islands (not to be confused with ANI)? While the balance of evidence currently points towards migration streams from the north-west to explain the appearance of ANIs and ASIs in the Indian subcontinent, these questions are likely to be answered more substantively only over the course of the 21st century through inter-disciplinary research spanning genetics, anthropology, linguistics, archaeology and the like.

Beyond the Aryan migration debate, migrations in India were historically shaped by specific geographical conditions and the technology available at different times to remould or surpass them. The mighty Himalayan Range in the north and north-east formed a natural barrier between China and the Indian subcontinent as did the Hindu Kush Range in the north-west against central Asia. The passes in the north-west mountains such as Bolan, Gomal and Khyber passes were the keyholes to unlocking entry into India for centuries and were used more often than the Himalayan passes as they were less snowbound. The passes would also affect the fate of towns such as Taxila, Kabul and Peshawar located in the vicinity.

The triangular peninsular region of the subcontinent consists of the land below the Vindhya Range and Narmada River in central India, including the Deccan Plateau made up of volcanic rock bounded on two sides by the Western and Eastern Ghats. The undulating nature of the plateau, the presence of a few navigable rivers or passes connecting the coasts gave it an isolated landlocked status for much of ancient Indian history, when the means for migration were still primitive. And while historical texts allude to the *dakshinapatha,* or the southern route through the peninsula, the northern rim of the Deccan Plateau around the Vindhyas itself became a sort of cultural barrier, demarcating the north from the south.

It is not entirely a coincidence that this northern rim and its extension in the Chhota Nagpur Plateau in the east is home to the bulk of India's tribal communities, known as the Scheduled Tribes (STs), less affected by developments and assimilations taking place around them throughout history. The STs constitute around 8 per cent of India's population today and they are also found in other hilly tracts such as the Himalayas, the hills of the Northeast and the desert landscape of west Rajasthan. It is their languages that make up the Austro-Asiatic group in central and eastern India and the Tibeto-Burman group in north-eastern India, two major language groups outside the Indo-European and Dravidian clusters, and which as per recent genetic research correspond to two distinct groups dubbed as the Ancestral Austro-Asiatic and Ancestral Tibeto-Burman.[11] Tribal migrations in ancient India ranged from nomadic hunter-gatherer formations to pastoralism and the exploration of greener pastures. At high altitudes, it also involved transhumance or the seasonal movement of people with their livestock between different altitudes.

If higher altitudes in difficult terrains restricted spatial mobility, or gave it a particular character in ancient India, the lower altitudes in conjunction with water through rainfall or rivers, supported more inmigration for agriculture-based settlements and the rise of rural population density, which as described in later chapters, had a definite impact in creating conditions for eventual outmigration. The coastal plains of India on both sides of the subcontinent, and especially the Kaveri delta of Tamil Nadu in south India, fall in this regional category, but they are miniscule in size compared to the great plains that lie between the Deccan Plateau and the Himalayas.

The Indo-Gangetic plain of over 600 million acres stretching from present-day Bangladesh in the east to Pakistan in the west is the most significant region from the point of view of the Indian subcontinent's political and demographic history. Most empires that have ruled the wide expanse of the subcontinent had their base there. It covers the fertile tracts of the rivers Indus and Ganga and their numerous tributaries, and is currently home to roughly 10 per cent of the world's population. The migrations that led to the settlement of this great plain before the Common

Era (CE) literally constituted a watershed moment in Indian and global history.

One of the earliest known agricultural settlements in the Indian subcontinent has been located in Mehrgarh, near Quetta in Baluchistan, and dates back to around 7000 BCE.[12] The settlement lived in mud-brick huts, grew wheat and barley and herded cattle, sheep and goats. These are typical features of a village as the emergence of agriculture and settlement marks a radical departure from the nomadic ways of living. That this occurred in Baluchistan is all the more remarkable because even as recently as in the 20th century it was known for its tribal communities and peripatetic ways of living. Commenting on their pastoral practices, a Census official in 1921 noted that the Balochi people had 'discovered the secret of perpetual motion' and that one third of the indigenous population were nomads, 'pure and simple'.[13] Nevertheless, in the ancient past, the region around Mehrgarh showed clear signs of continuous settlement over millennia and a gradual process of urbanization.[14] The first traces of rural to urban migration could potentially be traced to this part of the Indian subcontinent.

Mehrgarh and its surrounding region are considered to belong to the pre-Harappan era, dated between the late fourth millennium BCE and 2600 BCE. Between then and 1900 BCE, what we now call the mature Harappan civilization flourished along the Indus Valley and beyond, covering an area of roughly one million square kilometres from the Ganga–Yamuna doab (or land between rivers) in the east to the present-day Pakistan–Iran border in the west and extending to Gujarat and Rajasthan.[15] There is considerable evidence of large urban centres and trade, and hence the introduction of a new form of migration in the subcontinent involving mercantile links. The Harappan people were also of different racial types, pointing towards different streams of migrations. But the civilization remains a mystery even a century after its excavation and rediscovery due to its undeciphered inscriptions. Equally puzzling is its decline and the abandoning of many sites from around 1900 BCE. One theory for this decline, and presumably outmigration, are droughts or floods due to climate change.

The next major population group in India's great plains that finds a mention in historical records are the Vedic cultures, located around the *sapta sindhu* or the land of seven rivers identified with the tributaries of the Indus—the name which itself, and subsequently 'India', 'Hindu', and 'Hindustan', are derived from the root word 'sindhu', meaning river. The geographical location of the Indo-Aryans, as the Vedic people are referred to, is noted to have shifted eastwards over time. There are references to migrations into the Gangetic plains in the *Satapatha Brahmana*, a Vedic text. For instance, King Videgha Mathava is said to have led his people eastwards as far as the Gandak River, along the Himalayan foothills.[16] This could have been along the *uttarapatha* or the northern route described in ancient Indian texts, linking the Ganga and Yamuna river systems and Punjab to central Asia.[17]

The Indo-Aryans are usually considered to be pastoralists. They used the horse, mostly imported from outside the subcontinent, for equestrian activities, greatly increasing the speed of movement within the subcontinent. They spoke languages such as Sanskrit which would later be classified under the Indo-European category. Their most famous literary compositions are the Ramayana and Mahabharata, two classic epics that have deep resonance even today. Significantly, both the epics had exile and return as the central themes, conveying the circularity of migration.

Another important offshoot of the Vedic culture with a persistent legacy was a unique social structure called the varna or caste system. It divided society into four varnas: the brahmin (priest), kshatriya (warrior), vaishya (trader) and shudra (labourer), and an additional group of the outcastes or the untouchables. The system specified not only division but also hierarchy in terms of ritual status. The caste system may not have crystallized strongly in the first millennium BCE, and the numerous jatis or sub-castes may have emerged much later, but it did lay the foundations for strict endogamy or marriage within groups. Genetic studies show that around this time, there was a demographic transformation from a region where 'major population mixture was common to one in which mixture even between closely related groups became rare because of a shift to endogamy'.[18] It is a feature of Indian society that lasts till now as even today only 5 per cent of Indian marriages are inter-caste.[19] Endogamy would be closely associated with village exogamy or the practice of women leaving their villages upon marriage. In this way, marriage migration also became an important route for the circulation of ideas and practices.[20] And because the choice of partners was restricted due to caste, these migrations were not necessarily to the neighbouring village but could involve larger distances. Like the Brownian motion of random movement of particles in a fluid, the Indian subcontinent was also witnessing the spatial mobility of its mostly brown bodies in multiple directions to different villages.

Ancient Migrations: In, Out, Within

The history of migration in ancient India from the middle of the first millennium BCE to circa 1300 CE, covering nearly 2000 years, is one of immigration mainly from central Asia via the north-western passes, instances of emigration to the west and the east, and internal migration accompanying urbanization, colonization and deportation. It is a complex history, of a religion born in India—Buddhism—and exported, of another religion—Jainism—circulating within, and of other faiths such as Christianity, Judaism, Zoroastrianism, and Islam coming in. It is also a history of the rise and fall of countless kingdoms, among which the Mauryan (c. 320 BCE–200 BCE) and Gupta Empires (c. 300 CE–600 CE) stand out for their geographical extents. At the heart of this narrative is a region synonymous with migration in contemporary India's Bihar—but for inmigration, not outmigration.

As per available historical records, the centre of gravity in the political and urban sphere shifted between 2000 BCE and 300 BCE, progressively eastwards from the Indus Valley to the Ganga–Yamuna doab and then to the region surrounding Pataliputra, or present-day Patna in Bihar, eventually the seat of both the Mauryan and Gupta Empires. While there is evidence of human activity throughout the Indo-Gangetic valley even before 2000 BCE, the limited evidence on migration in the Vedic texts and other sources do convey an eastward migratory movement.[21]

One reason, therefore, for Bihar's ascendance around Pataliputra could be the culmination of an eastward drift of settlement. But another interesting explanation has recently been provided in terms of its unique environmental character based on aridity and rainfall.[22] Bihar forms a transitional zone between the humid areas in the east and the dry areas in the west which made it attractive as a site of interaction between two societies with different agrarian practices. In the dry zone, economic activities apart from agriculture included herding and horse-breeding whereas in the humid zones, agriculture, in particular rice cultivation, supported higher densities. If the eastward migration hypothesis is correct, Pataliputra would emerge as a strategic site as it had drier areas in the south and west suitable to the migrant's agrarian practices, access to the mineral resources of the Chhota Nagpur Plateau below and to bountiful agriculture supported by relatively more fertile soil in the north and east in the humid zones. Further, the southern banks of the Ganga around Patna formed a ridge that was amenable for the growth of urban markets, towns and kingdoms.

The earliest kingdoms of Bihar were the Magadha kingdoms, and it is there in the middle of the first millennium BCE that we encounter two of the most famous migrants of Bihar of all time—Buddha and Mahavira—who would forever be associated with the religions of Buddhism and Jainism.[23] Their life stories of the royal-turned-ascetic-turned-preacher were similar but the subsequent trajectories of their faiths were not. For many centuries in the first millennium CE, the Buddhist monastery in Nalanda was patronized by the Gupta Empire and later by Harsha, the Emperor of Kannauj, and attracted students and monks from as far as China. Buddhism travelled to some extent within India for a few centuries, but made more headway outside the subcontinent, travelling through merchants and monks along the Silk Road via the northern passes such as Karakoram and others, to places in East Asia. Jainism would make some headway down south but over time drifted westwards towards Gujarat. Today, these two faiths comprise less than 1 per cent of the Indian population. Both faiths popularized the wanderlust of asceticism and monastic ways of life, leading to new migratory circuits in addition to the pilgrimage routes associated with the pantheon of gods in Hindu philosophies. Also, both faiths were urban-based with a positive outlook towards trade and were heavily patronized by merchants.

Vibrant trade and agriculture in the transitional zone of the Indo-Gangetic plain eventually led to the birth of the Mauryan Empire with Chandragupta Maurya ascending the throne circa 320 BCE. He is said to have been assisted in this endeavour by his close adviser, Kautilya, and it is through his *Arthashastra,* a fine treatise on statecraft whose authorship and date of origin remains contested, that we glean more about migration in the ancient world.[24]

The first point to note in the *Arthashastra* is that ordinary people travelled considerably, for personal reasons, pilgrimages and fairs and festivals. This was in addition to those who led a life of travel such as traders and entertainers, though the latter were forbidden to travel in villages during the monsoon to avoid distractions during farm work. Most journeys were by foot, some on animals and carts, and there were official specifications on roads and charges for their use. Caravans of merchants paid escort charges and a road cess and boats could be hired for ferries. Special privileges were accorded to Brahmins who could travel free of charge. In fact, it was a punishable offence if they were made to pay the charges! Similar privileges were given to the *pravrajita* or wandering monks, men and women, though they had to carry a pass issued by the relevant authority.

Overall, migration was strictly controlled in the countryside and the fortified city through a chief passport officer, who collected a fee called *mudradhyaksha*. Different officers were appointed to oversee the safety of travellers and traders from thieves and wild animals. Village headmen were responsible for the traveller's safety inside villages. Officers had travelling allowances included in their salary structures and were liable for compensation in case of robbery within their jurisdictions. Villagers were supposed take turns in accompanying the village headman on tours related to official business. *Vanaprashta*s or forest recluses had allotments in the forests for habitation and were permitted to take salt free of charge for consumption. The *Chandala*s were the untouchables, governed by strict rules on segregation and movement.

The secret service or spies disguised themselves as ascetics and traders in other kingdoms, but there were also secret agents deployed to keep track of arrivals and departures within the kingdom. Lodging within the city was carefully monitored with merchants, artisans and artists allowed to accommodate visitors only from their own professions. Suspicious activity at eating places and brothels was to be reported to the authorities.

In the Kautilyan world, women's position was one of dependence on men. This was reflected in the curtailment of their movement as long as they were not courtesans, in which case they were encouraged to travel even during battle expeditions and motivate the men to fight. The wife had to take permission from her husband to go on pleasure trips and could not leave the house when he was drunk or asleep. The categories of punishment for various forms of leaving the house are listed in great detail in the *Arthashastra*. There were also detailed regulations regarding the absence of the husband for long periods, including oversight of the women left behind and punishments such as the nose and an ear being cut off in case the woman committed adultery. In case of domestic abuse, the wife could run away from the husband and it would be the responsibility of the village headman to give asylum to such women. She could always visit her own family on special occasions such as childbirth, death and illness.

Another aspect of migration was linked with the policies to counter famines, an age-old calamity in India that was the result of the failure of the monsoon that brought over 90 per cent of the rainfall to the Indian subcontinent between June and September every year. Kautilya recommended migration to different regions, and even the movement of entire populations including the king and court to places with abundant harvests or those near water bodies. Similarly, there were policies for new areas to be cleared and inhabited by Shudras deported from overpopulated areas.[25] This has also been inferred from the inscriptions of Ashoka, a Mauryan ruler in the 3rd century BCE, whereby some 1,50,000 people were deported from Kalinga in eastern India (around present-day Odisha).[26] Separately, as a matter of transportation policy, Ashoka took great pride in planting shady trees, digging wells and building rest houses along highways.[27]

The next major direct reference to migration in ancient India appears in the second half of the first millennium CE, in the context of the migration of the *Brahmanas* during the upward march of Hindu philosophies across most parts of the subcontinent.[28] Numerous inscriptions on charters across north India inform us about land and village grants being bestowed upon this social group, most probably the priestly caste, with special taxing privileges conferred on them in their newly found colonies. Migrants moved as individuals or in entire groups, in which case their *gotra*s or ancestries were also mentioned. The source regions were varied with charters noting places such as Varendri, Sravasti, Takari, Kolanca, Hastigrama, Hastipada and Madhyadesa in north India. They moved to live under the Rashtrakutas in Maharashtra, Palas in Bengal and Bihar, Paramaras in Madhya Pradesh, but by far most went to Odisha under different ruling houses. The migrations were long distance and often in search for new homes, though the exact reasons remain a bit of a mystery. As per one legend on the Kayastha community in Bengal, traditionally a scribal or administrator caste, the five *kulin* Kayastha lineages—Bose, Ghosh, Mitra, Datta and Guha—were descendants of Kayasthas who accompanied the migration of five Brahmins from Kannauj. Since the Brahmins were invited by a local king in Bengal in the 8th century CE, this suggests one possible explanation for their movement in this period. In fact, a recent study combined genetic research with family genealogies to ascertain weak positive evidence of this migratory link between Uttar Pradesh and Bengal.[29] More generally, all combinations of migration have been noted for the Brahmanas: rural–rural, rural–urban, urban–rural and urban–

urban.[30] These migrant networks potentially quickened the pace of standardizing varying Hindu practices by establishing Brahminical centres, a process greatly facilitated at that time by the wide travels of the philosopher Adi Shankaracharya, who is credited with unifying many different currents of Hindu thought.[31]

In ancient India, a couple of words were popularly used to denote outsiders. *Yona* or *Yavana* was used for foreigners from the west, derived from the Ionians or ancient Greeks.[32] Thus the large armies of Alexander of Macedon that reached the Indus in the 4th century BCE and turned back on account of homesickness would be referred to as the *yavana*s. So would Megasthenes, the Greek ambassador who visited the Mauryan capital, farther inland. The *Arthashastra,* like many texts before and after it, used the word 'mlechha' to denote the outsider, or those with foreign or even tribal origins. The word was historically used to describe outsiders from the west, and at times even those from the east.[33] It would be used to describe the Indo-Greeks, Parthians, Shakas, Kushanas and Hunas who appeared in north-west India, some of whom drove small ruling groups such as the *Gana-samgha*s of Punjab southwards or eastwards from their original inhabitations between the 2nd century BCE and 3rd century CE.[34] It would also be used to describe the invading Turko-Afghans from the north-west, made famous by the attacks of Mahmud of Ghazni in the early 11th century CE and Muhammad Ghuri in the last decade of the 12th century CE, which culminated in the formation of the Delhi Sultanate in 1206 CE.

The world 'mleccha' was also associated with a notion of impurity and, presumably sometime in the first millennium CE, with the codification of Hindu customs and laws, restrictions were placed on overseas mobility for fear of contamination on contact with the mlecchas.[35] These restrictions were placed because it was difficult to observe caste rules and rituals in distant lands, resulting in the notion of 'loss of caste upon return,' a notion that was fairly strong up to the late 19th century CE when the word *kaalapani* was in vogue to describe the forbidden dark waters.

Nevertheless maritime trade did take place in ancient India, usually separate from the Indo-Gangetic political empires and in regions less affected by caste taboos on long-distance mobility. The monsoon winds were used by sailors to cross the Arabian Sea. The west coast of India, especially the southern reaches of Kerala, were well-connected with West Asia and even the Roman Empire in Europe. The Syrian Christians and Cochin Jews of Kerala have a history of well over a thousand years due to these connections. Even with Islam, when the faith was founded in the 7th century CE, it arrived in the subcontinent through trade in Kerala, perhaps earlier than the Arab conquest of Sind in the early 8th century CE. Kerala, therefore, became the first point of contact for many foreign cultures in India. Keralites would return the favour by migrating overseas with great fervour in the 20th century.

Mirroring Kerala on the other side of south India, Tamil Nadu was home to a vibrant culture in ancient India, replete with sophisticated urbanization and magnificent temple building.[36] The Gupta Empire's patronage of Vedic culture influenced the religious outlook of south India to a certain extent in the first millennium CE. There were extensive links with South East Asia, such that since the 4th century CE, political states in South East Asia also began adopting many of these Indian cultural practices.[37] The Chola Empire (c. 850 CE–1250 CE) marked the pinnacle of Tamil achievements, witnessing raids by Rajendra I on Sri Lanka and the ports of Srivijaya in the Strait of Malacca in the 11th century CE and envoys being dispatched to the Chinese court as part of efforts to seek greater control over the east–west trade in the Indian Ocean.[38]

There were other instances too of outmigration from the
Indian subcontinent that were recorded in ancient India. The
returning armies of Alexander and other invaders took back
many Indians, and elephants, to central Asia and Europe.[39]
For centuries, overseas and overland links were principally
maintained by merchants, with textiles and spices as key exports
and horses and gold comprising key imports, though not much
is known about the merchants' activities outside India. Hindu
settlements of over 15,000 members were noted in Armenia
between the 2nd century BCE to the early 4th century CE,
with references to initial flight due to persecution in north
India and wars with early propagators of Christianity.[40] Their
disappearance remains unexplained. Buddhist missionaries from
India such as Dharmaraksa and Kasyapa Matanga were noted in
China around the beginning of the Common Era, followed by a
procession of artists and teachers. Later, Indian migrations were
also noted in Thailand, Vietnam and the Malay Peninsula.[41]
When Fa-Hien, a Buddhist pilgrim from China, arrived in India
in the 5th century CE, he returned by sailing from Tamralipti in
Bengal to South East Asia and observed the flourishing
Brahmanas in Indo-China.[42]

There is also a particular mention of the emigration and
settlement of a large troupe of 12,000 Indian musicians to Iran
in the 5th century CE, on invitation by Persian king Bahram
Gor.[43] A Hindu physician by the name of Manka has been
noted in Baghdad in the late 8th century CE, translating books
from Sanskrit to Arabic.[44] Such translations were important
for the transfer of ancient Indian knowledge in astronomy,
mathematics, medicine and other fields to the Arabic world.
Indian settlements were also noted in West Asia where they
were valued as accountants, artisans, gunners and cooks.[45] The
14th century Moroccan traveller Ibn Battuta, who now has a
Bollywood music track in his honour, found Indians in troops

and military establishments of the Byzantine Empire. But the most famous early Indian diasporic link comes from the Romas or Gypsies found across Europe today as relatively poor nomads and who trace their origins, with genetic evidence, to not just south Asia, but the low-ranking castes and indigenous tribes of north-west India.[46] The date of their dispersal has been placed in the late ancient period even as the exact causes for the outmigration remain shrouded in mystery.

Ancient India thus witnessed different types of migrations from outside and within, all contributing towards greater diversity and a better understanding of regional geography. This was manifested through vivid descriptions as expressed in poet Kalidasa's *Meghaduta,* or 'Cloud Messenger', and later by the purposeful locations of Hindu monasteries in four different corners of the subcontinent—Dwarka (west), Puri (east), Sringeri (south) and Badrinath (north).[47] Migrants—pilgrims, pastoralists, merchants, monks, soldiers and colonizers—were slowly connecting different parts of the Indian subcontinent, and to a lesser extent, the outside world.

Medieval Migrations: From Mlecchas to Firangis

In the medieval period, from roughly the 13th century CE to the early 18th century CE, there were three major changes that increased the overall spatial mobility. First, at the global level, there was an increase in people's mobility and widening of horizons in what has been referred to as the Arid Zone which comprised much of east, central and west Asia and Eastern Europe, with the successful march of pastoral nomads over relatively more sedentary peasant-based societies.[48] These mass migrations were linked with warfare across the region and made India's north-west an important site of battles among competing outside rulers for supremacy over the subcontinent.

Many people entered India as refugees from central Asia fleeing Mongol invasions. Even the arid zones within India, such as the Deccan, were affected. In general, a massive military labour market was created consisting of the Rajputs, Marathas, and many other groups including armed peasants, with lasting legacies for spatial mobility.[49] Some evidence of the scale can be understood from the fact that nearly 4,00,000 cavalry and over 4 million infantry served in the Mughal Empire under Akbar in the late 16th century, when the total size of his empire was pegged at over a 100 million.[50]

Closely related with these developments was the mass migration of hundreds of thousands of animals—horses, oxen, sheep, goats and dromedaries or Arabian camels—that carried humans and goods in large caravans mostly plied by the *Banjaras*.[51] The success of military campaigns in India depended in large part in securing access to grains and other supplies from the Banjaras. Similarly, Afghan traders and warriors positioned themselves in Rayalaseema, a semi-arid zone of south India, in the 17th and 18th centuries to control the supply lines of mercenaries and horses from the north, and also the Deccan pilgrimage route to Tirupati.

Second, India's roads and seas were more permanently integrated with the consolidation of Turko-Afghan imperial power in northern India through different rulers of the Delhi Sultanate (1206-1526), and then the Mughal Empire until the 18th century.[52] With Delhi as the centre of political authority and its vassals spread over a large distance, north–south, east–west and trans-Himalayan routes opened up further. More importantly, the expansion of the northern empires to the seas on both sides of the subcontinent opened up maritime trade by directly connecting the ports to the hinterland. In 1498, Portuguese explorer Vasco da Gama arrived in south India, sailing from Portugal via the Cape of Good Hope in southern

Africa, and opened a new route for Europeans to trade with Asia. Followed by the English, Dutch, French and even Danish merchants, Indian goods produced in the hinterlands, especially textiles, received a global market, ushering the migration of artisans and craftspeople towards textile centres. In the 17th and 18th centuries, another major realm of circulation straddled across the three powerful Muslim-ruled empires—Mughal (India), Safavid (Iran) and Ottoman (Turkey)—by land and sea.[53] Surat, a commercial port in western India, grew to be one of the largest cities in the country in the 17th century, housing numerous groups in trade, including the English, Dutch, Arabs, Persians, Turks, Armenians, Jews, Brahmins, Rajputs and Banias.[54] Before the rise of Surat, the largest cities of India were typically inland. With the establishment of English posts in Calcutta, Bombay and Madras in the 17th century, they too would grow to be among the largest cities of the subcontinent by the 20th century, indicating a major spatial shift in the concentration of economic activities to the coasts, thereby spurring coast-bound migration. From the coasts, Indians themselves began leaving for distant shores as lascars (sailors) and ayahs (nannies) to England, or even as Tamil teachers to Germany in the early 18th century.[55] Growing European contact led to a new word being used to refer to outsiders in India. Yavana and mleccha gave way to *firangi* in Persian, the language of the Mughal Empire, to denote foreigners from Europe. The word came from the root word 'franks', an ancient Germanic tribe.[56] It continues to be used to describe foreigners, mostly white, even today.

Third, pilgrimages of various faiths intensified during the medieval period. French traveller Jean-Baptiste Tavernier in the 17th century observed a band of 4000 pilgrims in India travelling without prior food arrangements, conveying both scale and logistical possibilities.[57] Pilgrimage-associated trade in south India led to temple-generated urbanization, benefiting merchants and artisans.[58] New routes were developed for more recent faiths such as the overseas Hajj pilgrimage from Surat for the Muslims and the Bhakti, Sufi, and Sikh religious and spiritual movements. There was also the immigration of Christian missionaries from Europe, initially to Goa which was ruled by the Portuguese since the 16th century. The share of the Muslim population in the Indian subcontinent rose substantially in the western and eastern wings due to the 'creative adaptation' of migrants and newly settled peasants who were not necessarily a part of entrenched Hindu societies, while the share of Christians in Goa rose on account of conversion.[59] Migrations in the medieval period were therefore at the intersection of complex military, commercial and religious networks. Some of these migrations, especially those of the military and merchants, are recounted in greater detail later, but there are a few direct references on migration in the medieval period that deserve special mention.

The first was to do with the rise and fall of cities in the medieval period. In the 17th century, at least nine cities were known to have populations exceeding 2,00,000 people: Agra, Delhi, Lahore, Thatta (Sindh), Ahmedabad, Surat, Patna, Dacca and Masulipatnam (a port on the east coast).[60] These were large city sizes for their time, drawing a large number of merchants and artisans. Since many cities were built from scratch, they also required migrants to populate their activities. In some places like Uttar Pradesh, there was an established practice of recruiting migrants from beyond the Indus.[61] There are records of migrants from Afghanistan and Bukhara (Uzbekistan) being brought to Shahjahanpur in the 17th century, and more from Afghanistan to Rohilkhand (around Bareilly) in the 18th century. There are also records of rulers willingly moving en masse to another place, as in the infamous case of Muhammad bin Tughlaq's move from Delhi to Daulatabad in the Deccan region of present-day Maharashtra in the 14th century.[62] When rulers were not building cities or moving away from them, they faced the threat of attacks, decline and desertion. Such a fate befell the magnificent urban settlement of the Vijayanagar Empire in the Deccan, which flourished in the 15th and early 16th centuries but was deserted soon after its defeat at the hands of the Deccan Sultanate in the Battle of Talikota in 1565 CE. The remnants of the empire can be seen today at Hampi.

The other noteworthy aspect of medieval migration was that of skilled labour. The Mughal court attracted nobles and scholars from beyond the Indus. It also brought in Persian painters, calligraphers and artisans by paying higher salaries, dubbed by some historians as a potential brain drain into India.[63] Skilled labour was often tied with specific communities and regions. The Dak Meoras, comprising the Meos of Mewat in north India, served as trusted post carriers for the Mughal Empire, while the Aiyangar Pattamars operated separately as couriers around the southern tips of the subcontinent.[64] Julaha weavers, Kagozia papermakers, Kashmiri shawl-makers and Persian carpet-makers were some of the many groups noted for migration.[65] In the 17th century, some Persian carpet-makers settled in Godavari district of Andhra Pradesh in south India and when, in the 18th century, Iranian king Nadir Shah sacked Delhi, Indian carpenters and shipwrights were taken back to Iran reportedly to build 1100 boats in 1740 on the banks of the Oxus. Stone-cutters, masons, goldsmiths and other craftsmen were also taken to build a city in Iran on the lines of the Indian city he had just plundered. If not war, artisans were also found fleeing from famines or unjust pricing regimes. In 1636, weavers left Baroda for Surat to protest against pre-dictated prices but were persuaded to return by the local

governor in scenes reminiscent of 21st century negotiations over
the Goods and Services Tax (GST) regime in India.

Weaver migrations in medieval south India were one of
those migrations that left a deep imprint in inscriptions and folk
traditions and have been brought to light by historian Vijaya
Ramaswamy in painstaking detail. These migrations were either
on invitation by local rulers or decisions made by the weavers to
escape famines and seek greener, or more aptly, silkier pastures.
Weavers in south India belong to specific communities with a
long history of migrations such as the Kaikkolar, Saliyar, Devanga,
Jedara or Pattunulkarar, the last also known as the Saurashtrar—
the largest group of weaver migrants in the Vijayanagar and
post-Vijayanagar periods, concentrated in Madurai.[66] They can
trace their origins to an inscription in Mandasor in the Malwa
region of Madhya Pradesh in the late 5th century CE. The
Mandasor inscription stated that Brahmin silk weavers migrated
as a group from a region in Gujarat into Mandasor, or Dasapura,
around the 3rd or 4th centuries CE, providing a clue as to why
they may be called the Sourashtrar. Subsequent migrations are
preserved in oral traditions called *boula*, a unique question and
answer session between the parties of the bride and groom at
every Saurashtra wedding. A sample translated dialogue from
the boula is as follows:[67]

Kay naa meneti [What I mean to say is]

'When we glance at the history of immigration of our
ancestors from times immemorial, they lived in a far-off
northern direction, in a region called Saurashtra. In that
district, they lived in the town of Devagiri.

'What I mean is, our gotra is . . .
Our country is Saurashtra,

Our town is Devagiri,
Our religion is the Vaishnava religion,
Our varna is the Gauda-Brahmin varna,
If you ask to which they proceeded
They came to Madurai . . .'

The other party would also begin with the first line and refer to a similar migration route. The ritual ended after an exchange of *tamboolam* and a concluding ceremony with people dressed in the silks for which they had acquired much fame.

Weaver migrations in medieval south India could involve distances of over a 1000 km staggered, at the community level, over centuries, and were usually permanent migrations of entire families. The language of the community was hybrid: that of the Pattunulkarar was called Patnuli, involving a mix of Gujarati, Marathi, Kannada, Telugu and Tamil. Like in Baroda, the weavers in south India were also known to 'vote with their feet' to less oppressive tax regimes. While these migrations were extensive, there was another kind of migration occurring in medieval India, within and between frontiers, and those migrants did not necessarily weave silk. On the contrary, they were sometimes traded in return for woven silk.

Slaves

Many people in India derive their conception of slavery from Hollywood movies depicting slaves in American history. Slavery was a defining issue in American politics, and its abolition in most places of the world in the 19th century was a major moral victory for humankind. Between the 16th and 19th centuries, an estimated 12 million slaves were forcibly transported from Africa to the Americas across the Atlantic, the majority in fact going to Brazil and the Caribbean, and not North America.[68]

The trans-Atlantic slave trade was enormous in scale and one of the largest forced migrations of all time, but it was not the first time the world had experienced slavery, nor was slavery unique to that part of the world.

Slavery existed in ancient India and is well-documented in the *Arthashastra* through the use of the words *dasa* (slave), *dasabhava* (the state of being a slave), *dasakalpa* (rules related to slavery) and *dasatva* (concept of slavery), representing the most unfree kinds of labour.[69] This was distinct from bonded labour where workers mortgaged themselves to their masters. There was even a four-fold categorization of slaves: those who were inherited, born in the house, bought, or procured by other means such as capture or gift. The punishment for slaves breaking the laws were harsh and those caught stealing male or female slaves would have both their feet cut off. There were possibilities of manumission, or obtaining freedom, on receiving redemption money, or in the specific case of a slave giving birth to a child of her master in which case both the slave and her child would be recognized as free. However, if a woman had sexual relations with a slave, the punishment was straightforward: death.

Historical research on slavery in India over the past millennium has revealed its diverse forms in military service and domestic work, and in contrast with the Americas, some remarkable avenues available for upward mobility.[70] Richard Eaton, a distinguished historian of medieval India, defines slavery in this period as 'the condition of uprooted outsiders, impoverished insiders—or the descendants of either—serving persons or institutions on which they are wholly dependent'.[71] Thus, we find that in the Chola Empire, female war captives were enslaved and served as 'reproductive pools' for bolstering a military cadre, the *kaikkolars*, loyal to the rulers.[72] Temple patronage in south India had also given rise to the phenomenon of female devadasis or temple-servants, which spread across India and could degenerate towards forms of harsh servitude.[73] Between the 16th and 18th century, female taken captive in war by the Rajput polity could serve as slave-performers and slave-concubines.[74]

In the 17th century, the Bengal delta became a major slave-raiding zone for the eastern kingdoms.[75] States like Assam, Manipur, Koch, Cachar and Tripura in the north-east were known to be slave-holding societies, but the major flow occurred between south-east Bengal and the Arakan (north Burma), the same passageway as that of the recent Rohingya refugee crisis. In the early 17th century, some 18,000 Bengali slaves were observed in just two small centres of the Arakan as it became a major slave-raiding state to manage the expansion of the Mrauk-U kingdom. The kingdom took the help of renegade Portuguese in these operations and also sold the slaves to Dutch-occupied Batavia (Jakarta). Growing contact with the Europeans made the Indian coasts a site of slave recruitment in the Indian Ocean world and was the precursor of the better-known mass migration of indentured labour in the 19th century, when slavery was abolished in many European colonies.

But for sheer scale and audacity, it would be the Turkish, Indian and Ethiopian slaves that would capture the imagination of west, central and South Asia. The Delhi Sultanate, under the Mamluks in the 13th century CE, is also known as the Slave dynasty because the rulers were originally Turkish Mamluks or soldiers with slave origins.[76] Slaves were reputed for their loyalty, as noted in the saying 'one obedient slave is better than three hundred sons, for the latter desire their father's death, the former his master's glory', though they would often revolt and usurp power themselves.[77] Qutb al-Din Aybak, after whom the famous Qutb Minar in Delhi is named, was originally a military slave of Sultan Ghuri, as was Shams al-Din Iltutmish, a successor and slave of Aybak.

In the warfare of subsequent centuries in the north-west, captives from India would also be taken to central Asia in large numbers, often traded for horses, giving rise to a saying of those times: 'Slaves from India, horses from Parthia.'[78] According to Ibn Battuta, the 14th century traveller who had noted the presence of Indians among the troops of the Byzantine Empire, the Hindu Kush range in the north-west frontier of the Indian subcontinent was called so because the name meant 'slayer of Hindus' who experienced high mortality due to the intensity of the cold when they were taken across as slaves.[79]

Between the mid-15th and mid-17th centuries, the slave markets of the Arab world began importing *Habshi* slaves from Ethiopia as servants or for re-export to meet the demand for military labour in the Deccan plateau, and sometimes in exchange for Indian textiles.[80] Arguably the most famous of these slaves, Malik Ambar, earlier known as Chapu, was born in Ethiopia in 1548 CE, taken to the slave markets of west Asia and exported to the Deccan where he was purchased by the Nizam Shahi of the Sultanate of Ahmadnagar (1496-1636 CE). The person who bought him, one Chengiz Khan, the peshwa or chief minister, was himself a former slave and a Habshi. He was only following what was by then a well-established practice of importing African slaves from the Persian Gulf region to the Deccan kingdoms via the Konkan seaports on the west coast. The Arab dhows would take a few weeks to cross the Arabian Sea to deliver the slaves, known as *ghulam*s in Arabic and *banda*s in Persian.

Ambar's subsequent upward mobility was stunning, mirroring the Turkish Mamluks of Delhi in the 13th century. Once his master died, he was freed by his master's wife, married, and then served with local troops. He raised his own cavalry which grew from 150 to 7000 in a short span of time and revitalized the Ahmadnagar kingdom by appointing puppet Sultans to thwart Mughal attacks from the north. By 1610, his army had 10,000 Habshis and 40,000 Deccanis. Over the next decade, he frustrated Mughal Emperor Jahangir, not only by the size of his army but also by the colour of his skin as race was an important marker that shaped Jahangir's perception of Malik Ambar. But when Ambar finally died in 1626, even Mughal chroniclers submitted that he had lived an honourable life and praised his guerrilla warfare that possibly inspired the Shivaji-led Maratha ascendance in the late 17th century. The Ethiopian military labour market by then had disappeared as the Ahmadnagar kingdom had fallen to the Mughals in 1636. The remaining Habshis, mostly men, were absorbed into local society.

The Siddi community of India, closely related to the Habshis, runs into tens of thousands of people today and is found in the states of Karnataka, Maharashtra and Gujarat. Among the masterpieces of Siddi craftsmanship in the 16th century is the beautiful and intricate window screen of the Sidi Saiyyed mosque in Ahmedabad, which inspired the logo of the Indian Institute of Management in the city (IIM-A). I often point this out to the students there, as an example of what the institute strives to achieve: creativity and the upward mobility of a diverse student body. Students, in turn, have pointed out an important difference: that they willingly submit themselves to a life of corporate slavery!

Modern Migrations: From Horse Power to Horsepower

This brief outline of Indian migration history over several millennia has thrown up a galaxy of actors. In alphabetical order, they are: accountants, animals, artisans, ascetics, ayahs, banjaras, colonizers, cooks, couriers, courtesans, entertainers, lascars, mercenaries, merchants, missionaries, monks, nomads, nuns, *pattamars*, pastoralists, pilgrims, priests, prostitutes, slaves, spies,

students, thieves, travellers, warriors, weavers, wives, and that
catch-all term 'workers'. As one historian noted: 'mobility was
at least as characteristic of pre-modern India as sedentarism'.[81]
The modern world would popularize words like 'coolie' and
'kangani', 'professional' and 'pardesi', and much more. It can be
separated into two phases: one from roughly the middle of the
18th century to the late 19th century in which the power of the
horse and wind still mattered, and the other since then till now,
in which the horsepower of the engine increased the speed of
travel over land, water, and most dramatically, air.

The first phase was closely linked with the disintegration
of the Mughal Empire after Aurangzeb's death in 1707 and the
gradual colonization of India by European powers, led by the
English East India Company after its victory in the Battle of Plassey
in Bengal in 1757. One direct impact of European colonialism
on spatial mobility was the effort towards settling nomadic
groups, which throughout history had been on the move, most
famously the Banjaras. Their lives were those of travel in *qafilas*
(caravans), progressing at roughly 10 miles a day, with thousands
of bullocks, each carrying goods weighing over 100 kg.[82]
They would be well-entertained during their long journeys
by jugglers, conjurors, astrologers, musicians and people with
trained monkeys and dancing bears accompanying them. But the
colonial authorities wanted to settle mobile groups, which were
often armed with weapons, into sedentary peasants as a matter of
surveillance and also as a measure to increase the land revenue tax
base. Their tightened control on mobile groups in the early 19th
century led to a small disruption which then intensified with
the introduction of the railways in 1853. A few Banjaras turned
to criminal activity, leading the authorities to brand them as a
'criminal tribe', while others settled down as local cattle herders.
Some Banjaras, also called *Vanjaris*, migrated to Bombay to work
as porters again, but this time on the platform of the technology

that had displaced them: the railways. In southern India, the Lambada community of Hyderabad, equivalents of the Banjaras in the region, under the Nizam state and indirect British rule underwent a similar process of occupational displacement and surveillance checks. They transformed into agricultural labourers and then bonded labourers, and their suffering eventually led to revolt and the Telangana armed struggle in the mid-20th century.[83] In the Great Indian Desert, also called the Thar Desert, in western Rajasthan, there was a similar outlawing of peripatetic groups in the 19th century to curtail mobility.[84] Another impact of colonization that reduced spatial mobility was the extensive demilitarization that took place in the 19th century such that the share of the military in the population fell from around 2 to 4 per cent during Akbar's reign to less than one-third of a percentage.

While some colonial policies were restricting mobility, others were increasing mobility in the late 18th and early 19th century. European ventures in gunpowder manufacture, indigo and opium involved factories and fields that used migrant labour and contributed to the goods traffic along the Ganga which employed as many as 3,50,000 boatmen by the 1830s.[85] The construction of canals and roads similarly led to the demand for migrant labour.[86] In places where harsh land taxes were levied, there was no option to play a cricket match and escape it, as depicted in the Bollywood blockbuster *Lagaan*. Migration was very much a strategy of resistance. Deindustrialization in the early 19th century due to cheap machine-made British cloth flooding Indian markets led to a realignment of textile manufacturing, triggering weaver migration from eastern Uttar Pradesh to upcoming centres like Bombay, Bhiwandi and Malegaon in western India.[87] The term 'Madanpura' or 'Mominpura' became a metaphor for Muslim Julaha weaver migrations as they settled in recreated Madanpuras of these three urban centres.[88] Internal barriers to trade were broken down in the 1830s and factories, plantations, ports and mines in India and outside began to beckon Indian labour and capital, centred around the colonial port cities of Calcutta, Bombay and Madras. The Crown rule took over administration of the country from the English East India Company after a revolt in 1857, and since then British India (including Burma since 1886) was more firmly entrenched in the global circulation of labour.

The introduction of the railways and steamboats played a decisive role in the next phase of modern migrations, increasing the speed of travel in the late 19th century. By the 1890s, one could cover a distance of 400 miles in the same time it took to travel 20 miles a century earlier. Transport costs per ton per mile had fallen by nearly 90 per cent.[89] Internal and international migration surged in the late 19th century alongside the wave of globalisation (and intense famines). The Census of India in 1901 revealed that over 2 per cent of the population was composed of inter-provincial migrants, not too far off from the number for inter-county migration in Britain eighty years earlier, by when Britain was already industrialized.[90] Similarly, India was also a part of the 'Age of Mass Migration' that is otherwise used to characterize the trans-Atlantic migrations from Europe during 1870–1914. Between 1834 and 1937, 30 million people emigrated from India, mainly towards Burma, Malaysia and Sri Lanka, of which nearly 24 million returned.[91] In terms of gross emigration flows, it was similar in magnitude to the trans-Atlantic migration wave, but in net terms, it was different as a large part of the migration was circulatory in nature, though it was similar to the experience of southern Europe. The two world wars in the early 20th century also drew a couple of million Indians to the battlefronts as circulating labour. The circulation that used to take place in India's north-west subsided for the first time in two millennia due to geopolitical reasons, but was replaced by circulatory labour moving towards the plantations in the north-eastern frontier, often assisted by immigration from Nepal. As historians Claude Markovits, Jacques Pouchepadass and Sanjay Subrahmanyam have pointed out, 'circulation has to be treated as a fairly general framework within which to look at Indian society and the transformations it underwent in the modern period, that is at least from the 18th century, if not from an even earlier period'.[92] It is a theme that is laid out in greater detail in the next chapter.

The Landscape of Contemporary Migration

Ancient, medieval and modern-day migrations of different faiths, castes and communities have led to the stunning diversity observed in India and the world, one that continues to be reshaped every day with the arrival of each train into a city and each aeroplane leaving the country. While it is difficult to quantify migrations before the late 19th century with great precision, the historical accounts narrated in this chapter show that they were substantive for specific regions and time periods.[93] They were almost always linked with global migrations—in prehistoric times with the human journey out of tropical Africa, in medieval times with the march across the arid zones of the world, and in modern times, in sync with the waves of globalization.

However, until recently, one of the peculiarities about Indian migration was that you saw migrants everywhere except in the data collected by the Census and National Sample Surveys. Official surveys asked people whether they were migrants, defined so if they were outside their usual place of residence for at least six months. Such an approach omitted many circular migrants who moved for shorter spells or whose residential sites were often not enumerated in the destination region, or those who reported themselves as non-migrants rather than return migrants in the source region.[94] It also undercounted female migrants for work as they would report themselves as migrants for marriage. As a result, migration escaped the attention of policy makers under incorrect assumptions of low spatial mobility in India.

Researchers have only now begun to evaluate critically the official statistical databases and have derived migration estimates that are several times higher than earlier estimates. Migration rates at the all–India level are no longer considered to be exceptionally low and are astoundingly high in many parts of India. The key to understanding migration in India is by looking at the reason and duration of migration.

One important reason for migration is 'forced migration' due to involuntary displacements caused by natural disasters, wars, riots, persecutions and development projects. The numbers for this kind of migration are difficult to come by in surveys, though in Chapter 5 we will observe that since Independence, more than 40 million Indians have been estimated to have moved in this manner. The number of internally displaced persons, and refugees in India from Tibet, Sri Lanka, Afghanistan, Myanmar and a few other countries currently stands at close to 1 million people. In specific episodes recounted later, such as the aftermath of the Partition in 1947 and the Bangladesh War of Independence in 1971, this figure had touched 10 million.

Among voluntary streams, marriage and movement with the household are important stated reasons of migration, amounting to over *300 million* people in India as per the Census of 2011, almost completely dominated by women in short-distance rural to rural movements. However, many of these migrations are also long-distance, especially from Bengal towards the north-west as the latter has very few females in the marriage market on account of strong norms such as preference for a son.[95] More women have moved permanently than men throughout Indian history due to the practice of village exogamy, and it is their connections and migrant links that constitute some of the major 'invisible threads' holding together Indian diversity.

Outside marriage migration, the Census of 2011 also revealed that nearly 10 million people had moved for educational purposes, mostly males and towards urban centres.[96] The data on pilgrimage is not directly available but the periodic Kumbh Mela attracts over 50 million people today, making it the largest human congregation to take place for a short period of time. Over 10 million Indians have moved abroad, primarily for work towards West Asia and North America, making India the world's largest recipient of international migrants' remittances.[97] Roughly the same number of people immigrated to India from Nepal and Bangladesh. Taking together the descendants of past emigrants, the size of the Indian international diaspora recently surpassed the 25 million mark. Correspondingly, in Chapter 4, I introduce the concept of internal diaspora based on language and conservatively estimate that figure to cross over 60 million.

Work-related migration is what most people associate 'migration' with. The Census of 2011 revealed that there were over 50 million internal migrants for economic reasons. The *Economic Survey of India* in 2017 estimated this figure to cross a 100 million when the limitations of the Census were fully taken into account.[98] That is, the migrant workforce has been conservatively estimated to comprise a fifth of India's total workforce. In some states, like Kerala and Bihar, outmigration rates are among the highest in the world. There is also clear evidence that work-related migration rates increased since the 1990s, coinciding with increased economic growth rates and the globalization of the Indian economy.

The duration of work-related migration matters greatly in understanding the geography of migration in India. The shortest duration migrations of less than a day or a week are called commuting and affect over 10 million people around major

urban centres.[99] Slightly longer duration migrations known as
seasonal migrations occur, by survey definitions, in spells of a
few months each, with no spell lasting more than six months.
The word 'seasonal' refers to the gap in the agricultural calendar
where people begin to migrate outside for work, usually between
November and April. These are India's most vulnerable migration
streams affecting 5 per cent of households and over 10 million
migrants.[100] Relatively poorer and landless households, STs and
the Scheduled Castes (SCs), are over-represented in this form
of migration that is often mediated by contractors.[101] Prominent
clusters of seasonal outmigration occur in India's tribal belts
in central India—at the borders of Gujarat, Rajasthan and
Madhya Pradesh, in southern Odisha and Telangana, northern
Karnataka, southern Rajasthan, Chhattisgarh and also in Bihar
and Jharkhand. In these areas, nearly a third of the households
are directly affected by seasonal migration. In Dohad in Gujarat
or Dindori in Madhya Pradesh, one in two households sends out
seasonal migrants. These migrations are both rural to rural and
rural to urban as a third of the seasonal migrants in India work
in the construction sector, a fifth in agricultural activities and a
sixth in manufacturing activities.[102] While seasonal migration is
male-dominated in nature, it is not uncommon to see women
and children working in specific sectors such as construction
and brick kilns. Seasonal migrants also live in makeshift tents,
huts and camps around worksites, if not in urban slums, under
informal contracts and with constant threats of eviction.

Permanent migration lies at the other end of the spectrum
of work-related migration, accounting for tens of millions
of Indians. Here, the movements are largely rural to urban
or urban to urban and are over-represented by the relatively
richer segments of the population and upper castes. In 2011, a
quarter of India's urban population was enumerated as being
migrants, and many of them were permanent migrants. These

are migrations of entire families as they want to raise their children in the cities.

The big story about work-related migration in India, however, lies between the twin poles of seasonal and permanent migrations. It mirrors what the British did in India, for in the late 18th century historian Gholam Hossein Khan had observed that:[103]

> The English have besides a custom of coming for a number of years, and then going away to pay a visit to their native country, without any one of them showing any inclination to fix himself in this land.

This is the world of semi-permanent migration, where migrants seem to have discovered that 'secret of perpetual motion'. The old adage of most Indians dying in their villages of birth may still be true, but most adult women die outside them as they leave after marriage, and for many men, between life and death, there is a whole new world that is explored. It is this phenomenon that has such a remarkable history that it deserves a separate chapter and a somewhat grandstanding title.

2

The Great Indian Migration Wave

Mere piya gaye Rangoon, kiya hai vahan se telephone,
Tumhaari yaad sataati hai, jiya mein aag lagaati hai.

—*Patanga*, 1949

Shamshad Begum's famous song in a classic Hindi film about a
wife bemoaning her migrant husband's absence in the middle of
the 20th century echoes the feelings of millions of women before
and since. The long wait, first for the postman to deliver letters
and then for fleeting reunions, has been a perennial source of
anguish for separated families. Rangoon in Burma, now Yangon
in Myanmar, happened to be one of the important places in the
world that saw many Indian migrants in the early 20th century,
but similar voices can be unearthed across the world in songs,
letters and books across eras. In the Philippines today, one can
hear of husbands bemoaning the absence of their wives who
head to the US for work.

What makes the Indian case unique is the sheer persistence
and magnitude of this phenomenon, one that has lasted for well
over a century now. It is also a phenomenon that affects regions
covering at least 20 per cent of the Indian population, currently

comprising over 200 million people. I call it the 'Great Indian
Migration Wave', and it ranks among the largest and longest
migration streams for work in documented history. It led to the
rise of cities like Kolkata and Mumbai in India and Yangon and
Dubai abroad. It produced a number of freedom fighters and
political leaders who went on to become Presidents and Bharat
Ratna awardees. It popularized various types of regional cultures,
cinemas and culinary delights. In short, it played a significant
role in shaping the history of modern India. Surprisingly, it is a
story that has never been told.

In order to understand the Great Indian Migration Wave
and see how it is different from other migration streams within
India, it is important to define its features. It is mass migration
that is male-dominated, semi-permanent and remittance-
yielding. Mass migration is considered to arise from a *source*
region where usually over 20 per cent of the households report
outmigration or over 5 per cent of the population is enumerated
outside.[1] By 'male-dominated', I mean that over 70 per cent of
the net outflow of migrants from a particular region comprises
men. Semi-permanent durations are those where migrants spend
a greater part of the year away from their homes and who do
not permanently settle in their destinations. They return after
working outside for a few years or even decades. Remittances
are the inevitable outcome of such migrations to support families
back home. Of course, some individuals and families do settle
away from home, but the bulk of the migrations do not lead to
permanent settlement.

The wave I refer to represents peaks and troughs in this
migration episode which occurred at different points in different
regions. Broadly, this wave mirrors India's engagement with
the global economy, rising from the late 19th century to the
1930s and then once again since economic liberalization was
introduced in 1991. These migrations have fundamentally

been labour migrations towards plantations, mines and cities, but they can include a variety of other skills and occupations. Geographically, the maximum source-region impact of the wave is observed in the coastal belts, lower Indo-Gangetic plains and the northern Himalayan range. A remarkable aspect of the Great Indian Migration Wave is the near constancy of the source areas but, literally, a sea change in the destinations from the Bay of Bengal towards the Arabian Sea. How and why did these migrations occur and why have they been so persistent? This question is best addressed by exploring the unique histories of districts, recruitment practices, railways, postal services, and maybe even dosas.

Mangoes and Man Goes: Ratnagiri in Maharashtra

Summer in India is incomplete without the sweet taste of mangoes, and the Alphonso variety, or *Aphoos* in Marathi, rules the roost in Maharashtra. Those who have grown up eating them attest to attaining nirvana at an early age and acquire an inevitable arrogance about its superiority over the numerous other varieties found in India. Legend has it that it was named after a Portuguese general of Goa, from where its cultivation spread up north along an undulating terrain between the Western Ghats and the sea. It is now grown mostly in the Konkan region and has been a constant export from the region for over a 100 years. But the Konkan has been exporting more than just mangoes for a long period of time. It has been exporting manpower as well.

Between 1872 and 2011, the sex ratio of Ratnagiri district in Konkan Maharashtra never fell below 1100 females per 1000 males.[2] In a country of 'missing women', where sex ratios hover around 900 and in some regions dip well below that due to the preference for sons and discrimination against daughters, this is an astounding statistic that has persisted for 130 years.

The 'missing men' phenomenon of Ratnagiri persists because men have been migrating for work in large numbers, primarily towards Mumbai which is around 300 km north. Even today, over a third of the households in Ratnagiri report outmigrants from whom they receive remittances. When did this mass migration wave in Ratnagiri begin and why did it persist over such a long period of time?

Migration was a 'well-established tradition' in Ratnagiri by the mid-19th century which affected all the three principal castes: Chitpavan Brahmins, Marathas and Mahars.[3] The migrations were initially directed towards Pune and beyond. Brahmins migrated first to secure administrative positions in the Peshwa court of the Maratha Empire and later towards newly established educational centres. These migrations were often family-based and permanent. By the early 20th century, these had produced an impressive list of political leaders and social reformers such as Bal Gangadhar Tilak (1856–1920), Dhondo Keshav Karve (1858–1962) and Gopal Krishna Gokhale (1866–1915). Marathas from Ratnagiri, the dominant land-holding caste, were recruited much earlier into Shivaji's army and, later, in the Bombay Army and police. Remittances and pensions brought in by these soldiers formed significant portions of the district's economy.[4] The British army was also the site for recruitment of Mahars, the outcastes or Dalits in today's parlance. Small sparks of upward mobility were lit up by these opportunities of exposure to different regions, customs and ideas. This gave rise to people such as Gopal Baba Walangkar, a pensioned soldier who began the first Mahar newspaper, and Ramji Maloji Sakpal, a subedar major and father of Bhimrao Ambedkar (1891–1956), who would in turn father the Constitution of India.[5]

Migration for military service and education was, however, quickly displaced in importance by the rise of Bombay's cotton textile industry in the late 19th century. A pernicious land tenure system known as the *khoti* system had already strained agriculture. The collapse of the Deccan trade after its connection with Bombay by rail in the 1850s triggered the impulse for mass migration from Ratnagiri. By 1881, 15 per cent of those born in Ratnagiri were working in Bombay.[6] Migration for mill work was not through the medium of contractors but an extensive kith–kin based social network dominated by the Marathas. Mill work gave a new sense of identity to workers but woeful and expensive housing led to little permanent settlement in the city. The chawls that sprung up were male ghettoes as migration was overwhelmingly male-dominated. Migration flows were temporarily reduced or reversed during bouts of plague in the early 20th century and economic slowdown induced by the Great Depression of the early 1930s. Mass migration towards the textile industry held sway until the closure of the mills in the 1980s following prolonged labour strikes, after which it diversified into other service sectors and destinations such as Surat and the Gulf countries.

To understand the persistence of a phenomenon like the Ratnagiri migration, one has to understand the psychology of the children growing up in the Konkan region. Young boys grew up in a place where virtually every second male member of the village worked outside. They were brought up in a culture of adult male absence punctuated by return visits during Ganpati and other festivals. Their grandfathers would recount stories of their experiences of migration, the adventure of living outside the village and the thrill of being able to retire amidst the lush green hillsides of Ratnagiri. Young girls on the other hand were taught from an early age the value of looking after one's land in the absence of men and the premium in the marriage market for the 'Bombay boys'. When these children grew up, they enacted the same rituals that they had carefully observed during their childhood. It did not matter therefore if a major employment sector like the textile industry collapsed as migration routes quickly adapted to new sectors. It did not matter if regions within Ratnagiri got better amenities as they were associated with even higher rates of outmigration.

These migrations led to considerable upward economic mobility within each caste but left existing inter-caste inequalities unchanged. Migration of the lowest castes was dented in the late 19th century itself due to a sudden change in army recruitment practices. Subsequently, migration rates were lower among the lowest castes and, over several decades, the distribution of village land holdings remained the same.[7] The mango orchards themselves are no longer looked after by local labour but by tens of thousands of Nepalese immigrants. Those who settled outside Ratnagiri were those who had earned enough money to secure their own house, though they rarely snapped all connections with the village. A common phrase in Ratnagiri is *'Jyechi kholi, tyechi Mumbai* [Mumbai belongs to those who can own a room].' The Ratnagiri diaspora today is several million strong and every other village has a diasporic association at the destination site. Its contribution to Indian public life has been immense as over 10 per cent of all awardees of the Bharat Ratna, India's highest civilian award, have been given to people directly or indirectly associated with the mass migration from this region.[8] Historical legacies of migration for military recruitment are etched in the vocabulary of the Indian army as 'Maratha' and 'Mahar' continue to be mentioned in the names of two infantry regiments. Mass migration from Ratnagiri has also contributed immensely to the rise of Mumbai. The interconnections are best viewed from the prism of village names in Ratnagiri. Dadar and Borivali are important train stations in Mumbai but are also names of villages in Ratnagiri. Similarly, many surnames ending with 'kar', such as Ambedkar and Mangeshkar, refer to ancestral villages in the greater Konkan region.

Ratnagiri is known to Indians for its famous Alphonso mangoes but its migration history suggests that it should also be known for *man goes*. In fact, Ratnagiri's export of mangoes and manpower often collided with each other on the busy ferry steamers that plied between Mumbai and the Konkan. In the 1930s, a legislative debate took place on how passengers were being displaced by mango parcels in the month of May![9]

Brahmins, Bunts and Butter Dosas: Udupi in Karnataka

If you walk into a south Indian restaurant outside south India, there are high chances of you being in an Udupi restaurant. The look and feel of these restaurants is similar. The cashier sits at the entrance with a photograph of the founder or pictures of gods and goddesses on the wall behind him. A young man clears used utensils from the table into a bucket in one swoop as you take your seat and inspect the varieties of dosas and idlis on the menu. The waiter briskly memorizes your order and passes it on to the kitchen and a dish magically appears before you within five minutes. What you witness is not just fast food at its finest but also a product of the Great Indian Migration Wave which originated in Udupi district of coastal Karnataka.

Between 1901 and 2011, the sex ratio of Udupi district never fell below 1090 females per 1000 males, reflecting over a 100 years of mass male outmigration. Migrations on a large scale were triggered in the late 19th century by lower-caste *Holeya* labourers towards the coffee plantations of Kodagu (then Coorg) and the Malnad region of Karnataka. By the early 20th century, the migrations were wide-ranging, affecting a variety of castes as observed by the district gazetteer of 1938:[10]

The emigrants are labourers, mostly men who are recruited for the plantations in Coorg and Mysore territory, but they return to their native villages every year when the crop is harvested. There is of course the usual emigration of the professional and middle-classes in search for employment in other parts of India, besides a considerable number of 'Udupi' Brahmin cooks who are to be found employed in households or engaged in running restaurants outside their own native district.

What were Brahmins doing as cooks and why did they start migrating in large numbers to run restaurants? Udupi is known in religious circles for its famous Sri Krishna Temple, founded after Madhvacharya in the 13th century. To propagate his philosophy of *Dvaita Vedanta,* eight *matha*s or monasteries were set up, and over time a vibrant temple culture took root in nearby places. Brahmins came to comprise 10 per cent of the region's population, three times higher than elsewhere in south India.[11] The temple culture manifested itself in periodic ceremonies where food was served to big gatherings of the temple staff and pilgrims.[12] It was in this setting that K. Krishna Rao, the son of a Hindu priest and founder of the Woodlands group of hotels, began his career in food service as an attendant. In 1922, family squabbles led him to move to Chennai where he worked his way up the ladder in the food business and started his own Udupi Sri Krishna Vilas within a few years. The 1920s proved to be a watershed moment in Udupi's migration history as a major flood devastated the region in 1923.[13] Mass migration of male workers and professionals to large cities led to the rising demand for low-cost public eating spaces. Several prominent Udupi food outlets such as Dasaprakash in Mysore and Udupi Sri Krishna Bhavan and Mavalli Tiffin Rooms (MTR) in Bangalore were set up in the 1920s to cater to this demand. These public eating spaces were famous for being 'pure vegetarian', employed middle to upper caste folk from the

Udupi region and, in the initial decades, had segregated seating spaces on caste lines. Migration from Udupi was unique in that it involved a considerable number of child migrants in search of work and the key destination—the restaurant—provided free food and accommodation.[14] This led to substantial cost savings in the city and prospects of dramatic upward mobility whereby cleaners could rise up to start their own restaurants.

Chennai, Mysore and Bangalore were important destinations for the Udupi migrants, but it was Mumbai that would capture the imagination for the next century. Matunga in Mumbai became a veritable bastion of south Indian migrants, and Udupi restaurants with Ramanayaks, Café Madras and several others established in the 1930s and 40s. Land reforms in the 1970s stimulated greater migration of Bunts, a dominant peasant caste of Udupi, who took on the mantle from the Brahmins to run the bulk of Udupi restaurants, often taking over old Irani restaurants. Vegard Iversen, an economist with an anthropological streak, studied the evolution of the Udupi migration and restaurant phenomenon and noted the strength of caste networks in sustaining restaurant proliferation and food practices and its interaction with urban cosmopolitanism.[15] Only in big cities did employment opportunities in Udupi restaurants significantly widen to accommodate other castes and religions. In Mumbai, night schools for restaurant staff were a prominent feature in the initial years, and working conditions improved substantially after the labour rights movements of the 1950s and 1960s championed by George Fernandes, himself a product of the coastal Karnataka migration wave. The invasion of north Indian and Chinese dishes into the menus in the closing decades of the 20th century helped diminish the notions of purity associated with traditional vegetarian south Indian food. In smaller towns, and even in Bangalore to some extent, orthodoxy in menus and the workforce continued to prevail.

The common factor across locations was the high rate of return migration. Working outside the district was a rite of working life, but retirement took most migrants back home. Until now, Udupi's economy continues to be sustained by migrants' remittances, much of which goes towards temple trusts. These remittances clash with remittances from many Muslim emigrants working in the Gulf countries, leading to a communal and caste-based display of wealth and violence. However, despite persistent mass outmigration and remittance related woes, Udupi is not the characteristic basket case of underdevelopment. Instead, it outperforms all other districts of Karnataka, barring Bangalore, on the Human Development Index.[16] Migration is an important reason behind this relative prosperity.

Several decades before the establishment of McDonald's in the US, the Udupi fast food restaurant model began to spread its tentacles around India. Eventually, it breached national boundaries and reached key Indian diasporic hotspots around the world. Expansion did not occur through franchises but migration and community networks.

Migration avenues have widened in recent years to include more destinations and occupations, including the underworld, but the intensity of mass male migration from coastal Karnataka continues unabated. Ironically, the region's two most famous migrant personalities are not men but women—Bollywood actors Aishwarya Rai and Shilpa Shetty, both of whom were born in Tulu-speaking Bunt families in Mangalore, just south of Udupi.

Density and Destiny: Saran in Bihar

Perhaps no other region in India evokes such a picture of migration in contemporary and historic times as Bihar. Situated in the lower part of the Gangetic plain, it has witnessed the rise and fall of some of the greatest dynastic civilizations in Indian history. The cities of yore, including Pataliputra, now Patna, would have drawn numerous migrants over many centuries, at least since the 4th century BCE. South of Patna, the famed Buddhist monastery at Nalanda attracted students from as far as China for several centuries in the first millennium CE. Over the next millennium, secure with water supply in the Gangetic basin and safe from the periodic wars around Delhi, the population of Bihar grew steadily under different rulers. Continuous habitation over time led to high population densities, particularly in the Bhojpuri-speaking part of modern-day west Bihar and east Uttar Pradesh. By the late 19th century, districts in this region were among the densest rural tracts of the world. Saran district, located west of Patna, emerged as the leader of the pack.[17]

It is possible to trace outmigration from Saran and its surrounding regions to as far back as the 15th century. The historian Dirk Kolff has shown how this region became a major recruiting ground for 'peasant-soldiers' over several centuries, serving Sher Shah Suri, the Mughal army, the British, and other local rulers, zamindars and warlords.[18] Some migrants were recruited into Robert Clive's sepoy battalions in Bengal in the 1770s and the district was providing over 10,000 sepoys by the mid-19th century.[19] It is possible that harsh rents and unsuitable conditions of indigo cultivation prompted peasants to look at options beyond the district in the early 19th century.[20] It is possible that this was triggered by streams of emigration to plantations in Mauritius and the Caribbean islands, for which recruitment took place in the mid-19th century. Be that as it may, by the late 19th century, colonial officials were noting the 'usual exodus' of not thousands but hundreds of thousands of migrant workers comprising over 15 per cent of the district's population going *purab* or east.[21] By 1901, Saran's sex ratio had risen to 1200 females per 1000 males, reflecting mass male outmigration as workers headed towards opportunities in 'mills, factories, docks and coal mines, or on the roads and railways, or in harvesting the crops of other districts'.[22] These opportunities lay in various parts of Bengal (including present-day Bangladesh), from Darjeeling in the north to Kolkata in the south and offered daily wages that were three to five times higher than what was available in Saran. Migration peaked between November and May which was the slack season in the agricultural calendar of Saran. Initially, migrants would 'tramp every foot of the way out and home' taking one or two months to reach their destinations.[23] With the advent of the railway line linking north Bihar to Kolkata, the volume and flexibility of migration streams grew as travel time was shortened to a few days.

Migration from Saran affected all the numerically significant castes—Brahmins, Rajputs, Ahirs, Koiris, Kurmis and Chamars—as well as Muslim communities. The occupations, however, varied with the upper castes being predominantly engaged in service professions in towns and cities and the lowest castes working predominantly as agricultural labourers. The jute mill towns that sprung up around Kolkata became an important destination for Saran's migrant workers in the 20th century. Migrant networks were crucial to secure jobs in the urban labour market and consolidated over the 20th century in particular sectors and firms. For instance, Saran's share of weavers in the Titaghur Jute Mill rose from a third in 1902 to three-fourths in 1991.[24] Female migration was not altogether absent but since the early 20th century, a combination of forces such as ideas of domesticity, male-dominated trade union politics and maternity benefit legislations led to the reduction of women's contribution to the jute industry of Kolkata.[25]

On the other hand, the women of Bihar were haunted by the women of Bengal amidst doubts that the *Bangaaliniya Sunnri*, or beautiful Bengali women, would seduce their husbands.[26] This theme is embedded in a rich culture of Bhojpuri folk songs on separated existence where the *purab* (the east) is portrayed as a dangerous site full of temptations. Celebrating the ideal loyal wife, Bhojpuri folk songs also lamented a life of exile, paradoxically for the woman of Bihar as she waited for her husband. The songs also talk of money and remittances and the gifts in store for those waiting and virtues of migration espoused by the migrants themselves. As noted by an official in the early 20th century, 'every coolie who emigrates, on his return becomes an apostle of it.'[27]

While Saran's migrant connection with Kolkata continued into the 21st century, it had also diversified its destinations like many other regions of Bihar. No longer was the male migrant only purab-bound. Kolkata's relative economic decline and the loss of agricultural fields to Bangladesh on account of Partition led migrants to seek new destinations west of Bihar. First, the fields of Punjab beckoned as the Green Revolution had led to a surge in demand for agricultural labour in the 1970s. Next, Delhi emerged as a powerful magnet for Bhojpuri-speaking migrant workers in the late 20th century for a variety of informal sector jobs. Economic dynamism in west India led to yet another option for migration. Finally, the Gulf countries have emerged as attractive destinations.

Unlike Ratnagiri and Udupi, Saran found itself among the poorest parts of India and the world in the 21st century. Mass migration had led to a widening of opportunities and a relatively secure source of income but could not dent poverty significantly at the regional level due to corrupt governance and persistence of unequal land holding patterns. The migration wave had given India its first President in Rajendra Prasad (1884–1963) and the activist Jayaprakash Narayan (1902–79) whose political movement defiantly opposed the Emergency imposed in the 1970s. But apart from this, it had little to celebrate as circular migrations rarely eased the pressure on the land and, in fact, sustained it. For Saran, its density, it would appear, was its destiny.

Cyclone Psychology: Ganjam in Odisha

In the middle of the 19th century, Henry Piddington (1797–1858), an English merchant who eventually settled in India, coined a new word—cyclone—to describe the peculiar pattern of circular wind movement witnessed during storms in the Bay of Bengal.[28] Having its roots in the Greek word 'kukloma', which meant a wheel or the coils of snakes, cyclones would cause intense damage and had a particular affinity for Ganjam district on India's east coast. Here, they would arrive with great thunder in 1864, 1887, 1909, 1938, 1942, 1968, 1972, 1981, 1984, 1999 and 2013.[29] How does one eke out a livelihood when your house and crops are destroyed once in fifteen years?

The Ganjami response to circular wind movements since the late 19th century has been simple: circular migration. To be more precise, it was circular mass male migration as the district's sex ratio rose from 970 females per 1000 males in 1872 to over 1100 in 1901 and hovered at that number for another six decades. The 'missing men' of Ganjam found a destination across the Bay of Bengal, long known to the people on India's east coast as *suvarna bhumi* or land of gold.[30] Boarding a steamer from the district's port of Gopalpur, they would head for Rangoon, the capital of Burma. Here, they would disembark and take up a multitude of occupations across lower Burma. Nearly half of them worked in the transport sector—railways, road and water—and another 15 per cent were engaged in rice pounding.[31] Burma had become the rice exporter of the world.

Rice harvesting and processing operations required labour which the Ganjamis were able to provide as Ganjam itself was known for its rice fields. Earthwork was another sector where the Ganjamis excelled and, according to one general manager of the Burmah Oil Company in the 1930s, the native Burmese efficiency level in earthwork was only 60 per cent that of the Odiya migrant worker.[32]

Ganjam district, part of the Madras Presidency, was predominantly Odiya-speaking but also had a fair share of Telugu speakers as it lay at the border of modern-day Odisha and Andhra Pradesh. Migration was prevalent across both these language groups and a variety of castes: Brahmins, Kalingis, Kapus, Malas, Velamas, Bavuris, Kollas and more. Migrants' social networks would often transcend caste barriers as entire villages were depopulated of men of working age. Between 1911 and 1921, the district experienced negative population growth rates on account of extensive migration. Over 5 per cent of its population was found to be working in Burma.[33] However, Ganjami outmigration rarely led to permanent settlement in Burma with departures occurring between October and December and return migrations observed between March and May. But in many sectors, migrants would return only after three or four years of work.[34] Remittances served as a lifeline for the district, increasing during times of distress induced by natural disasters.[35]

The turmoil in Burmese politics ejected the Indians out of the country in the middle of the 20th century, causing Ganjami migrants to seek new destinations. They would eventually turn a full 360 degrees, to the west coast of the Indian subcontinent. Gujarat replaced Burma and Surat replaced Rangoon as the city of disembarkation. The Gopalpur–Rangoon steamer line gave way to the Puri–Okha Express that snaked its way across India, covering over 2500 km in fifty-odd hours.

How or when this switch occurred remains a bit of a mystery. In the 1970s, there were migrants who were referred to as 'malias' in Surat, suggesting that they were first employed in the gardening and horticulture sector.[36] But by the end of the 20th century, they were firmly located in the powerloom sector in the city, weaving synthetic *kapda* (cloth) amidst clanging machines in small *karkhana*s (workshops). Today, even the most conservative estimates place the number of migrants from Ganjam district in Surat to be over a 1,00,000. More generally, over 5 per cent of the district's population works in Gujarat. Remittances, for a while, were sent through *tappawalla*s, an informal money transfer service run by the migrants themselves, until modern methods arrived. Migration continues to be male-dominated and sub-districts of Ganjam continue to have elevated sex ratios that they experienced a 100 years before. Just like in Rangoon, the Ganjami male migrant worker continues to save on accommodation costs by sharing his room in Surat with five to ten other workers in congested housing sites.[37]

Ganjam is not the poorest part of Odisha and the households that send migrants are not the poorest households either. Migration has evolved over a century as an important response mechanism to periodic natural disasters, embedded in a cyclone-related psychology. The returns to migration have been higher than in Saran but not as high as in Udupi or Ratnagiri. Ganjam also faces an additional health hazard of HIV-AIDS linked with the promiscuity associated with mass male migration to Surat. Yet, Surat is still seen as the new 'land of gold'. As one Ganjami migrant worker explained, 'Nobody leaves the city poorer than when they first arrived.'

Ganjam's labour contribution to the economies of Burma and Gujarat has been immense. It is perhaps fitting that one of its leading contributions at the national level was also on labour issues, from a son of its soil, V.V. Giri (1894–1980), first a labour activist, then a labour minister and finally President of India. Ganjam figures today on the tourist map as a crossover point to the spectacular Chilika Lake, which hosts nearly half a million migratory birds, some who visit all the way from Siberia, during the Indian winter months. Birds or humans, the Ganjami tradition of circular migration appears to be truly all encompassing.

Clusters and Corridors along the Coasts

Ratnagiri, Udupi, Saran and Ganjam are only some of the representative districts of the Great Indian Migration Wave. I estimate that over 150 of India's 600-odd districts belong to this migration wave at present, and most of these have experienced mass outmigration for several decades, if not centuries. In a few districts, outmigration has waned in intensity, while in some others the intensity has picked up only in recent decades. There are also districts left untouched by the migration wave, with many other regions acting as destinations, namely plantations, towns and cities. The Great Indian Migration Wave can be disaggregated by geographic regions, and the starkest divide occurs between the coasts and the hinterlands.

We begin our exploration of India from a particular part of the west coast that stretches from Ratnagiri to Kerala, bounded by the sea on one side and the Western Ghats on the other. It is a scenic destination and figures on many recommended road and rail trips. If you travel there today, you will also notice the proliferation of Western Union boards and the general lament about the shortage of labour. That is because this stretch of land is one of the most remittance-dependent regions in the world. That this stretch also constitutes a relatively more developed part of India in terms of incomes and education levels suggests that it is not just a simple story of poverty driving migration.

What unites this region is the historic connection with Mumbai via steamers since the late 19th century and the evolution of a tradition of migration eventually transcending that city.

For instance, few people would associate Goa, of all places, with outmigration. However, Portuguese Goa, like the Konkan, had turned from an 'agrarian to a remittance-based economy' in the late 19th century.[38] Sex ratios were elevated, reflecting mass male migration, and remittances financed Portuguese Goa's trade deficit with British India. Next to those beautiful beaches, people lined up at the ports to head towards Mumbai and other destinations to meet the 'demand for personnel who could meet European tastes in food, drink, music, dress and medicine' and where Christian migrants worked as 'cooks, stewards, butlers, musicians, tailors, ayahs and bakers'.[39] Baking was such a significant activity that Goan Catholics earned the sobriquet of being *maca paos*, a phrase still commonly used in Mumbai.

After Independence from the British in 1947 and Portugal in 1961, many traditional occupations of Goan migrants in the Indian subcontinent were curtailed. The Goans increasingly began to migrate outside India. Over the next five decades, overall outmigration intensities reduced but were still high in traditional hotspots such as Bardez and Salcete, where 30 per cent of households received international remittances. In recent years, nearly 60 per cent of Goan emigrants were reported to be working in the Gulf countries and many men were found to be working in no man's land—the oceans—as part of the merchant navy.[40]

Below Goa lies the Canarese region, which includes Udupi, and farther south is Kerala, now known for high circular migration just like the circularity of its language: Malayalam, a palindrome. While the 'Mallu' connection with outmigration is the butt of far too many jokes today (mass migration, after all, is quite the pheno*menon*), Kerala surprisingly entered the Great Indian Migration Wave relatively late. For a while in the early 20th century, Kerala was a region of net inmigration due to the plantations in Wayanad and Idukki.[41] Other forms of mobility existed, for instance, the settlement-based migrations from Travancore–Cochin in the south to Malabar in the north, or migrations towards Sri Lanka. Since the 1930s, male-dominated outmigration picked up towards various Indian cities, especially Mumbai. The first authoritative account of Mumbai's migrants was written in 1968 by one such male migrant, a Syrian Christian Malayali demographer, K.C. Zachariah, who would become the doyen of migration research in India.[42] But the floodgates of mass male migration from Kerala opened only in the 1970s with the surge in demand for labour in the Gulf countries following a hike in oil prices. Kannur and Thrissur districts were early entrants to the wave but by the end of the 20th century all districts participated in the migration wave and nine out of ten emigrants went to the Gulf. Within the Gulf, Saudi Arabia and the United Arab Emirates each absorbed a third of Kerala's emigrants. The others were distributed across Oman, Kuwait, Bahrain and Qatar.

We know more about Kerala's mass migration wave than any other part of India because of a series of pioneering migration surveys conducted by Zachariah and S. Irudaya Rajan over the past two decades. They showed how in a highly educated state with low prospects of employment, migration 'contributed more to poverty alleviation than any other factor, including agrarian reforms, trade union activities and social welfare legislation'.[43] They estimated that there were over 3 million non-resident Keralites in 2008 and showed how Muslims were over-represented in the migration wave, the variety of occupations the emigrants worked in—from construction to commercial plazas— the social costs of migration in terms of loneliness of the women left behind and, above all, the extent of money and gold that flowed from the Gulf to 'God's Own Country'. If Kerala were to be a country, it would rank among the five most remittance-dependent nations in the world as its remittance to GDP ratio stood at a staggering 30 per cent.[44] As I have pointed out, this is not a Kerala-specific story. It applies to the entire west coast below Ratnagiri in internal and international migration streams.

As we go around the tip of the subcontinent, we enter a new world of Tamil mass migration from the coastal plains of Tamil Nadu. Tamil migrations towards South East Asia have a long history but labour migration picked up only in the early 19th century, trotted in the late 19th century and galloped in the early 20th century with over a 1,00,000 people migrating annually. Migration was highly circular and fluctuated as per conditions in destinations as well as local crises such as the Great Famine of 1876–78 that led to a surge in migration volumes.[45] But Ceylon, now called Sri Lanka, Malaya and the Straits Settlements, now part of Malaysia and Singapore, and Burma attracted the bulk of migrations from the Tamil-speaking region. By 1930, Tamils represented around half of all overseas Indians as these three regions hosted nearly 70 per cent of all overseas Indians.[46]

From the southern cluster of districts, earlier called Tanjore, Tinnevely, Madura and Ramnad, migrants would head for Ceylon to work on coffee plantations. After the 1880s, it was tea plantations. From the heartland of the erstwhile Chola Empire that exported martyrs and merchants, labour would now flow at a steady pace to, literally, make tea. Crossing the sea would take a couple of hours, but it would take days to reach the plantation hills before the advent of the railways. These migrations were initially male dominated but became more gender-balanced over time to reflect the demand for female labour on tea plantations. They were also over-represented from the lowest castes, especially the Paraiyan caste.[47] From the north-eastern cluster of districts closer to Madras, migrants would head for the region comprising present-day Malaysia with a relatively more mixed caste and religious profile to work in rubber, sugar and oil palm plantations, and other assorted jobs. Towards Burma, Tamil migration was dominated by the Chettiar mercantile caste. World War II and the Japanese occupation of Burma and parts of South East Asia curtailed opportunities for migration. Later, thousands of workers were repatriated from Ceylon as well. These mercantile connections and mass expulsions will be discussed in greater detail in subsequent chapters, but suffice to say that when India re-engaged with the global economy in the late 20th century, Tamil labour outmigration resumed from the same clusters as before and with considerable intensity towards the Gulf countries and to a lesser extent, Malaysia and Singapore.[48]

Upwards on the east coast, after a momentary pause, the memory of historic mass male migration lies in the elevated sex ratios of districts north of the Godavari river basin—Vishakapatnam, Vizianagaram and Srikakulam—in the early 20th century.[49] This region, like Ganjam, was cyclone-prone and set off mass migrations of Telugu-speaking people who would comprise a major part of overseas migration to Burma and also form a small part of the Indian community in Malaya. The majority would work in Rangoon's vast informal economy and send home considerable amounts of money. Migration was important for many lower-caste labourers to improve social and economic mobility.[50] While outmigration involved a mix of castes and was male-dominated, women also went to Burma, working either as domestic helps or prostitutes.[51] Mass outmigration from this region is no longer as intense as it was, partly because of the rise of Vishakapatnam as an important port city in the 20th century. Coastal Andhra migrations towards Hyderabad, and later America, picked up in the second half of the 20th century. This was strongly reflected in Telugu cinema but those migrations were of a different nature, involving the elite classes.

Farther up along the east coast and past Ganjam, mass migration was firmly in place by the early 20th century in Puri, Cuttack and Balasore, then constituting the three districts of coastal Orissa. But unlike Ganjam, these Odiya-speaking migrants from the land of the majestic Konark Sun Temple set off for Calcutta to work as day labourers, palanquin bearers, doorkeepers, cooks and domestic servants and even in Assam's tea gardens.[52] Much of this migration wave was famine-induced and subsided in the middle of the 20th century. It revived later towards Gujarat—in industries and ports. Today, Odisha's entire coastal belt is a hotspot for outmigration with over a quarter of households receiving remittances from Gujarat and other major Indian cities. The remaining tract of the east coast, north of Odisha, was closely linked with migrations towards Kolkata and Dhaka but was not noted for high outmigration in the past. The other coastal tract that eluded the Great Indian Migration Wave was in the west—the region between Mumbai and Surat that would over time become a powerful industrial corridor. Amreli and Bhavnagar on the coast of Gujarat became major suppliers of migrants to Surat's diamond industry in the late 20th century, while Kachchh sent a large number of migrants to Mumbai and East Africa. The enclave of Diu, too, faced consistent outmigration. But, by and large, the coast of Gujarat stayed clear of the mass migration wave. Yet, as described above, over 60 per cent of India's vast coastline experienced persistent mass migration like the world had rarely seen.

Clusters and Corridors in the Hinterlands

Bounded by the Western and Eastern Ghats, the Deccan Plateau below central India was shielded from the sound and sights of mass migration at the ports. Though the region was ravaged by famines in the late 19th century, mass migration did not materialize here as it did in the coastal tracts. It escaped the net of colonial recruiters as it was governed largely by princely rule in the erstwhile states of Mysore and Hyderabad. Migration to towns and cities in this region was fairly gender-balanced and gradual. The recent growth of Pune, Bangalore and Hyderabad was largely based on migration from other urban locations and therefore these cities did not experience intense male-dominated labour migrations from rural areas as witnessed in Mumbai, Kolkata, Delhi and, more recently, Surat. The Malnad and Coorg coffee plantations and Nilgiri tea plantations in the south were important destinations of the Great Indian Migration Wave, but they often attracted labour from the coastal plains. Migration to the Kolar Gold Fields near Bangalore was mostly family-based and not very large in magnitude. Today, there are important tracts of short-term seasonal migration such as west Odisha, Raichur in Karnataka, Khandesh in Maharashtra and Mahbubnagar in Telangana which are slowly showing signs of joining the semi-permanent movements of the Great Indian Migration Wave.

Like the Deccan, much of west, central, and north-east India never became important source regions of the migration wave. Rajasthan has only recently emerged as a major hotspot for remittance-based migration towards Gujarat, Delhi and other major cities, but historically, labour outmigration was limited. Assam in the Northeast emerged as a major magnet for over a million Indians by the early 20th century by providing jobs on tea estates and construction works, among others. Five populous source region clusters in the hinterlands deserve particular attention: the Bhojpuri-speaking tracts of east Uttar Pradesh and west Bihar, Jharkhand, parts of Chhattisgarh, east Punjab and the Himalayan belt.

Density was a burden not only for Saran but the entire Bhojpuri-speaking belt, and this would in turn lead to similar migration destinies if not similar destinations. Their destinations were purab but many of the erstwhile districts of the eastern United Provinces, now Uttar Pradesh, such as Ballia, Ghazipur, Azamgarh, Fyzabad, Basti, Gonda, Gorakhpur, Banaras, Mirzapur and Jaunpur would became key recruiting areas for overseas migration to Mauritius, Fiji, Suriname, South Africa (Natal), the Caribbean and many other parts of the world in the late 19th century. Apart from density, this region also had pre-existing migratory links in military service and had what some have called a 'spirit of adventure'.[53] Commenting on the Bhojpuri's adventurous spirit, one scholar-official, in 1906, pointed out:[54]

> As fond as an Irishman is of a stick, the long-boned stalwart Bhojpuri, with this staff in hand is a familiar object striding over fields far from his home. Thousands of them have emigrated to British colonies and have returned rich men.

Rich or not, there were nearly 2,00,000 people, almost all men, from this region in Calcutta in 1901 and tens of thousands more in Assam, Bengal and Burma.[55] The region's outmigrant to population ratio was above 10 per cent, higher than what it is for Kerala today. Weaver migrations, especially of Momin Muslim communities, towards the textile towns of Malegaon, Bhiwandi, Dhule and even Bombay in the 19th century, contributed to the emergence of a new corridor being established towards Maharashtra by the end of the 20th century.[56] Today, Bhojpuri mass male migration extends in all directions within the Indian subcontinent, especially westwards and southwards, with a new line opening to the Gulf countries. Annual migration to the Gulf from Uttar Pradesh and Bihar now exceeds that from Kerala.

Unlike the Bhojpuri world, the Chhota Nagpur Plateau of Jharkhand is a hilly region with significant tribal or adivasi populations and is also rich in mineral resources. As a result, its migration history is quite different. The 'hill coolies', or Dhangars or Oraons, of this region were said to be good workmen on indigo plantations in the early 19th century. They were among the first recruits for the sugar plantations of Mauritius in 1834.[57] Overseas migration continued only for a couple of decades and was a tiny fraction of overall seasonal migration within the region. Between 1880 and 1920, two significant migratory routes opened. One was a gender-balanced stream towards the tea gardens of Assam that led to more permanent migrations, and the other was a male-dominated stream towards the Jharia coalfields in Dhanbad, over-represented by landless caste groups.[58] Ranchi and Hazaribagh divisions had extremely high outmigration rates of over 10 per cent in the late 19th century, but over the next century these rates declined to more moderate levels. Today, migration is directed towards the industrial towns of Jharkhand and other major Indian cities.

In Chhattisgarh, in the late 19th century, there was a small cluster of districts around Durg and Rajnandgaon that was noted for extremely high rates of outmigration towards the Berar cotton-growing belt of present-day north Maharashtra and for construction work for the railways, among other occupations and destinations.[59] They continue to have high outmigration rates even today. Similarly, mass outmigration from east Punjab towards the Gulf countries and Canada has deep roots. In 1956, historian K.L. Gillion observed that:[60]

> Of the Indians who went to Fiji outside the indenture system, the largest group was from the Punjab and most were Jat Sikhs from the adjacent districts of Julundur, Ludhiana and Hoshiarpur . . . They were almost entirely young male cultivators or herdsmen and many were younger sons. They

came with the intention of making money in agriculture or
trade and *returning*. [Emphasis added].

. . . most of them returned with money which had
important economic results in the villages, giving peasants
capital for the first time, as well as social results which were
also beneficial.

Sikh and Punjabi migration was closely tied up with the army,
police and government service in the early 20th century.
A similar case was observed in the Himalayan states of
Uttarakhand and Himachal Pradesh, but not so much in Jammu
and Kashmir, where outmigration intensities began climbing
over the 20th century to extremely high levels today. Today,
these migrations are overwhelmingly towards government
jobs and the large informal sector of Delhi.[61] The Great Indian
Migration Wave has therefore touched the Himalayas, the
Gangetic plains and the coasts and collectively covers over 20
per cent of the Indian population in the source regions. In
these regions, once the migration bug set in, people seemed to
acquire a madness to move.

Adventure, Indenture and Nomenclature

The Great Indian Migration Wave has, for the most part, been
voluntary in nature. It represents an adventure, the ability to
break out of the family's gaze and yet be able to support it, to
enjoy the city lights and the company of friends and relatives, and
finally to return home with the satisfaction of a life well spent, at
least in the eyes of the others. For many though, this would not
be the case as life would have cruel twists in store. The nemesis
could be a worldwide recession leading to unemployment. It
could be the landlord threatening to evict on account of delayed
rent payments, or it could be a simple piece of paper with the

word 'indenture' marked on it, a pre-passport visa to a new world of hope and, often, despair.

Organized emigration in India was initially associated with indentured migration that began in the 1830s. The system entailed fixed-term contracts of intensive labour, usually for three or five years, with no option to change the employer or terms of employment. The labourer was free to leave after the contract period ended. It came up in the 17th and 18th centuries to recruit poor Europeans for work in North America and played a major role in the 19th century colonial plantation economy after the formal abolition of slavery in some parts of the world. Charles Darwin was in Mauritius, a sugar plantation colony that used slaves, at this momentous time in 1836. He observed how little people cared about the abolition of slavery 'feeling confident in a resource in the countless population of India'.[62] When he did get to see Indians for the first time on the island, he keenly jotted down his observations, as he had done only a few months earlier on the finches in the Galapagos Islands that would eventually lead him to theorize on the evolution of species:[63]

> Before seeing these people I had no idea that the inhabitants of India were such noble looking men; their skin is extremely dark, and many of the older men had large moustachios and beards of a snow white colour; this together with the fire of their expressions, gave to them an aspect quite imposing.

Between 1831 and 1920, 2 million people were transported across continents through indenture contracts: one-third towards the Caribbean, one fourth towards Mauritius, a tenth towards South Africa and the rest scattered in numerous islands and regions including Fiji, Cuba, Peru and Hawaii. As many as 20 per cent of these migrants were sourced from China while 70 per cent

were sourced from India.[64] Within India, Calcutta was the
leading port of embarkation followed by Madras and, very
rarely, Bombay. By the late 19th century, of those who left from
Calcutta, two-thirds were recruited from present-day east Uttar
Pradesh, a fifth from central India, a tenth from Punjab and very
few from Bihar even though it was an important site initially.[65]

Closer home, indenture was used initially in migrations to
Ceylon and the Malaya region but it would fade away by the late
19th century, before the massive surge in migration volumes.[66]
A less known but equally significant stream of indentured
migration took place within India, towards the Assamese tea
plantations, with an estimated 2 million people moving over
several decades in the late 19th and early 20th centuries.[67] The
worst aspects of indenture were felt there as mortality rates were
exceptionally high and special legislations were introduced to
allow the planters the right to take penal action.

Overseas indentured migration from India was initially
overwhelmingly male-dominated, and it came to a point
where colonial officials had to forcefully mandate laws on
gender-balanced voyages in the 1840s. This led to just a slight
improvement as the share of female emigrants rose from next
to nil to around 25 per cent.[68] Women and men on indenture
would be dubbed 'coolies', a word whose origins could either lie
in the Tamil word 'kuli', which means 'wages', or the Turkish
word 'Quli', which means 'slave', or even the Chinese words
'k'u' (bitter) and 'li' (strength).[69] Indentured migration would
start with a recruiter, known as the *arkati,* scouting 'markets,
caravanserais, railway stations, bazaars, temples and urban
centres' for likely candidates who could be persuaded to embark
on the long journey.[70] In the first few decades of indenture,
this would often include extreme coercion, if not outright
kidnapping, as the concept of overseas travel was still new to the
labourers. To overcome this, the entire process of emigration

was brought under legislation with lasting legacies. In the 1840s, legal provisions introduced a 'protector of immigrants' at the port of disembarkation and a 'protector of emigrants' at the port of embarkation. The latter now survives as a department in India's ministry of external affairs. As per an Act of 1844, the protector of emigrants would ensure that 'no emigrant shall embark without a certificate from the Agent, countersigned by the Protector' leading to a curious phrase that is now imprinted in Indian passports as 'Emigration Check Not Required'.[71] After frequent protests and a long-protracted debate led by Indian political leaders, indenture was abolished to give way to the Emigration Act of 1922, which was again replaced in 1983 to govern contemporary labour emigration.

In the late 19th century, with better regulations and word of mouth advertisement of returning emigrants, indenture transformed into a kith-kin based system of migration that would be the hallmark of the Great Indian Migration Wave.[72] It is also worth emphasizing that indentured migration formed less than 10 per cent of all work-related migration during its period of existence.[73] Indenture has been seen as a 'new system of slavery' by some but was also an escape from an older system of slavery or domestic bondage induced by caste, and other pressures.[74] This is why the abolishment of the system did not stop migration from the key recruiting districts as they continued to supply migrants to different places for another 100 years.

The dominant form of labour recruitment of the Great Indian Migration Wave in the late 19th and early 20th century was through a contractor, with a wide-ranging nomenclature. Called Kangany in Ceylon and Malaya, Maistry in Burma, Sardar in other places, or Jobber in English, he would often be a production site foreman, labour recruiter and community headman who would bring in people from his village or neighbourhood to the doorstep of his employer, be it a mine, mill, port or plantation.[75] He spoke the same language as the labourers and had the confidence of capitalists. He could be a saviour, in which case his role would survive for decades, and in other places he would turn out to be a debt-raking villain leading to his eviction. Elements of this figure still survive in many seasonal migration streams in contemporary India, but for the most part, the Great Indian Migration Wave today operates less on indenture and nomenclature and more on a kith-kin based notion of adventure.

Railway Manic and Postal Magic

The railways played an important role in facilitating the Great Indian Migration Wave, but this was remarkably unforeseen at the time of its inception. During the hectic rounds of lobbying by private British companies in the 1840s, it was observed that Indians were 'poor' and 'thinly scattered over extensive tracts of country' and that revenue from railway services would be drawn mainly from goods traffic and 'not from passengers'.[76] Nothing could be further from the truth. In the first 100 years of the railways after its inauguration in 1853, annual earnings from passenger traffic were greater or almost equal to the earning from goods traffic.[77] Annual passenger traffic grew exponentially from 13 million in 1865 to 250 million in 1905 and over a billion in 1946, faster than the growth in population or size of the track network.[78] This fact, however, did not change the material conditions of travel in the Indian train and 90 per cent of passengers travelled in badly ventilated third-class carriages, tolerating the congestion in reward for speed.[79] A third-class carriage usually had fifty-six seats with each passenger getting less than seventeen inches of sitting space when twenty inches was thought to be permissible.[80] Toilets appeared in these carriages only in the 1900s.[81] For some decades, passengers were made to cram into goods wagons with livestock during peak traffic, even after the practice was banned in Britain.[82]

The blame for the disorderliness was inevitably passed on to the Indians. In 1929, journalist H. Sutherland Stark wrote a piece called 'Educating the Third-Class Passenger' which noted that Indians would 'hurl themselves at a half-open doorway in a suicidal effort to board a moving train' and were 'insufficiently taught how to travel like sane human beings'.[83] As a long-time traveller on the Indian Railways, I share some sympathies with such stark observations, but in reality the supply of services consistently fell short of the demand. Not surprisingly, this was one of the first issues Mohandas Gandhi (1869–1948) raised when he returned from South Africa in 1915 and embarked on a two-year discovery of India, often travelling in third-class railway carriages.[84] When political protests gathered steam, passengers slowly began asserting their rights. 'To stop train, pull chain', a common sign and rarely used service in trains even today, was popularized in the early 20th century as a way to alert authorities about the problem of overcrowding.[85]

Over the past century, the comforts of railway travel have improved but the high density of railway trains continues to haunt the migrant worker. As a commuter in Mumbai, I would watch passengers travel in the wrong direction for ten minutes in order to grab a seat for their hour-long journey. Similarly, in Odisha's Ganjam, I have seen migrant workers travel two hours in the wrong direction to Puri in order to get a seat for the fifty-three-hour journey of the Puri–Okha Express, that too after dutifully seeking blessings at Jagannath Temple. The third-class carriage is now called the 'general compartment' and moves with deafening silence, carrying the dreams of countless migrant workers.

The railways did not only move migrants from home to work. They were also the source of migrant work. Between 1853 and 1900, an estimated 8 million workers in south Asia were put to work to construct the railways.[86] The construction of the line in Bhor Ghat in the 1850s, which opened up Bombay to the Deccan, required over 3000 rock-cutting migrant workers, 6000 bullocks and 1000 carts to work in the hills on any given·day, and 42,000 workers in all to complete the project.[87] Millions of circulatory migrant workers have since then contributed towards building the railway network from scratch to over 90,000 km today.[88] The railways itself grew to be one of the largest employers of the world with over one million people, many of them migrants or made to move due to official transfers.

The railways, it is often argued, facilitated mobility that for the first time brought about a sense of unity in the subcontinent. Gandhi, a bitter critic of the railways, opposed this view but even he had to concede that it had brought Indians 'assembled under one roof'.[89] Bhimrao Ambedkar argued that caste practices were momentarily paused only during rail journeys and foreign travel.[90] However, for all its sheen, it should be remembered that the railways did not introduce the concept of travel in India and that it wasn't present in many of the corridors of the Great Indian Migration Wave—where carts, steamers and motor transport operated. The railways were not the most important institution in the lives of migrant workers. That distinction fell to the post office.

The Post Office of India, formally established in 1854, rapidly wove its way into the lives of migrant workers across the subcontinent.[91] Letters and telegrams were useful, but not so much for the illiterate migrant. It was the birth of the Indian postal money order in 1880 that dramatically changed the life of migrant workers by allowing a cheap, secure and reliable means of remittances. The money order was the first formal financial instrument used by the masses and was quickly lapped up in all the migration corridors within and outside India. It, however, posed a unique problem to the postal department in the initial years. Since most migrant workers were men, and remittance recipients were women, it was difficult to disburse cash from the regional post offices as prevailing gender norms restricted women's mobility. In 1884, the post office radically altered the money order system to provide home delivery of cash, a unique practice that survived until very recently. It also gave the postman in every village the position of being not just a harbinger of letters and news but also money. In the early 20th century, east Uttar Pradesh, the position of the postman was elevated to just below that of a policeman's, where he could exact 'a high price of undoing the straps of his money-order bag'.[92]

Compared to the railways, the postal department was unusually active in addressing migrants' concerns. Illiteracy was combated through innovative postal services. A class of professional letter writers emerged to assist remitters in filling up money order forms. Since 1896, thumbprints of payees were taken as marks of acknowledgment for the remitter. This slip was dubbed as a 'magic slip of paper' that for the first time served as an 'indisputable proof of payment' for labourers.[93] New types of money orders to make payments of rents also emerged. These postal innovations caught the attention of global media outlets. In 1898, an article in the *New York Times* pointed out the 'originality and vigor' of the Indian postal department and observed that:[94]

> The sepoy on active service, the coolie from distant provinces on the Assam tea gardens, and the domestic servant following his master's fortunes over the length and breadth of India, are as sure that their monthly wages will punctually reach their remote homes as if they paid over the money with their own hands.

Postal money order traffic grew so much that it amounted to 2–3 per cent of the Gross Domestic Product (GDP) between 1900 and the 1960s. In the Bombay of the 1930s, 'the practice of sending money orders had proved to be so disruptive' due to breaks taken from work that the Bombay Mill Owners Association approached the postal authorities to arrange for remittance services directly from the mill premises.[95] International postal money orders would pour in from overseas Indian emigrants who also had the option to remit through facilities provided by the protector of emigrants. Postal money orders gradually lost out to bank transfers and private money transfer operators in the last quarter of the 20th century and rapidly lost market share in the past decade.

Between 1880 and 2010, the post offices of India issued 7 billion postal money orders and formed the financial lynchpin of the Great Indian Migration Wave. The word 'money order' became an adjective as recipient regions were labelled as money order economies. Money orders supported the migrants' families and enabled them to stay away from home for longer periods. The trust in the postal service was supreme. I recollect a money order sent to my mother reaching my grandmother in a neighbouring house, only because the postman thought it wise to do so in my mother's absence!

The Wave Continues

It would be difficult to write the history of Europe in the late 19th century without acknowledging the significance of the 'Age of Mass Migration' between Europe and the rest of the world. Similarly, it would be hard to omit the 'Great Migration' of African–Americans within the US in its 20th century history. And yet, the migrations that I have described in this chapter, of greater scale and enduring significance, are rarely featured in historical works on modern India. This has happened because of a curious oversight whereby all historical labour migration of the colonial period has been associated with the indentured system that ended in the early 20th century, and a failure to acknowledge internal and international migration within a common framework.[96]

The framework presented here, in contrast, reveals the Great Indian Migration Wave, which stands tall among the big migration episodes of global history. The trans-Atlantic slave trade lasted for centuries but was coercive in nature. The migration of Europeans in the age of mass migration was intense, but not coerced, and lasted for less than seven decades. The on-going migration linked with Chinese urbanization is more voluminous than the Indian one but is also of much more recent vintage. In India, migration for marriage affects virtually all adult women, but most often it is not directly related to work. Compared to these episodes, the Great Indian Migration Wave is arguably the largest and longest non-coerced migration stream for work in documented history.

The social composition of the wave has varied across space and time, but it appears to be over-represented by the relatively richer folk today. Likewise, the initial causes of the migration were complex and varied. They include factors like cyclones and famines, unequal and unjust land tenure systems, new trade routes, better transportation, wage differences, aspirations and an opportunity to escape social restrictions. But as a general pattern, regions with high population densities, often sustained by easy access to water and pre-existing migratory networks either through military service or global trade, were crucial factors in determining why some regions were more likely to participate in the wave than others.[97]

What explains the tremendous persistence of the Great Indian Migration Wave even in the 21st century? To answer this question, one has to understand why most Indians chose to return home after working outside for many years, sustaining long-lasting circulatory paths. This was because of factors arising in both the source and destination regions. In some destination regions, permanent settlement was and is simply not possible due to horrendous and astronomically priced housing options, as in congested cities, and strict legislations on citizenship, as is the case with Gulf countries. The inability to settle due to hostile conditions in the destination regions automatically structured circulatory migration strategies. An even more powerful reason occurred in the source regions and revolved around gender norms. If caste norms had the ability to restrict one's movement overseas for certain periods in Indian history, gender norms almost always restricted women's mobility apart from marriage. This was noted by the post office when it was forced to change its money order delivery practices in the late 19th century. It was noted when I would ask the most awkward question on my interview schedule as part of research in 2011: 'Why don't you bring your wife to the city?' The answers or counter-questions of the migrant workers were nearly unanimous: 'Who will look after my parents back home?', 'What will she do here?'[98]

Not surprisingly, many migrants who had moved to the cities with their families had done so because their parents were either dead or did not require support. The second counter-question also points towards the demand for female labour in the destination region. Departures from the general pattern of the Great Indian Migration Wave occurred precisely when women could also work in destination regions such as the tea plantations of Assam and Sri Lanka and garment knitting textile hubs across India.

The regions affected by the Great Indian Migration Wave now have rich migration cultures embodied in songs, festivals and conversations. If you grew up in these regions, you are more likely to migrate during your lifetime and get infected by the adventurous spirit as it appears to be the general norm. These regions are also remittance economies with strong consumerist cultures, little manufacturing and a booming service economy. Women in particular gain considerable autonomy in nuclear families given the absence of their husbands but not so much in other family structures. They also have to look after the agricultural land and are less likely to participate in other sectors.[99] Most importantly, the Great Indian Migration Wave has restricted further impoverishment, even if it has not always been successful in raising standards of living dramatically. It is a unique model of development where entire regions become residential sites and work is located at some distance.

The clusters and corridors of the wave shifted over time and also criss-crossed the world. At times, two unrelated clusters would accidentally cross each other. For instance, Ratnagiri's political star, Tilak, would serve out a term of imprisonment in Burma between 1908 and 1914 at the same time that the last King of Burma—Thibaw—was serving his life in exile in Ratnagiri. Today, both Tilak's house and Thibaw's palace are on exhibit in the quaint town of Ratnagiri. In other times, two corridors could unexpectedly meet through a marriage alliance. The Rai-Bachchan name signifies as much the union of two acting talents as the union of families linked with two distinct migratory corridors, one from coastal Karnataka and the other from east Uttar Pradesh, both meeting in Mumbai.

Such unexpected interconnections between clusters will continue in the 21st century as there is no terminal date in sight for the Great Indian Migration Wave. Declining birth rates could dampen population growth and weaken the impetus for outmigration.[100] Increasing female outmigration for work, either individually or with family, could potentially change the nature of mass migration in India. Yet, it is quite likely that the persistent zones, especially in the Gangetic belt, will continue to send out migrants for several more decades, maybe even a century, just as they have been doing so in the past. If the Bihari migrant went purab in the 19th century and *paschim* (west) in the 20th century, *dakshin* (south) may be a major calling in the 21st century as large wage differentials overcome previous linguistic barriers. The north–south corridor within India will be the latest addition to the Great Indian Migration Wave, already reflected in the fact that over 2 million north Indians work in Kerala today. This will imply the continuation of a life of separated existence between father and child, and husband and wife, for millions of families. The migration songs will continue. After all, in that eternal song, Shamshad Begum's lyrical words of longing were matched eloquently by the male voice that regretted leaving home and wife:

> *Hum chhod ke Hindustan, bahut pachhtaye, bahut pachhtaye,*
> *Hui bhool jo tumko saath na lekar aaye.*
> *Hum Burma ki galiyo me, aur tum ho Dehradun,*
> *Tumhari yaad sataati hai, tumhari yaad sataati hai.*

3

Merchants and Capital

'As long as there remain opportunities for business among his own countrymen, there the Indian merchant will be found.'

—Mohandas Karamchand Gandhi[1]

M.K. Gandhi, born into a traditional Gujarati business community, experienced the Great Indian Migration Wave at close quarters during his long stay in South Africa. He saw that the Wave affected not only labour but also the capital and business enterprises that moved with it. These enterprises were closely linked with particular business communities whose migration trajectories started much earlier and whose destinations at times differed from those seen in the Great Indian Migration Wave. These communities were often perceived as villains, similar to how Shakespeare portrayed Shylock, a Jewish moneylender, in *The Merchant of Venice*. Nevertheless, in 2014, over 60 per cent of India's hundred most rich business leaders belonged to these communities that formed less than 5 per cent of the country's population.[2] Understanding the history of migration of these communities is critical in explaining their dominance in the world of Indian business. Who comprised these communities, where did they go and what did they do? To answer this, we must enter the fascinating world of the *Parsis*, *Chettiars*, Punjabis, Sindhis, Marwaris and Gujaratis, among others, and along the way even encounter the occasional Scot from Britain and the Jew from Baghdad.

Parsi Emigration and Efflorescence

The Parsis 'are probably the smallest community in the whole world, for they number scarcely a hundred thousand'. Thus began D.F. Karaka's majestic *History of the Parsis* in 1884, documenting the history of a community that would go on to have an outsized influence in shaping modern India. The community gave rise to India's first articulate economic nationalist, Dadabhai Naoroji (1825–1917), the first cotton mill entrepreneur, C.N. Davar (1814–73), and also the largest business conglomerate of the past century—the Tata Group. It gave rise to women stalwarts such as the pioneering lawyer Cornelia Sorabji (1866–1954) and freedom fighter Bhikaiji Cama (1861–1936) in the early 20th century, at a time when women rarely entered public life. Later, the community's contributions came in a variety of fields ranging from the armed forces (Sam Manekshaw) to science (Homi Bhabha) to law (Nani Palkhivala) and music (Zubin Mehta). By the end of the 20th century, the Godrej brand became synonymous with locks and steel cupboards. This remarkable Parsi efflorescence over 200 years has a unique migration history, linked in popular memory with sugar and ships and, perhaps not so popularly, with narcotics.

Parsis have bittersweet memories about their origins. They are bitter because they left Persia—hence the word 'Parsi'—after the collapse of the Sassanid Empire in the 7th century CE due to the persecution of their Zoroastrian faith that was founded in the first millennium BCE.[3] It is sweet because of the legend that on being asked why they [Parsis] should be accommodated in a land filled to the brim, they explained to the local ruler, Jadi Rana, who reigned over a part of present-day Gujarat in the 8th century CE, that they would be like sugar in milk—enhancing but not overwhelming.[4] Impressed, the ruler gave them permission to reside in Sanjan on the west coast, today equidistant between Surat and Mumbai, but on the condition that they learn the local language, wear no armour and that the women wear the local attire.[5] They did this, along with building a Parsi fire temple that dates back to 721 CE. For the next 300 years, their tribe would grow and move to other parts of India such as Cambay, Anklesvar, Surat, Variav and Vankaner north of Sanjan and Thana to the south. However, the sources are not clear about whether these migrations took place from Sanjan or directly from Persia. In 1142 CE, they were traced to Navsari and a few other parts of the Indian subcontinent in subsequent centuries. References to Parsis in historical records often come from travellers' observations about their distinct cultural practices such as that of Oderic, an Italian monk in India in the early 14th century:[6]

> The people thereof (Thana) are idolaters, for they worship fire and serpents and trees also, and here they do not bury the dead, but carry them with great pomp to the fields and cast them to the beasts and birds to be devoured.

War-related disturbances saw the Zoroastrian 'sacred fire' move to different places: Navsari in 1419, Surat in 1733 and Udvada in 1742, where it burns till date. In the 17th century, when a doctor was visiting Bombay in 1671, the Parsis were documented there for the first time. The doctor had noted a Parsi tomb on top of Malabar Hill.[7] The English East India Company had acquired Bombay in 1668 after the Portuguese ceded the islands

to England in 1661 as part of a dowry when the Portuguese
Infanta Catherine and the English King Charles II got married.[8]
The link between the Parsis and the Company, and Surat and
Bombay, would be crucial in the next phase of Parsi migration
as the economy of Surat declined compared to that of Bombay
in the 18th century. These links would be forged in shipping,
trading and tax farming.

The records of the East India Company mention Cursett,
a Parsi shipbuilder, in Surat in the late 17th century.[9] Much
later, Lowjee Nusserwanji Wadia, a Parsi foreman of a shipping
agent in Surat, was brought over to Bombay by the Company
to build the Bombay dockyard. The dockyard built over 350
wooden ships between the middle of the 18th and end of the
19th centuries and drew in a large number of carpenters and
artisans.[10] As the Company wielded greater power, cotton,
textile trading and tax farming—the practice of the government
outsourcing revenue collection—also attracted Parsi enterprise
in the 18th century. Weaving and liquor distillation were other
sectors of Parsi interest.[11] All these activities entailed Parsi
migration from the Navsari–Surat region to Bombay. Later,
their descendants would spur the industrial world of cotton
mills in the late 19th century.

In between these two epochs, the opium trade with China
'played a major role in making wealthy merchants out of Parsis'.[12]
The Readymoneys, a Parsi family, would be the first to settle
in China, but there were hundreds of Parsi traders who would
ply between Bombay and Canton by the middle of the 19th
century. The phenomenal rise of Jamsetjee Jejeebhoy (1783–
1859), the trading magnate, occurred due to a chance encounter
with William Jardine on a ship and the subsequent collaboration
with Jardine Matheson Company, the largest company involved
in the opium trade. He would defray much of this opium-driven
wealth during his lifetime by pioneering secular philanthropy

towards public institutions. In contrast to Jardine Matheson, a firm that continues to dominate the corporate world of Hong Kong and South East Asia, Jejeebhoy's business does not have a strong legacy, but his philanthropic contributions still dot the city of Mumbai with several institutions bearing his name, best known by his initials 'J.J.'

The opium and cotton trade was initially important for the Tata family too, but by the end of the 19th century J.N. Tata (1839–1904) was focussed on cotton mills and his dream project—a state-of-the-art steel plant.[13] He would not live to see the steel plant in action in 1911, but two months after his death, his nephew, J.R.D. Tata (1904–93) was born, who grew up to oversee the dramatic expansion of the Tata Group in the 20th century. J.R.D. Tata's migratory links included Paris, the city he was born in to his French mother, as well as his pioneering contributions to India's air passenger service that finally became Air India.

At the turn of the 20th century, there were over 80,000 Parsis in British India, more than half of them in the city of Bombay, 6000 in Surat and 2000 in Bharuch.[14] They formed 7 per cent of Bombay's population, which exceeded 7,00,000. They were quite a settled population by then as 70 per cent of them were born in the city. In Bombay, twenty-six of the forty-six shipbuilders and boat-makers, and thirty-three of the eighty-four civilian engineers, were Parsis. Not a single Parsi was enlisted in the army, a fact perhaps compensated for several decades later when Sam Manekshaw commanded India to victory in the Indo–Pak war of 1971. Some 3000 Parsis outside British India, many in the trading ports of China, and 8000 people in Persia were said to profess the ancient Zoroastrian faith.

Over the next century, the size of the Parsi population in India would peak at over a 1,00,000 in 1941 and then remarkably *decline* to less than 60,000 today according to the

most recent Census. The factors for this decline include low
fertility, outmigration to other countries combined with little
internal migration and conservative Parsi community laws on
interreligious marriage. What Karaka had written in 1884 still
holds true—the Parsis are probably the smallest community
in the world today—but one can add that as long as Bombay
House, Tata's head office, remains powerful, they will always
be in the news.

Chettiar Credits

Chettinad in south India is famous for exporting its mouth-
watering cuisine, which involves a rich variety of spices and
curries, to major metropolitan kitchens around the world. The
cuisine blends local ingredients and styles with those observed
outside India. The kavuni arisi, a black sticky rice pudding,
is said to have a Burmese flavour while the idiyappam, or
string hopper, has a Sri Lankan influence. These multicultural
adaptations occurred because Chettinad, home to less than a 100
villages, was until recently the headquarters of a large financial
empire straddling both South and South East Asia.

Located in southern Tamil Nadu, Chettinad lies in a region
spanning the erstwhile princely state of Pudukkottai and Ramnad
district. It is the land of the Nakarattar or Nattukkottai Chettiars, a
prominent merchant–banking caste, whose population rose from
10,000 at the turn of the 20th century to around 1,00,000 at the
turn of the 21st.[15] The first historical record of this community
dates back to the 17th century when they were documented
as salt traders in south India.[16] In the 18th century, they were
identified as traders of pearls, arrack, cloth and rice in places like
Sri Lanka and Calcutta. Around 1808, they established their first
banking firms in Malacca, followed by Penang and Singapore.[17]
These firms served small Indian and Chinese traders by providing

medium- and long-term credit. The Malaya region was emerging as an important junction in the global trading system, especially in the lucrative opium trade between India and China. By the middle of the 19th century, the bulk of this trade in Singapore passed through Chettiar hands.[18]

The stunning rise of Chettiar wealth would occur in the early 20th century thanks to the tea, rice and rubber fields of Sri Lanka, Burma, and Malaya respectively. In these places, the Chettiars formed a unique migratory chain that financed the expanding frontiers of the cultivation of these products. This involved agents, associations and a certain amount of asceticism.[19] Chettiar families would send out agents to remote places and occupy the position of the local village moneylender. Almost all the big villages of lower Burma, for instance, had a financial connection with Chettinad through these agents. Agents were young men who worked for three years and tried to maximize their returns from lending. After accumulating profits over several terms, they would become independent and have their own agents. Chettiar associations would coordinate these activities in different places, especially the setting of interest rates that ranged from 10–40 per cent per annum. Money was rarely spent in the places the Chettiars migrated to as they practised a life of austere living. Savings were either re-invested into business or remitted back to India as profits. Remittances would finance the upkeep of the Shaivite Chettinad temples and the construction of grand mansions and palaces that still survive. Chettiar migration, therefore, closely followed the pattern of the Great Indian Migration Wave as it was male-dominated, semi-permanent and remittance-based.

At the peak of their power in the 1930s, estimates suggest that the Chettiars had 1650 firms in Burma, 1000 each in Malaysia and Singapore, 500 in Sri Lanka, 200 in French Indo-China (Vietnam, Laos and Cambodia) and 150 in other East Asian regions.[20] The

Great Depression was the first shock that knocked the wind out
of these sails. The collapse in world trade affected the peasants'
ability to repay debts and, overnight, the Chettiars became
owners of large tracts of land that they held as collateral. In lower
Burma, they came to occupy a quarter of the rice-cropped area.[21]
In the past, the Chettiars would sell the land back when trading
conditions improved, but the Great Depression was far more
intense than previous crises. Nationalist outpourings against them
in Burma and the Japanese invasion of South East Asia sealed the
deal for the Chettiars, who returned home empty-handed.

The big Chettiar groups—Rajah Sir Muthiah, M.A.
Chidambaram, M.Ct. Muthiah, A.M.M., Karumuthu,
Somasundaram—turned inwards and started investing in sectors
beyond banking such as cotton textiles, fertilizers and engineering
goods. Most Chettiars turned towards government jobs and
other occupations. The heyday of the Chettiar financial empire
is over. What remains in Chettinad are the grand mansions
built using Burmese teak, and an occasional reminder to the
Burmese government about their past migration and business.
In 2007, the Chettiar-run Burma Investors Group was formed
to stake claim on assets worth over Rs 1 lakh crore remaining
in Burma.[22] If that ever materializes, there will undoubtedly be
celebrations in Chettinad, that too with a lot of kavuni arisi.

Punjabi Wanderlust

Bollywood cinema routinely takes its audience to lands they
cannot visit, mountains they cannot climb and lavish weddings
they can never afford. Escapist cinema requires imagination, but
above all it requires capital and experience. Bollywood's escapist
ideals have been influenced by the Punjabis, especially those
belonging to business communities that enjoy an extraordinary
migration history.

Punjabi mercantile migration is synonymous with the Khatri community which includes surnames such as Kapur, Chopra, Mehra and many others that have routinely made their way into Hindi cinema. Historically, the caste position of the Khatris has been ambiguous with their claims of Kshatriya status clashing with a robust Vaishya culture of trade. Ambiguity also lent itself to complexity as Khatris transcended religious boundaries during the 16th and 17th centuries, when Sikhism came up as a new religious doctrine. The spread of Sikhism itself in Punjab was facilitated by the growth of the Khatri merchant network in this period.[23] The Sikh gurus were drawn from the Khatri community, and the Sikh philosophy welcomed mercantile ideals leading to a steady uptake of the new religion among the Khatris.

The Khatri merchant network is ranked among the earliest Indian diasporas outside the subcontinent. Between the 16th and 20th centuries, the Khatris spawned a mercantile diaspora of over 20,000 people across the Hindu Kush—in Afghanistan, Iran, central Asia and even Russia.[24] They would also migrate eastwards from Punjab into the Gangetic heartland cities such as Delhi, Agra, Lucknow, Allahabad, Mirzapur, Varanasi and Patna. From the late 19th century, along with other Punjabi communities, they would spread out to set up shop practically everywhere in the world.

An important source of these migrations was Multan, a part of greater Punjab that is now in Pakistan, a key trading node between the Mughal and Safavid (Persian) empires, and also central Asia. Multani Hindu traders, essentially Khatris, had close links with Persia. According to a French traveller's account in the 17th century, they had the same occupation as Jews and surpassed them in their usury.[25] Khatri merchants were not only traders of textiles, spices and horses along the caravan trade between India and central Asia, but they were also important moneylenders and played a role similar to that of the Chettiars in South East Asia. Moneylending was an important way to invest idle money received on completion of a trade, and over time was critical in supporting the agricultural economies in parts of Iran, Afghanistan and central Asia. The other important trade in this region was the slave trade, but evidence of Khatri involvement in this sector is scant or undocumented, though it cannot be ruled out given the sheer scale of the trade.

According to historian Scott Levi, Hindu merchants enjoyed considerable state protection in Islamic central Asia, a factor integral to the growth of their commercial network.[26] A 17th century farman, or official ruling, in Bukhara, now in Uzbekistan, stated as much:[27]

> We are thinking about the condition of the greater community of people . . . The goods and property of these people should not become ruined; they are protected. Their protection will come from here and their hopes should be directed to Bukhara. Regarding the Hindus who live in the territories of Bukhara, Balkh, Badakhshan, Qunduz, Taliqan, Aibek, Ghuri, Baghlan, Shabarghan, Termiz, Samarqand, Nasaf (Qarshi), Kish, Shahrisabz, and wherever else they may live: who knows the *aqsaqal* (community elder) must obey and respect him as he is working in their best interest.

Khatri merchants lived in caravanserais during their long sojourns that lasted several years and lived separately in quarters marked for Hindu merchants.[28] They could celebrate Diwali and Holi and follow other religious practices inside these quarters with rites being performed by Brahmin migrants who circulated with the mercantile diaspora. They could also participate in other celebrations by consuming alcohol and narcotics which were prohibited for the local population. This caused some friction, but more than liquid it was smoke that caused resentment among the locals who simply could not fathom the Hindu cremation ceremony.[29] The ashes would then come back to India on the return journey, perhaps giving a new interpretation to the Hindu belief in 'transmigration' of the human soul.

Khatri merchant migration was male-dominated and semi-permanent in nature.[30] The principal directors of the trade were based in greater Punjab and entrusted their wares and capital to agents who would return after several years, if not decades. Returning agents would have to produce their *bahis*, or books of accounts, to their directors to square trading positions, repay debts, or deposit a part of the profits. In the interim, information would flow across towns through travelling merchants and *hundis*, sophisticated financial instruments that limited the use of physical currency.

The merchant network flourished until it received its first jolt around the middle of the 18th century with the collapse of the Safavid Empire and Nadir Shah's invasion of Delhi. This led to significant relocations towards the east and south, especially to Shikarpur, where merchants slowly began to reassemble their mercantile strength. The connections with central Asia remained strong and extended till Russia, in the port city of Astrakhan by the Caspian Sea. With the Russian conquest of Tashkent in 1865, a new administrative policy was drawn, one that seriously restricted the scope of Indian mercantile activities.[31] This attitude was shaped by concerns of growing Indian ownership of agricultural land, much like the later experience of the Chettiars in Burma. Along with the expansion of the Russian empire in central Asia, the mercantile diaspora of Punjab began to recede to negligible numbers by the middle of the 20th century. Unlike the Chettiars, however, they were able to relocate their wealth in time.[32] The Partition in 1947 was the next shock that led to much devastation and the influx of a large number of entrepreneurs into the Indian side of Punjab as refugees, who then played an important role in establishing manufacturing clusters in Punjab, especially the bicycle industry.[33]

A different wave of Punjabi migration around Hoshiarpur began to extend within the Indian subcontinent, and to the world in the second half of the 19th century, often tied up with the Great Indian Migration Wave of labour. In addition to mercantile groups like the Khatris and Aroras, this included the Jat Sikh and non-Sikh peasant groups who migrated as soldiers, traders and entrepreneurs. Punjabi mercantile migration within India in the 20th century was associated with commercial towns and big cities such as Mumbai. The migration of Punjabi capital was instrumental in the development of Bollywood and the establishment of several industrial enterprises, such as Mahindra's automotive venture. From the beginning of the 20th century, and accelerating towards the end of it, Canada and the US also became major magnets of Punjabi migration. There, the road from agriculture and labour work towards entrepreneurship was slow and uneven but not uncommon.[34] For instance, Didar Singh Bains, a descendant of a family drawn from Hoshiarpur to the US in the early 20th century, would emerge as one of the largest peach growers in California by the end of the century. Thus, Punjabi wanderlust sent people and money far and wide across the world. The spirit was infectious and certainly caught on in neighbouring Sindh.

The Global Sindhi Stereotype

Sindh lies where the Indus meets the Arabian Sea, and is now a province in present-day Pakistan. It was earlier a part of the Bombay Presidency from 1847 to 1936.[35] With riverine origins, the Sindhis have meandered across the world through different circular migratory paths over the past few centuries. Within India, the Sindhis usually refer to Hindus who migrated from Sindh either before or after Partition with a high proclivity of having surnames ending in 'ani', as in Advani, or 'ja', as in Raheja.

The Hindu Sindhis are today seen as offshoots of the disintegration of the British Empire, but the community has historically been mobile and was itself a creation of the messy disintegration of the Mughal and Safavid empires in the 18th century.[36] To escape violence and declining commercial opportunities, many Khatri merchants from Multan, and the broader Punjab region, headed south towards Sindh. Here, they would lose some of their pre-migration identities and be absorbed into the Lohana caste which would over time dominate the Hindu population of Shikarpur and Hyderabad towns in Sindh, and form a fifth of the Hindu population in Karachi.[37] Within the Lohana grouping, two important sub-castes were the *Amil*s in administrative services and the *Bhaiband*s in trade and commerce. Outside the Lohana group were the Sindhi Bhatias and Brahmins, and they collectively exhibited a multicultural ethos which respected Guru Nanak, the founder of Sikhism (most Hindu Sindhis are *Nanakpanthi*s), the pantheon of Hindu gods, especially their beloved Jhulelal, and Sufi pirs.

From the middle of the 19th century, Sindhi men began migrating to set-up an unusually wide transnational mercantile network stretching 'from Bukhara to Panama'.[38] Bukhara (Uzbekistan), central Asia and later the Indian subcontinent would be destinations for the Shikarpuri bankers to finance trade. The *Sindworki*s of Hyderabad would sell products from Sindh, mainly handicrafts, in all leading ports of the world which served as popular stops for travellers, going as far as Panama in Central America in the west and Kobe and Yokohama in Japan in the east. Closer home, Bombay attracted a number of Hindu Sindhis for trade and entrepreneurship.

Chicago Radio, the loudspeakers on which the Indian freedom movement was relayed to the masses, was the brainchild of one such Sindhi migrant entrepreneur—Nanik Motwane (1902–70).[39] His father, Gianchand Chandumal Motwane (1878–1943), worked with the telegraph department of the Sind government for some time, set up Eastern Electric & Trading Co. in Sukkur in 1909 that dealt in imported torchlights and telephones, and moved to Karachi in 1912. After setting up more branches and widening his import base to include the US, he moved to Bombay in 1919 to increase the scale of his business. Here, he set up the Chicago Telephone Supply Co., mimicking the name of an American company, after taking due permission, to deal in the growing business of telephone installations. One day in the 1920s, Nanik Motwane saw Gandhi struggling to make his voice heard from a public platform. He took it upon himself to supply loudspeakers for the political movement. Henceforth, Motwane's most important client would be the Indian National Congress, even supporting the 'Congress Radio' used during the Quit India movement of the 1940s. The Sindhis' global migratory and trading links, entrepreneurship in India and penchant for electronic goods were visible well before 1947.

Partition only extended these lines farther by pushing out a large number of Hindus from Sindh to India and around the world. The Sindhis' love for trading in electronic and radio goods accelerated and formed a veritable stereotype of the community abroad. Manohar Rajaram Chhabria, a small radio parts dealer in Bombay, would go to Dubai in the 1970s and start a firm that would be one of the world's largest distributors for Sony, a Japanese electronic goods giant.[40] Outside electronics, the Hinduja family from Shikarpur set up a commodities trading base in Iran, but like the displacement caused by the downfall of the Safavid regime two centuries earlier, the family had to relocate, this time due to the 1979 Islamic Revolution.

The Hinduja group, then headquartered in London, went on to become one of the largest transnational business groups with an Indian heritage, owning firms such as Ashok Leyland and Gulf Oil. Sindhi business tycoons came up in the Persian Gulf (Micky Jagtiani), Uganda (Madhvani), Nigeria (Chanrais), and virtually every country where they had a significant base.

The global Hindu Sindhi diaspora outside India is spread over 100 countries with estimates varying between a 1,00,000 and a million people.[41] Within India, the Raheja and Hiranandani groups are big names in real estate. The connection with electronics goods—Gulu Mirchandani of Onida TV fame—also persists, as does the house of Motwane. Sindhis constitute 0.2 per cent of the Indian population but accounted for 7 per cent of the hundred richest Indian business leaders in 2014.[42] The Sindhi diaspora within India consists of well over two million people, a third of them residing in Maharashtra, a fifth in Rajasthan and a sixth each in Gujarat and Madhya Pradesh.[43] Almost all Sindhis live in urban areas and are generally associated with trade and business. Apart from Mumbai, Thane and Ahmedabad, which host hundreds of thousands of Sindhis each, they also live in sizable numbers in Jaipur, Barmer, Ajmer, Indore, Bhopal, Raipur, Pune and Nagpur. In 2001, as many as 135 of India's 593 districts had over 1000 Sindhis while 465 districts had at least one Sindhi speaker, reflecting the march within the country. Migratory links have also extended southwards with over 30,000 Sindhis now living in parts of south India.

Hyderabad, in particular, has a special connection with the Sindhis as it was a post-Partition migrant Sindhi entrepreneur, Khanchand Ramnani, who started the Karachi Bakery in 1953. The brand value of this confectionary has grown so much that it has become synonymous with the city of Hyderabad itself. The franchise has now reached Delhi airport too where it greets hundreds of thousands of travellers and migrants every day, a gentle reminder to the city that migrant Sindhi contributions can come not only in the form of political leaders such as Karachi-born L.K. Advani but also through delightful plum cakes and biscuits.

Marwari Migration and Dominance

In 1844, the *Bombay Times and Journal of Commerce*, now known as the *Times of India*, ran a brief piece titled 'Beware of the Marwaries', exhorting their readers to pay 'special attention' to the account of one Mr Punditrao:[44]

> These Marwaris leave their own country for the purpose of trading, and they are spread all over Hindostan. A Marwari's shop may be seen in a hamlet, consisting of only four or five cottages; in fact, were you to search all Hindostan, it would be difficult to find an agricultural village without a Marwari. When they arrive here they commence by selling gram, and, in the course of four or five years, they become opulent bankers. The causes of this are their unjust dealings . . . Therefore, my advice to my countrymen is this, that they avoid entering into any transactions of this nature with such deceivers as these.

The newspaper did not take its own advice seriously. A century later, its ownership fell into the hands of a Marwari family. By then, the Marwari community and its power had extended beyond trading and moneylending to dominate the world of industry and big business. They would emerge as the most enigmatic, celebrated and vilified business community of India.

The puzzle about the Marwaris begins with the name. Marwar belongs to the western part of Rajasthan around Jodhpur, and yet a large number of Marwaris outside Rajasthan do not trace their roots to this region. Most Marwaris are, in fact, Shekhawatis, referring to a region in northern Rajasthan, close to Jaipur. It is here, for instance, that you will come across Pilani, the roots of the famous Shekhawati, or Marwari family, the Birlas. Further, Marwari in popular lingo does not refer only to a region but also to Banias or those who engage in commercial occupations. This is closely tied up with the Vaishya caste within the Hindu fold and the Jains outside it. Within them, there are three main divisions—Aggarwals, Maheshwaris and Oswals—which comprise around 6 per cent of Rajasthan's population with distinct regional variations.[45] The Aggarwals are more prominent in northern Rajasthan while the other two are relatively more prominent in the western and southern parts of the state.[46] One could therefore be a Kolkata-based Shekhawati Aggarwal Jain or a Mumbai-based Jodhpuri Oswal Hindu. Such sub-group identities often matter in the close-knit marriage market. Today, they are generally known to outsiders as those engaging in commercial occupations and having roots in Rajasthan.

The term 'Marwari' dates back to the founding of business houses outside Rajasthan, in Bengal, Bihar and Orissa during the Mughal rule.[47] These links are said to have been established through the Rajput army on the Mughal side as many traders and *modis* (suppliers to the army) accompanied them. Over time, they established themselves along key towns of the Gangetic waterways and also extended their network towards central Asia. Apart from trading, banking was also a prominent activity as land revenues in many regions were paid in cash. As Mughal power declined in the 18th century, merchant-bankers became important for exchanging coins, financing trade and brokering political power. According to one historian, 'from Astrakan [in Russia] to Dacca, finance and commerce came to be dominated by the Marwaris in the first half of the 18th century.'[48] The most famous firm was the house of Jagat Seth ('banker of the world'), the Oswal Jains who were most likely from Bikaner and served the Nawabs of Bengal in Murshidabad and financed European trade before eventually playing a key role in securing victory for the British in the Battle of Plassey in 1757.[49] The subsequent decline of Murshidabad and the rise of Calcutta in eastern India, mirroring the decline of Surat and the rise of Bombay in western India, led to a new wave of Marwari migrations to both upcoming cities. The number of Marwaris in Calcutta rose from eighty in 1813 to 600 in 1833.[50]

As British rule slowly consolidated over the Indian subcontinent, Marwaris participated in the cotton, cloth and opium trade in north Indian urban centres, financed through the intricate hundi system of bills of exchange. In the Maratha and Hyderabad courts, they worked as bankers and contractors. With commercialization of agriculture in the 19th century, Marwaris also found a role as moneylenders in rural areas. Just like the Chettiars, the Marwari network began to expand in the hinterland between Bombay and Calcutta, through agents, associations and a certain amount of asceticism. Young men would set forth to new towns, live in congested *bassa*s or collective messes run by Marwari firms and associations, and learn their first trading skills through apprenticeships.[51] Shivnarain Birla (1838–1910), for instance, set forth from his village of Pilani for Bombay in 1858. It took him a twenty-day camel ride to reach Ahmedabad, the nearest railway station, and then a train to Bombay. Child marriage was a common practice, which meant that when these men left they would already be married and their wives would be left behind. Agents and sub-agents would settle in villages, live austerely and remit money back to their birthplace. In the 19th century, Shekhawati migration had increased considerably while remittances facilitated the building of community wells, local temples and now famous grand havelis. Marwari migration in the 19th century represented the Great Indian Migration Wave of capital, accompanying the labour routes towards mill towns and plantations as far as Assam and Burma.

At the turn of the 20th century, there were around 15,000 Marwaris in Calcutta, working almost exclusively in the Burrabazaar, as large firm owners, brokers and speculators in the cloth and jute trade.[52] There were over 10,000 Marwaris in Bombay, clustered around Bhuleshwar and Crawford Market. Hyderabad in the south was home to several thousand Marwaris who had first come as jewel and shawl merchants in the early 19th century. Madras and Rangoon hosted 500 Marwaris each while another 10,000 were distributed across the fourteen districts of Assam. But the biggest concentration of Marwaris was in the region that is present-day Maharashtra. As many as 60,000 Marwaris worked as traders and moneylenders here. It was here that the first major violent uprising of peasants against moneylenders would occur in the form of the Deccan Riots of 1875 in the districts of Poona and Ahmednagar.[53] High interest rates and strict discipline enforced in repayment were the reason to spark off protests. Similar protests against Marwaris in Bengal and Assam in the late 19th century would cast a negative image on the community that took time to shake off. Bengali nationalist P.C. Ray, in fact, would go to the extent of calling the Marwaris 'parasites' who were draining the wealth from Bengal, much like the British.[54] Perhaps spooked by such views, in the early 20th century, Marwari engagement in the public sphere grew through charity, philanthropy and above all, the freedom movement. If Marwari capital had 'placed the feet of the English' inside India in the 18th century, it would also ensure their departure as it played an important role in financing the activities of Gandhi and the Indian National Congress.[55]

Marwaris made the transition from trade to industry, famously into Calcutta's jute mills, relatively late, in the early

20th century. Post-Independence, the significance of Calcutta in
the Marwari world declined. Militant trade unions led to capital
flight and the Marwaris began leaving Calcutta in large numbers
for other Indian cities, especially Delhi and Bombay. Marwaris
also left earlier settlements in the Gangetic belt and the Assam
valley towards places with better opportunities. Significant
female migration had begun with speedy and safe passage assured
by trains after the completion of a railway corridor linking
Shekhawati and Calcutta in 1916. Over the 20th century,
Marwari male-dominated semi-permanent migration gave way
to more permanent migration of families.[56] By the end of the
20th century, the Marwari diaspora exceeded 2 million, a third
of which was located in seven major cities. Mumbai now hosts
the maximum number of Marwaris with other metropolitan
cities such as Pune, Chennai, Hyderabad and Bengaluru catching
up with Kolkata. The largest concentration, however, continues
to live in the districts and smaller towns of Maharashtra such
as Nashik, Jalgaon, Dhule, Ahmednagar, Solapur, Aurangabad,
Chandrapur and more. Collectively, this region hosts nearly a
million Marwaris who continue to be associated with trading
and moneylending but have also moved into other sectors
such as cultivation, irrigation, construction and real estate. The
rise of Nandlal Dhoot, founder of the billion-dollar Videocon
Group, is an example of successful Marwari entrepreneurship
from this relatively unheard of Marwari diaspora. He studied in
Ahmednagar and Pune, made profits from sugarcane and cotton
cultivation and set up a sugar mill in 1955 before becoming one
of the first industrialists from the Marathwada region.

Marwari migrations have been closely linked with state
patronage, a flair for spotting opportunities in new regions and
also moving out early from regions with declining opportunities.
In the early 20th century, the largest Chettiar firms were
richer and more global than the Marwaris, but by the 1960s

the prominence of these firms had fallen and Marwaris formed a fourth of the business elite.[57] By 2014, there was only one Chettiar name among India's hundred most rich business leaders compared to a staggering thirty-two Marwaris, the maximum from a single community.[58] Socially conservative and financially brilliant, the Marwaris today dominate the world of big business, and also small business in specific sectors such as trade. The core Marwari investment and diasporic network grew within India, arguably because Rajasthan was not a coastal region with historic international trading connections. This set them apart from the other community synonymous with the world of Indian business: the Gujaratis.

The Enterprising Gujarati

Compared to Marwari commercial brilliance that was achieved by a few groups in Rajasthan with a large internal network, Gujarati commercial success has been more secular and transnational. Gujarati entrepreneurship stretches widely from Assam to Tamil Nadu and East Africa to the US. It goes beyond the traditional *Vaish*–Jain folds and also cuts across religions as it had hosted the Parsis, as discussed earlier, and commercially successful Muslims, discussed in a later section. It also touches most areas within Gujarat, from Kachchh in the west to Saurashtra in the middle and Ahmedabad and Surat in the east.

Gujarat's coastline of over 1000 kilometres is an important part of this story. The coastal towns of Mandvi, Dwarka, Porbandar, Somnath, Diu, Bharuch and Surat have historically been conduits of spatial mobility for merchants and pilgrims. The towns of the hinterland were equally important for internal trading routes, especially for cotton. Since the 15th century, Ahmedabad, and its famous Manek Chowk, began to gain commercial prominence. This long history of trade and exposure to traders from other parts of the world allowed for the idea of business to be associated with respectability. A French traveller in the early 19th century commented that trade was not taboo in Gujarat, and even Brahmins were 'excellent men of business'.[59] The cotton textile industry of Ahmedabad in the late 19th century was started by one such Brahmin, Ranchhodlal Chhotalal, after which the traditional Vaish–Jain trading communities such as the Sarabhais and Lalbhais entered the fray.[60]

The Gujaratis' love for business transcended linguistic boundaries through mercantile and entrepreneurial migration. It has been so widespread that it is difficult to single out a period or event, or even a destination, as the initial wave of migration. The first Gujarati migrations are usually associated with the Arabian Sea, extending downwards along the coast of Africa and the Indian Ocean, similar to Chettiar migration along the Bay of Bengal.

Apart from these, another migration stream has branched out within the subcontinent over the past three centuries. More recently, in the 20th century, Europe and the US have drawn in hundreds of thousands of enterprising Gujaratis. These three broad migration waves were often interconnected.

The Gujarati Jains were arguably the first movers. They traded with Arab merchants in the Indian Ocean during the Solanki period between the 10th and 13th centuries. Later, they received preferential treatment in Portuguese-occupied port towns in East Africa in the 16th and 17th centuries.[61] European travellers clearly marked the presence of Gujaratis in Muscat and Zanzibar by noting their lifestyles of strict vegetarianism and effort to preserve all life forms, including insects.[62] Like the Marwaris, their march within India accelerated in the 19th century with Bombay emerging as the key destination for the cotton and trading businesses. According to one account from

the 1930s, Jains ran over 40 per cent of the grocery and provision
shops in Bombay even though they comprised less than 2 per
cent of the population.[63] Unlike the Marwaris, however, they
also reached important textile hubs in south India, especially
those around Coimbatore. The Jains usually migrated from
the principal urban centres in Gujarat, such as Ahmedabad and
Surat, to form new businesses whereas some migrated from other
places. The Jains of Palanpur, for instance, were well versed
with the jewellery business and their migration, noted later in
this chapter, had a spectacular impact on India's international
trade. The Jains around Jamnagar on the other hand engaged
in agriculture and left for East Africa amidst social ostracism.[64]
Away from the gaze of the Jain community in Gujarat, they
would rise to produce several business tycoons in East Africa by
the end of the 20th century. According to one family member
of the Chandaria business group in Kenya:[65]

> The Oswal Jains of Jamnagar migrated to East Africa in the
> beginning of the 20th century . . . At home, we eat business,
> drink business, we talk business at the breakfast table, at
> lunch, at [the] dinner table. It is a penetrating induction, and
> is backed up by a much bigger capital base for our young ones
> to start from.

Business success was closely tied up with migration of families
through kinship, a pattern observed across different communities
in Gujarat.

The migration of Bhatias and Lohanas, two other prominent
business-oriented communities of Gujarat, tracks closely with that
of the Jains in recent times. Both claim descent from warrior castes
in north-western India, migrations to Sindh to escape invasions,
and later movements into Kachchh and Saurashtra in Gujarat.[66]
The timing and exact nature of these movements is uncertain, but

by the late 16th century the Bhatias had converted to Pushtimargi
Vaishnavism, a Hindu sect started by Vallabhacharya that placed
less taboo on overseas travel and adopted commercial occupations.
Their presence was noted in Muscat, Aden and Zanzibar in
the subsequent centuries with trading bases at the Mundra and
Mandvi ports. The overseas migration of Lohanas started later.
In the interim, their internal migration led to shopkeeping and
moneylending activities within Gujarat. A migration stream to
Poona to finance the activities of the Peshwa court in the 18th
century has also been documented.[67] But the major destinations
for the Lohanas and Bhatias in the 19th and early 20th century
were Bombay and East Africa. In both cases, the migrants were
drawn heavily from Kachchh.

For long, Kachchh had hosted a vibrant culture of trade,
banking, insurance and shipbuilding, consistently patronized
by rulers over many centuries.[68] In the second half of the 18th
century, the Kachchh fleet comprised over 400 ocean-going
ships of different types and names: *Kotia, Navadi, Machhava,
Dhan, Tar* and *Hodi*.[69] Kotias were fast ships designed to resist
strong winds and measured less than 150 feet in length. With
the use of Kotias, Kachchh's tryst with Muscat grew in the 19th
century under the Omani Sultanate and eventually extended
its reach to Zanzibar in Africa. Merchant circulation between
Kachchh, Muscat and Zanzibar was common as part of the trade
of dates, pearls and ivory in the 19th century with counterparties
based as far away as the US. The trading season would begin in
the middle of September, when the south-west monsoon would
fade, and end in May or June with the return of the monsoon.
Apart from the Jains, Bhatias and Lohanas, Kachchh also hosted
the Goswamis, worshippers of Shiva, with monasteries scattered
across multiple locations. Remarkably, these monasteries also
acted as banks and handled advanced financial instruments that
supported the spirit of business and migration.

If Kachchhi mercantile migration was the highlight of Gujarati migration in the 19th century, Patidar migration from central Gujarat emerged as a major phenomenon in the 20th century. Patidars were traditionally rooted in agriculture and formed the dominant caste in many parts of Gujarat, usually carrying the surname Patel. Vallabhbhai Patel (1875–1950), independent India's first home minister, and arguably the most famous Patel, was a prominent migrant from central Gujarat who spent several years in London, Ahmedabad and Delhi. The Charotar Patidars of Kheda district began migrating to East Africa in the late 20th century to open shops and soon began pulling their brethren there as new opportunities were opened up by colonial investment.[70] They were associated with retail and wholesale trade, but they also came to dominate the ginning industry in Uganda, where they were heavily concentrated. By 1970, there were around 50,000 Patidars in East Africa, but nativist policies pursued by the decolonized African states led to many of them moving to the United Kingdom and North America. Thus began an extensive chain migration of Patidars from central Gujarat to the UK and North America in the late 20th century, often using links formed by the relocation from East Africa.[71] In the UK, the Patidars ran small stores and conducted trade around London and Leicester. The community was close-knit, so much so that in one local cricket match in Bradford in 2001 all twenty-two players on the field were Patels.[72] The scorekeeper, himself a Patel, had the fairly amusing job of recording a scoreboard on the lines of Patel c. Patel b. Patel, Patel b. Patel, Patel run-out Patel, and so on.

In the US, the Patels scored big in motels. Starting from just two motels in the 1950s, the Patels comprised over half of all the moteliers in the US by the end of the 20th century.[73] They would start by purchasing a run-down motel, renovate it and provide professional hospitality services. Patidar women would also participate in this business as the worksite was the same place as their home. Children would grow up to extend business lines or venture into other businesses in the US, especially those that catered to the requirements of high-skilled Indian professional migrants. Thus, the Gujaratis enjoyed commercial success in the US just like they had in East Africa and India.

In 2014, sixteen Gujaratis ranked among India's hundred most rich business leaders, second only to the Marwaris.[74] More significantly, they figure on the rich lists of many countries other than India. This has been possible due to the migration of Gujarati merchants and capital over centuries. This migration was gradual, transnational and widespread across communities and sectors. The image of a Gujarati family, sitting on a *chattai* and enjoying khakra practically anywhere in the world, including airports, is a sight to behold. The chances are high that they belong to a long line of illustrious entrepreneurs who call the world their home.

The Muslim Merchants

The Islamic faith first arrived in south India through trade and forged close and enduring connections along the west coast. Dating back to 7th century CE, the Moplah Muslims of Kerala arguably reflect the earliest of these connections. Today, they constitute a major share of the total number of Muslims in Kerala, who in turn constitute about a quarter of the state's population and are highly concentrated around Kozhikode, earlier called Calicut, and Malappuram. The presence of Moplah or Mappila merchants has been noted in the Indian Ocean world through the centuries. However, the mass migration wave to the Gulf since the 1970s gave birth to a new set of traders and entrepreneurs with businesses of substantial scale.[75] North of Kerala, the Konkani Muslims also had historic trading ties with the Arab world and started coming to Bombay in the 19th century for shipbuilding. Some Konkani Muslim families like the Roghays, Ghattays and Kurs amassed wealth by exporting cotton to China in partnership with the Parsis.[76] More recently, since the Gulf boom, they have been migrating to the Arab world again.

The Maraikkayars are a Tamil Muslim community living along the Coromandel Coast between Nagore and Karaikal with deep migratory and trading traditions.[77] The word 'marakkalam' means 'boat' in Tamil, and this community has been associated with substantive trade across the Bay of Bengal, where they settled in some of the leading ports and were known to many as the *Chulia*s. They also traded in horses with West Asia and, at one point, were accused of horse-trading in the political affairs of the Melaka court in South East Asia.

In north India, Islam arrived over many centuries, through conquest and trade, conversion and assimilation. Three Muslim communities that stand out in the world of migration and business are the Sunni Memons, and the (mostly) Shi'ite Khojas and Bohras. All of them hail from the region spanning Sindh and Gujarat in the west and had converted from Hindu trading castes such as the Lohanas around the 14th century.[78] Some of their cultural practices, such as those on inheritance, are closer to Hindu customs which reduce the dispersal of wealth. The migratory trajectories of all three communities were extensive in the 19th and 20th centuries both within the subcontinent and towards East Africa and South East Asia.

The Memons migrated from Sindh to various towns in Gujarat, and then using those towns as bases, migrated across the subcontinent in the first half of the 19th century to trade in commodities. They would, in fact, stake a large claim on the lucrative rice trade along the east coast and Burma, using the credit facilitated by their Sindhi counterparts—the Shikarpuri bankers of the Lohana caste.[79] Muslim business rarely ventured into industry in the early 20th century, but there were exceptions like Adamjee Haji Dawood (1880–1948), a Memon from Jetpur in Gujarat who set up a large matchsticks factory in Rangoon and later a jute factory in Calcutta. Like most Memons, he migrated to Pakistan after the Partition based on advice from his friend Jinnah, who was born into a Khoja Muslim family.

The Khojas included prominent Muslim business families such as the Currimbhoys and Habibs.[80] The former would rise through shipping and the opium trade to become the largest indigenous group after the Tatas for a short while before going bust during the Great Depression. The Habib banking and finance group had a Gujarati–Bombay connection before migrating to Pakistan and becoming the country's largest financial institution. The most famous Khoja in Indian business today—Azim Premji of the software company Wipro—hails from a Kachchhi Muslim family with links in Burma; his father was known as the 'rice king of Burma'. The Bohras were prominent shipping merchants in Surat since the 17th century at least when Mulla Abdul Ghafur, a merchant prince, ruled the roost during the heyday of the Mughal Empire.[81] Prominent Bohra families from the early 20th century include the Tyabjis and Valikas, and the Akbarally family of the departmental store fame who migrated from Palanpur in Gujarat to Bombay in the late 19th century. Bohra and Khoja migrations to Oman and East Africa also led to their overseas business flourishing.

Shi'ite Khoja and Bohra Muslims constituted only 10 per cent of British India's Muslim population but comprised nearly 50 per cent of the Muslim business elite.[82] In the 1960s, Memons constituted 0.16 per cent of Pakistan's population, but owned 25 per cent of the factories.[83] Like the Parsis and the Gujarati–Marwari Vaishya–Jain combine, the contribution of the Gujarati Muslims to big business in Pakistan's formative years was disproportionate to their share in the population. Migration networks remained a key part of their rise to the top.

European Christians and Baghdadi Jews

The migration of European colonists to India is usually seen in terms of military and administrative services, but it also included a significant number of traders and entrepreneurs. It was the English East India Company that acquired taxation revenue rights in the 19th century, but it was chiefly Scottish enterprise that dominated British business in India by the end of the 19th century. These migrants were mostly Christians and drawn from Scotland towards Calcutta in the jute, tea and coal sectors. A few of those firms such as Balmer Lawrie, Andrew Yule and Duncans have survived, owned either by the Indian government or migrant business communities such as the Marwaris. Scottish, and more generally European Christian, migration to India for business was very similar to the Indian pattern of temporary settlement, remittance of profits and eventual return to the native place. Just like Indian merchants and entrepreneurs felt the need to cater to the requirements of overseas Indian migrants, European military and administrative presence in India was well served by a similar class of European origin. The first major retail outlets and chains established in India in the late 19th century, such as Spencer's in Madras, arose precisely because of this shopkeeper migration from the 'nation of shopkeepers' to the land of bazaars.[84] Nor was entrepreneurial migration confined to Britain. Larsen & Toubro, one of India's largest engineering firms today, was started by Danish migrants. Monginis, a popular pastry and bakery chain in Mumbai, was started by migrants from Italy.

Apart from Europeans, the Baghdadi Jews were a small but influential business community in India. Initially based in Surat, and later in Bombay and Calcutta, they were Jews from Ottoman Mesopotamia who spoke the Judeo–Arabic language and had roots not only in Baghdad but also in towns such as Basra in Iraq and Aleppo in Syria.[85] State persecution, an age-old method of harassing Jews, led to an initial spurt in migration in the 18th century, thrusting them into the trade routes of the Indian Ocean and the South China Sea. Baghdad-born David Sassoon (1792–1864) started an eponymous firm in the 1830s that would dominate the lucrative textile and opium trades between Britain, India and China, from its base in Bombay. The Sassoons have been labelled the Rothschilds of the East after the famous Jewish banking family of Europe. Interestingly, they were linked to them through a marriage alliance in the late 19th century. The Sassoon family business would grow to own dockyards, oil mills and numerous cotton textile mills and make it a major promoter of the Bank of India that was founded in 1906. Sassoon's global operations led to further migration of Baghdadi Jews, and India soon became a stepping stone for them to receive an English education and protected status before migrating to other places, especially China. For instance, Silas Aaron Hardoon (1851–1931) worked for David Sassoon and Company in India in the late 19th century, before moving to China and amassing a real estate fortune, dying as the richest foreigner in Shanghai.

The Baghdadi Jews distinguished themselves from the Bene Israel Jews of India by claiming to be more 'European, white and loyalist' in a bid to secure protection under the British.[86] After India became independent and the British Empire collapsed, the Baghdadi Jews began to leave for Israel. Today, their numbers in India have dwindled from a few thousand to a few hundred, just like the Scots. With this wave of outmigration, ownership of firms was transferred to Indian hands. Their memory lives on only because of their firm commitment to philanthropy, witnessed for instance at the beautifully restored David Sassoon Library in south Mumbai.

Apart from European Christians and Baghdadi Jews, immigrant traders and entrepreneurs from many other regions have been attracted to India. Among these are the Armenians in Surat, the Burmese and Chinese in Calcutta, and the Iranians in Bombay who, since the late 19th century, have been running inexpensive cafes that enjoy an iconic status now.

The Migration of Capital, c. 1600–2015

If the Great Indian Migration Wave is a narrative of the migration of labour over the past century and a half, the migrations described in this chapter refer to the migration of capital over the past four centuries. They revolved around the family firm, a system whereby sons and nephews first worked as apprentices and then migrated either as agents or entrepreneurs to manage the business elsewhere. The family firm worked on the basis of trust, reputation and reciprocity. Those who would cheat or steal were punished by the community, and this threat alone was strong enough to persuade people to fall in line. More crucially, capital stayed within the family and the community, allowing both to accumulate substantial wealth over time through migration and the discovery of new business opportunities.

Not everyone in the family migrated, as daughters and wives generally stayed at home. Merchant migrations before the 20th century were male-dominated, semi-permanent and remittance-based, much like the nature of circular migration observed in the Great Indian Migration Wave. These migrations, however, occurred from different regions, such as the north-western areas of the Indian subcontinent and a few coastal tracts. Claude Markovits, a historian of Indian business, provides one possible explanation for the exceptional selectivity of merchant migrations from the region comprising Punjab, Rajasthan, Gujarat and Sindh.[87] His ecological argument credits the 'dry zone' for honing skills in risk management, which provide a comparative advantage in trade and finance, over regions with more reliable access to water. However, much of central India is also semi-arid and dry in nature and did not witness major mercantile migrations whereas the coastal tracts well-endowed with water did witness mercantile migrations.

A more complete explanation would include factors that shaped attitudes towards trade and spatial mobility. The *Arthashastra*, India's most famous treatise on statecraft compiled over 1800 years ago, mistrusted traders arguing that that they were 'all thieves, in effect, if not in name' and that 'they shall be prevented from oppressing the people'.[88] The caste system itself accorded the trading caste the third position, ritually lower than the priests and the warriors. Further, taboos on overseas travel were pervasive. In such a milieu, the trading castes were not likely to be in a position to expand their network or gain acceptance among other castes.

The north-western regions of the Indian subcontinent, however, differed substantially from other parts of India in having four major religious and philosophical traditions, outside orthodox Hinduism and Islam, already present or emerging around the 16th century: Zoroastrianism, Jainism, Sikhism and Pushtimargi Vaishnavism. All four belief systems were vital in dispelling conservative notions about trade and overseas travel. Interaction with people and exposure to these ideas led to a much greater acceptance of trading as a legitimate activity and migration as a means of expanding business and securing a livelihood. Merchants affiliated with these schools of thought generously paid back to construct shrines and places of worship, which in turn legitimized their way of life. In some of the coastal tracts, Muslim merchants were also free from taboos on travel. In Chettinad, closer to the coast, it would appear that a long history of regional trading connections between Tamil Nadu and South East Asia had dented notions about the loss of caste upon travelling overseas. Social acceptance of trade and travel is thus important to explain the geographical selectivity of merchant migrations in India before the 20th century. These migrations were also directed towards regions that were demographically marked by an absence or low share of trading castes in the Gangetic heartland and the Deccan. They filled the void in many places as the Mughal Empire began to fall apart in the 18th century and they grew under British protection in the 19th century. By then, Calcutta and Bombay had come up as major attractions thanks to commercial opportunities and the provision of a modern legal system that resolved cross-community disputes, thereby facilitating greater trade.[89]

For migrant merchants, social acceptance was important within their respective communities even if it was not prevalent in the regions that they migrated to. The migration of capital was often related to the opium and slave trades. When ethical attitudes to these trades changed, the merchants were slow to shift away from their lucrative practices. Migrant traders, financiers, entrepreneurs and moneylenders would also cause suspicion because of their capacity to generate wealth. The Chettiars in Burma, Marwaris in north Maharashtra, Gujaratis in East Africa and Punjabis in Russia, or for that matter the Baghdadi Jews and Scots in India, all benefited from state protection initially but were affected by local discontent at various points of time that manifested from a perception that they were parasitic outsiders.

In the 20th century, the migration of capital hitched on to the Great Indian Migration Wave, leading to the evolution of transnational Indian business. It was evident in the banking and diamond sectors, and also in the way Indian multinationals expanded in the second half of the 20th century.[90] The Indian Overseas Bank and the Bank of Baroda, for instance, followed the south Indian and Gujarati migrant trails towards South East Asia and East Africa respectively to cater to their financial needs. More spectacularly, Gujarati Palanpuri Jains began migrating to

centres of the diamond trade in the early 20th century, established
a presence in Antwerp in Belgium—a major wholesale diamond
market in the 1950s—and worked their way up to dominate the
market by the end of the 20th century. They would outsource
the rough diamonds to cutting and polishing centres in Mumbai
and Surat to avail lower labour costs and re-export them to
the world. Their strong migrant links firmly placed India in
the global diamond supply chain. Today, 70 per cent of the
diamonds in the world are estimated to pass through India at
least once with diamonds accounting for nearly 10 percent of
the country's exports.

Bankers and diamond merchants also played an important
role in financing overseas Indian investment between the 1960s
and 1980s, an era of strict controls on foreign exchange. For
instance, A.V. Birla's investment in a plant in Thailand in 1969,
one of the first major overseas Indian investment projects, was
partly financed by the Indian Overseas Bank and a non-resident
Indian (NRI) diamond dealer based in Bangkok. Over half of
the overseas joint venture agreements in the 1980s had people
of Indian origin as investment counterparts in the destination
country. In the software and healthcare sectors, investment flows
were closely related to the migration of Indian professionals to
the US. Mass labour migration to the Persian Gulf was also
accompanied by the creation of a class of Indian entrepreneurs
catering to Indian needs. Five of India's hundred most rich
business leaders in 2014 owed their wealth to the Gulf migration
wave. Migration and investment, therefore, moved in tandem
across the 20th century, first towards South East Asia and Africa
and later towards the US, Europe and West Asia.

Along with a greater transnational presence, the social
base of entrepreneurship in India has also been widening.
Community-based migration appears to be an important route
towards success for the latecomers. The migration of Gounders

around the cotton textile hub of Tiruppur or the migration of Saurashtra Patels towards the diamond hub of Surat in the late 20th century have been short-distance migrations that led to considerably upward mobility as workers became entrepreneurs. The agricultural landowning caste of coastal Andhra Pradesh—the Kammas—used agricultural wealth to move to nearby towns and Hyderabad, and eventually the US, as doctors and engineers to form a transnational community network with substantial capital.[91]

With the emergence of management education, many people found a new stepping stone towards becoming rich, as managers could rise to become directors or even owners of firms. Migration for education and professional reasons was not necessarily linked to caste groups per se, but those who invested first in education had a substantial edge. Here, the Brahmins, historically associated with the education sectors were natural first movers and stormed the trading–community bastion of corporate India. In 2010, as per one study, 45 per cent of the directors of India's 1000 largest companies were Brahmins, a figure close to that of the traditional trading castes.[92] That is, over 90 per cent of the leading corporate directors were Brahmins or Banias who formed less than 10 per cent of the Indian population. Historical migration, networks and the ability to exploit these to gain information about new jobs and business opportunities are important factors that explain this dominance. Conversely, relatively lower long-term spatial mobility and smaller information sets have reduced the chances of acquiring capital among many social groups, including the Dalits and Adivasis, and also stunted the development of their diasporas.

4

Diasporas and Dreams

'Not one single person came here with the idea that they'd get married, settle down; they just wanted to earn money for a couple of years and go back.'

—Palanisamy Kumaran, on migrating to the Malaya world in the 1930s[1]

Palanisamy Kumaran travelled from Nagapattinam in present-day Tamil Nadu to Penang in present-day Malaysia in 1937. He left with few possessions and a Rs 27 ticket for the steamer journey. He would live there for over seventy years but his initial memory of migration, as narrated and recounted before Sunil Amrith who recorded it in his magisterial book *Crossing the Bay of Bengal*, was not one towards permanent settlement. While Kumaran was initially a part of the Great Indian Migration Wave, he differed from the others by settling down in his destination instead of returning. Similar decisions by other migrant workers for a variety of reasons have, over time, contributed to the emergence of a vast Indian diaspora of over 25 million people across the world.[2] Depending on the vintage, it competes closely with the British and the Chinese in their claim to being the largest regional diaspora in the world.

The word 'diaspora', originally used to refer to the dispersal of Jews around the world, entered the Indian bureaucratic lexicon only in 2001 with the release of the *Report of the High Level Committee on the Indian Diaspora*. The report used the word to refer to NRI citizens and People of Indian Origin (PIO) who did not hold Indian citizenship but were linked to the country up to four generations, or by marriage, with caveats on the countries of destination. It is this definition, of relatively recent emigrants and their descendants, which I use in this chapter.

There is one Indian diaspora that is popular in the public imagination, but it is also the amalgamation of sub-national Indian diasporas defined principally by language. One can therefore talk about a Tamil diaspora, a Bengali diaspora or a Telugu diaspora. Most crucially, these diasporas reside *within* and *outside* India. In fact, when viewed from this prism, the internal diasporas of India are double the size of the international diaspora and are closely linked with each other. As we will see, the evolution of India's internal and international diasporas have popularized the very idea of Indian diversity.

Tiding over the *Kaalapani*

To understand the evolution of the international Indian diaspora, it is useful to begin with a brief statistical overview. Before the 19th century, few people born in the Indian subcontinent were found in the Americas, Europe or West Africa. India and Indians had captivated the imaginations of the others, but the reverse was not necessarily true. As described in the previous chapter, traditional destinations of merchants outside the Indian subcontinent included central Asia, South East Asia and East Africa. The numbers involved were small, perhaps less than 50,000 in total.[3] The fear of the kaalapani (black waters) constrained migration choices for the vast majority.

With the advent of organized indentured labour migration to Mauritius in 1834 as part of the colonial economic system, the number of emigrants began to increase. Migration to British Guiana, now the independent nation of Guyana, began in 1838 and to Trinidad and Jamaica in 1845. By 1850, the international Indian diaspora had crossed the 1,00,000-mark. The majority lived in Mauritius with its roots in the Chhota Nagpur Plateau and the lower Gangetic plains. The fear of the kaalapani began to wane. If the legend of the kaalapani promised the loss of caste upon return, this was precisely what the lower castes wanted and served to prompt them to experiment with overseas migration. Thus, from the middle of the 19th century, there was a distinct shift that occurred in overseas migration volumes as Indians began to move through indenture and more so, for adventure.

Between 1850 and 1910, overseas migration surged, powered by globalization and the steamboats, taking the size of the Indian diaspora to over 2 million people, or close to 1 per cent of the Indian population. As Table 1 at the end of this chapter shows, in 1910, nearly two-thirds of the Indian diaspora was located in Asia itself, mainly in the regions of present-day Sri Lanka, Myanmar and Malaysia. A fifth of the diaspora was based in Mauritius, South Africa and East Africa, though migration to Mauritius had tapered off by then. While all these regions were associated with the British Empire, Indians from the French colonies of India went to French-ruled territories such as Réunion Island, some 200 km southwest of Mauritius in the Indian Ocean. Around 10 per cent of the Indian diaspora was based in Latin America and the Caribbean Islands, in regions of present-day Trinidad and Tobago, Guyana and Suriname. Europe and North America attracted students, but restrictive immigration laws ensured that the Indians were kept out. Since the 1870s, the Pacific island of Fiji also rose to prominence as a destination.

Between 1910 and 1930, the diaspora rose by a million, mainly due to migration towards South East Asia, but not much changed otherwise. By then, Indian communities had begun to settle down in many places and natural growth, more than migration, mattered to their demography. In the next five decades, the collapse of the British Empire, decolonization and return migration led to a tectonic shift in the composition of the Indian diaspora away from Myanmar and Sri Lanka—two regions covered in other chapters of this book—and towards new destinations that had opened up in Britain, North America and Canada after the relaxation of immigration laws there. This migration wave consisted of professionals, instead of labourers, towards places outside the Great Indian Migration Wave which itself was reshaping away from South East Asia towards West Asia in the 1970s.

In the last quarter of the 20th century, West Asia, North America and Europe grew in prominence with more settlement taking place in the latter two regions. By 2010, a fifth of the Indian diaspora was based in North America and a tenth was based in Europe. The diaspora in the old hotspots of Africa and Latin America grew naturally, with little further immigration. With Nepal, migration across the porous border continued on both sides, especially for marriages. In recent decades, Singapore and Australia have emerged as important destinations for professional migration, while Italy has attracted over a 1,00,000 Indian immigrants, mainly in its agricultural sector.

The contemporary Indian diaspora of over 25 million people represents around 2 per cent of the Indian population. More than a third of this number is based in the English-speaking world. It forms less than 5 per cent of the local population in most countries: between 5 and 10 per cent in Malaysia and

Singapore, between 10 and 20 per cent in some of the smaller Gulf countries and over a third of the population in many of the old sugar plantation-based economies. The Indian diaspora is large, diverse and complex, and spans the entire world. The old adage about the sun not setting on the British Empire now holds true for the Indian diaspora.

Sweet Dreams and Nightmares: The Sugar Plantations

It is often said in jest that when the sun did rise on the British Empire, it did so on a tremendous sugar rush.[4] The sugar plantations in the distant European colonies in the Caribbean islands and Latin America, the islands of the Indian Ocean such as Mauritius and Réunion, and the islands of the Pacific Ocean above Australia, such as Fiji, were important centres for the growth of colonialism and capitalism. Most of these colonies began with slave labour, only to be replaced by indentured labour in the early 19th century.

Indian contact with Mauritius began as early as the 17th century when the Dutch brought convicts and slaves from Indian settlements.[5] The 18th century saw more contact as Mauritius came under the French rule, when Indians from Pondicherry were brought in as slaves, workers, craftsmen, companions and servants to the island, known then as the Isle of France, which served as a strategic trading post for the French in the Indian Ocean. There were Indian women as well, as slaves and single migrants who could become property owners through liaisons with the colonists. In one remarkable case, Marie Rozette, a slave of Indian origin, was freed, secured a large fortune through moneylending and trading and owned property and twelve slaves by 1790, making her one of the richest women on the island.

British rule in Mauritius commenced in 1810 during the Napoleonic Wars, at a time when slavery was declining. From

1815, Indian convicts were brought in to work on road and bridge projects. In 1825, Mauritius received sugar tariff parity on the output from the West Indies entering Britain, setting the stage for it to become a major sugar exporter. By 1830, there were around 70,000 slaves on the island, of which around 3000 were Indians. With the formal abolition of slavery in British colonies in 1833–34, the decision to import indentured labour for the sugar plantations was taken by estate-owners, some of whom were Indians. In the initial years, the recruitment methods were considerably criticized. Emigration was prohibited in 1839, only to resume in 1842 on a greater scale and under new controls. *Sirdar*s emerged as key intermediaries in the recruitment process by bringing labour from among their own kin and villages.

Between 1834 and 1900, around half a million Indians were brought to Mauritius as indentured labour, the highest for any colony, of whom a third returned to India. After the expiry of their indenture contracts, many of them moved away from the estates into the 'Indian' villages in Mauritius. The descendants of these indentured migrants still live on the island and now comprise two-thirds of the million-strong population, making it the most 'Indian' country outside South Asia. Unsurprisingly, the Indo-Mauritians have controlled political power after Independence from the British in 1968. They witnessed decent economic prosperity in the 20th century and, by 2010, the per capita income of Mauritius was three times that of India and several times higher than Bihar, the place where most Indo-Mauritians trace their roots. While most people speak Creole, a mixture of many languages, Bhojpuri is also spoken widely. At a smaller scale, even Hindi, Tamil, Telugu and Marathi are spoken, reflecting considerable cultural preservation. The Indian contact continues through tourism and investment as Mauritius is a popular honeymoon destination and also a tax haven that channelizes foreign portfolio investment (and illicit money transfers) into and out of India.

Mauritius is a part of the Mascarene Islands, which also includes Réunion and Rodrigues, the latter being an autonomous part of Mauritius. Réunion, earlier called Bourbon Island, is a French overseas department even today. In the 18th and 19th centuries, it imported Indian labour, mostly Tamilians, from the French settlements in India.[6] Slavery existed until 1848, and in 1860, under a treaty with the British, it began importing British Indian labour to expand sugar plantations. More than 20,000 Indians were brought in before migration was suspended in 1882 amidst growing chants of ill-treatment of labour. Gujarati merchants, Hindu and Muslim, also migrated in this period. In the 20th century, Indians assimilated within the French culture, such that three quarters of the population now identify themselves as having mixed origins. In fact, for some time, Indian-origin people even had to take Christian first names to meet the integrationist policies of the French. Today, churches, temples and mosques dot the island and people of Tamil descent make up a quarter of the population. Thus, the demographic and cultural evolution of Indians in Réunion differed from neighbouring Mauritius.

Most of the sugar consumed in western Europe during the colonial era was grown in the Caribbean islands and along the northern coast of Latin America. These were colonies of competing European empires whose political rule kept changing hands after several battles. In the 17th and 18th centuries, the sugar plantations depended heavily on African slave labour and from the middle of the 19th century, on Indian indentured labour. This part of the world was farther away from Mauritius, leading not only to higher concerns about mortality en route but also lower return migration rates. Sailing trips around the Cape of Good Hope would initially take up to three months but this reduced to one or two months after the Suez Canal opened in 1869. Ship rations included dal, ghee, mustard oil, vegetables, fish or flesh, salt, 'curry stuff' and rice for the rice-eaters and flour for the flour-eaters, reflecting India's north–south dietary divide.[7] Ships were most often named after famous people. During 1856–57, the ships that left Calcutta for the West Indies were the *Wellesley, Bucephalus, Robert Seppings, Adelaide, Roman Emperor, George Seymour, Maidstone, Eveline, Merchantman, Granville, Burmah* and the *Scindian*. They were not always named after European rulers—one ship was called Shah Jehan, but as luck would have it, it caught fire in June 1859 and all 300 people on board died.

The abolition of slavery in British colonies across the Atlantic led to the first batch of indentured Indian labour arriving in British Guiana in 1838. The terrain of Guyana was not particularly conducive to sugar plantations, but the Dutch had reclaimed and irrigated the land to make the coastland habitable in the 17th century, replete with dykes and dams.[8] The African slave labourers who worked on the sugar plantations resisted the governing elite after their emancipation from British rule in the 1830s, leading to the search for alternate labour, and the eventual entry of Indians, or East Indians as they were called, to differentiate them from the Native American Indians. Since Africans subsidized the introduction of Indian indenture labour through tax payments, their resentment also grew against the Indians.

Between 1838 and 1917, over 2,00,000 Indian labourers migrated to British Guiana, and less than a third returned to India. Almost all the migrants traced their roots to the Bhojpuri-speaking tracts of the Gangetic plains, a core area of the Great Indian Migration Wave. A sixth of the migrants were Muslim, another sixth were upper castes, a third were low-caste or outcaste and another third were middling artisan and agricultural castes. They were mostly men, but were over time accompanied by their wives and even single women. In her memoir, *Coolie Woman*, Gaiutra Bahadur traced the journey of her great-grandmother, a Brahmin woman from Bihar's Saran district, who sailed from Calcutta to the Caribbean in 1903 as a 'coolie', pregnant and alone, to work on a sugar plantation in British Guiana.[9]

Along with indenture contracts, the Indians took with them the world of the Ramayana, and the flavours and spices of the Indian subcontinent.[10] Outside the sugar plantations, the Indians began to cultivate rice on their own lands. They resisted the brutalities of the plantation world by organizing strikes on the sugar plantations in the early 20th century. From the 1940s, when malaria was brought under control in Guyana, Indians witnessed a demographic, economic and political upsurge as they moved away from the plantations. Faced with common adversaries far away from home, the caste system began to disappear as identities were reshaped along racial lines.[11] People of Indian origin now make up around 40 per cent of the Guyanese population, similar to those who trace their origins to Africa. It is tensions between these two groups that defined politics before and after Independence in 1966. If India has been an important part of the Guyanese imagination, Guyana entered cricketing folklore in India through Clive Lloyd, one of the most successful captains of the stylish and dominant West Indies cricket team of the 1970s, and two brilliant cricketers of Indo-Guyanese heritage: Rohan Kanhai and Shivnarine Chanderpaul.

A few hundred kilometres off the coast of Guyana are the islands of Trinidad and Tobago, the birthplace of Nobel Laureate V.S. Naipaul, whose writings were a hallmark of 20th century literature. His grandparents had moved from a place near Gorakhpur, a key north Indian centre in the Great Indian Migration Wave, to Trinidad in 1894 aboard a ship called the *Hereford* and indentured as coolies at Woodford Lodge estate.[12] But Naipaul was not among the first emigrants as indentured migration to Trinidad had begun four decades earlier. Between 1845 and 1917, around 1,50,000 indentured labourers were shipped to the plantations of Trinidad, sharing similar characteristics with the emigrants to Guyana.[13] Less than a quarter of them returned to India. On arrival after a long sea journey, the workers were lodged at Nelson Island for a medical examination. Then they spent a few days or weeks at a local depot before heading for the plantations. In addition to sugar, the cocoa plantations of Trinidad also absorbed a part of the Indian workforce. Once indenture contracts expired, many Indians began cane farming in the late 19th century. By the 1920s, they had started supplying a third of the produce to the sugar mills. Subsequently, Indians moved out of agriculture in greater numbers and began to assimilate with the wider society, experiencing marked upward mobility in education, occupation and employment in the 1970s and 1980s.[14] Representing 40 per cent of the million-strong population, people of Indian origin have held all major political offices in Trinidad and Tobago after it attained Independence in 1962. The country's per capita income grew to stand seven times higher than India's in 2010 and higher than any of the plantation economies that the Indians had migrated to.

In the late 19th century, a few thousand Indians were also brought to other Caribbean islands such as Grenada, St Vincent, St Lucia and St Kitts. Farther north, Jamaica received 40,000 Indians who worked on sugar and banana plantations. The French-ruled Guiana and the islands of Martinique and Guadeloupe collectively received nearly a 1,00,000 Indians, many of whom were from south India and had sailed from the ports of Pondicherry, Karaikal and Madras. These numbers were relatively small, and in all these regions, people of Indian origin today constitute less than 5 per cent of the local population.

Apart from the British and French colonies, Indians also migrated to Dutch Suriname, now known as the Republic of Suriname. The Dutch government abolished slavery in the

Caribbean islands in 1863 and like the British and French before, planters faced the quandary of labour shortage as the freed slaves now had more bargaining power. After experimenting with labourers from different nationalities and a labour agreement being signed by the British and the Dutch in 1870, the indentured Indian workers arrived for the first time on board the ship *Lalla Rookh* in 1873.[15] They were followed by around 30,000 more Indians in the next four decades, of whom only a third returned to India. The Indians in Suriname were referred to as the Hindustanis. Thus began a slow process of assimilation into local society over the next 100 years. The Verenigde Hindoestaanse Partij (VHP) was formed in the middle of the 20th century, and under Jagernath Lachmon, gained prominence in Surinamese politics. However, tensions with the Afro-Surinamese on the question of social integration led the VHP to prefer continued Dutch rule as a form of mediation. Then, unlike anything that had happened in the British or French Caribbean, more than a 1,00,000 Surinamese Indians migrated to the Netherlands in the early 1970s, given the uncertainty about their future in post-Dutch Suriname. After Independence in 1975, political affairs descended into military rule for a brief period before stabilizing, leading to less Hindustani emigration. People of Indian origin now constitute around a quarter of the local population, but more significantly, a new Hindustani diaspora has emerged in the Netherlands.

In addition to the Caribbean and Mascarene world of sugar plantations, Indians also migrated to the remote Pacific islands of Fiji in Oceania, thanks to the brainwave of one colonial official. Arthur Hamilton Gordon, Governor of Fiji, had previously served as the Governor of Trinidad and Mauritius and seen how effective the Indian indentured system was on sugar plantations.[16] When the British acquired the Fiji islands in 1874, Gordon replaced cotton with sugar as a way to develop the islands and began negotiations for indentured labour. The first batch of nearly 500 Indians soon arrived aboard the *Leonidas* in 1879.

Between 1879 and 1916, around 60,000 indentured Indians migrated to Fiji, and less than a half returned to India. Three-fourths of the migrants were from north India while the rest were south Indians. All of them came from the zones identified with the Great Indian Migration Wave. The five-year indenture contract was called the *girmit* and the migrants were called *girmitiya*s who worked for nine hours a day for five and a half days a week. Girmitiyas were of all castes and became *jahaji bhai*s during the month-long sea crossing, a bond that lasted for a long time in the remote islands where caste identities would eventually dissolve. The main sugar planter in Fiji was the Australia-based Colonial Sugar Refining (CSR) Company, with practices that were not particularly tuned to modern-day notions of CSR. High mortality, and even suicides, plagued the fate of Indian labourers in Fiji. These problems led to growing calls to end the indenture system, spearheaded by Gandhi's close associate, Charles Freer Andrews, who true to his name, campaigned vigorously to free the Indians from the perils of indentured labour.[17]

In the early 20th century, Punjabi and Gujarati agriculturalists and traders arrived as free migrants, adding to the Indian diversity in Fiji. The Indo-Fijians began to cultivate their own sugar and identity and moved to other occupations. However, unlike the Caribbean and Mascarene worlds, interaction between the Indians and the native Fijians was minimal and regulated by the government through a native policy. The growing prominence of the Indo-Fijians inevitably caused friction with the native Fijians and these have persisted till date. Fiji gained independence in 1970 but slid into periodic bouts of turbulence with growing cries of 'Fiji for Fijians' and the severe harassment of Indo-Fijians after a coup in 1987 and more recently in 2006. While the Indo-Fijians still make up a third of the local population, many have fled to Australia, New Zealand, Canada and other countries. Brij V. Lal, a Girmitiya descendant and an Indo-Fijian academic who edited the seminal *Encylopedia of the Indian Diaspora*, was one such person expelled from Fiji for voicing his views.

From Fiji to Jamaica, the Indian world in overseas sugar plantations has had a varied experience. In all places, Indians experienced upward mobility as they began to move out of plantations, and in all places the economic performance of the destination countries was greater than the source region. Yet, this process was associated with challenges of racial conflict with other groups, similar to what the Indians faced in South East Asia, albeit on a far greater scale.

The Land of Gold: South East Asia

The greatest influence of cultures evolving in the Indian subcontinent has undoubtedly been on South East Asia. It is here that you see temples, mosques and shrines with a distinct Indian flavour owing to cross-cultural encounters over a period spanning millennia. It is here that an Indian language—Tamil—counts as an official language of another country, Singapore, whose etymological roots lie in the Sanskrit word 'singha pura' or lion city. South East Asia is to India what America is to Europe—a land once ruled from a distance, a magnet for trade and ultimately a destination for mass migration.

Suvarna Bhumi, or the land of gold (and the name of Thailand's airport), receives short shrift in Indian history, obsessed as it is by events in north India. But for south India, and especially the eastern coast, its significance is enormous. In coastal Odisha, people still celebrate *Bali Jatra* or the voyage to Bali, a festival to commemorate historic merchant migrations

to South East Asia. By the late 19th century, the Great Indian
Migration Wave had firmly cast its web around the region that
constitutes present-day Myanmar, Malaysia and Singapore,
although in the latter two areas, migration over time became
relatively more permanent in nature.

Between 1844 and 1910, the Malaya world received around
2,50,000 indentured Indians, mostly Tamilians and Telugus, to
work in construction, transport lines and of course, plantations,
though not necessarily sugar.[18] Oil palm plantations also attracted
Indian workers. By the early 20th century, rubber had emerged
as the most important product of the Malay economy and
Indians would comprise over three-fourths of the workforce on
the plantations that grew it. The living and working conditions
of plantations were harsh and women and children were paid
substantially lower wages than men. The unskilled workers
worked on the fields while those who were slightly more skilled
were involved in rubber tapping. Indians were preferred over
the Chinese, who worked in the tin-mining sector, as their
reservation wage was much lower. They were also preferred
over the Javanese in Dutch-ruled Indonesia because British
India provided simple negotiation-free access to labour.

A major migration wave occurred in the first three decades
of the 20th century, by when indenture had given way to the
kangani system of headman-mediated migration and then from
the late 1920s to unassisted and more permanent migration.
Another migration stream was towards the services sector. From
north India, especially Punjab, people were recruited for the
security forces, while the Malayalis and Ceylonese Tamilians
from the southern rim migrated for clerical and administrative
positions. Finally, as previously noted, the Chettiars and other
merchants migrated to set up trading and moneylending posts.
By the 1940s, Indians comprised around a sixth of Malaya's
population, gradually falling to less than a tenth by the end of

the 20th century as the labour pipeline was shut down in the 1950s due to restrictive immigration policies. The latter two migrant groups did well for themselves but the plantation or ex-plantation workforce that comprised the majority of the 2-million-strong Indian diaspora continued to lag at the bottom of the social and economic pyramid.

There were several reasons for this predicament. The Malay world was different from Burma because of a sizable Chinese immigrant population and colonial policies that were tuned towards creating divisions between the Indian, Chinese and indigenous Malay population, now referred to as the *bumiputeras*, literally the 'sons of the soil'. If caste had given way to race in Trinidad, in Malaysia it moved to consolidate on ethnicity, sowing the seeds of ethnic tension that persist till date.[19] Previously, plantation life involved a high degree of social and geographic exclusion which led to strengthening of the Indian or Tamil group identity, but over the 20th century this failed to corner economic gains because of low representation in business and politics. The medium of education in the schools for plantation workers was Tamil, which did little to foster integration or equip workers with skills demanded by the global economy. Further, the takeover of plantations by the state after independence in 1957, and enforcement of nativist employment policies, displaced many Indians to live in urban slums and in greater poverty.

A completely different Indian world exists right opposite the Johor Strait that separates Malaysia and Singapore. In Singapore, the Indian diaspora of over half a million comprises around 10 per cent of the local population, and is more diverse and economically successful than in Malaysia. The Indian connection with Singapore began right from its formative stage. Modern Singapore was founded by Thomas Stamford Raffles (1781–1826) in 1819 with the assistance of Bhojpuri-speaking soldiers serving in the Bengal Native Infantry.[20] Within five years, over 500 Indian merchants referred to as the Chulias arrived in Singapore, followed by Indian convicts, after a detention facility was set up. The first mosques and temples were also established in the 1820s.

Singapore was a part of the British-ruled Straits Settlements from 1826 to 1942. For the first four decades, it was governed as an extension of British India. During this period, it developed as a port and site for plantations producing spices, sugar and eventually rubber. As in Malaya, Tamil indentured labour was brought to work on the plantations, Punjabi Sikhs were brought in to staff the police, and mercantile castes from different parts of India came in as traders. One such trader, of spices and cotton, became an extremely famous personality in Singapore's history. Rajabali Jumabhoy (1898–2001) was one among the few individuals who lived through all the years of the 20th century.[21] Born into a Kachchhi Khoja Muslim family, he moved from Kachchh to Singapore in 1916. Within a few decades of trade and real estate investment, his firm rose to become one of the wealthiest business houses of Singapore. He also helped establish the Singapore Indian Association in 1923, Singapore Indian Chamber of Commerce in 1935 and Singapore Indian Congress in 1945. He arranged for the evacuation of Indians during the Japanese occupation in World War II, at a time when the island attracted followers of the Indian National Army (INA) to mobilize violently against the British forces. But as with many family businesses in India, his business dynasty disintegrated in the 1990s.

In the 1950s, some 40,000 Indians in Malaya migrated to Singapore to escape Emergency rule, but restrictive immigration laws soon constrained further Indian migration to the city. After independence in 1965, Singapore witnessed astonishing economic growth amidst sustained efforts to preserve its multiethnic demographic composition. As a result, Indians became Indian-Singaporean and shared the benefits of economic growth, supplemented by the migration of highly skilled professionals since the 1990s. The emphasis on English in the Indian community also paid rich dividends. Serangoon Road, the historic hub of Indian activities, is today called Little India and serves as a reminder of the diverse Indian diaspora of Singapore.

Indian presence in other South East Asian regions was demographically not as significant as it was in Burma, Malaya and Singapore. Despite Indian connections with Thailand since ancient times, late 19th and early 20th century migrations were only a trickle, representing traders or labour deflections from Burma, Malaya and Singapore. Aditya Birla's overseas investment in Thailand in the latter half of the 20th century boosted the image of Indians in the local community, while Thailand itself became a major destination for Indian tourists. The experience of Indians in Indonesia mirrors that of Thailand, but with an important exception: Bali, a Hindu enclave with deep historic roots tracing back to India but not usually counted as part of the Indian diaspora generated through migrations of the past two centuries. French ruled Indo-China or modern-day Vietnam, Laos and Cambodia had connections to south India through the French Empire and therefore received Tamil Muslim and Chettiar capital in the 19th century, while the Philippines received traders in the 20th century. What is common today across the South East Asian world is a large Sindhi trading diaspora, similar to the Gujarati experience on the other side of the Indian Ocean.

Ghosts, Gujaratis and Gandhi: Africa

East Africa, representing the modern-day countries of Uganda, Kenya and Tanzania, was not a new destination for the Indians when they began migrating there in large numbers in the early 20th century, given that they were bound by historic ties to the Gujarati Hindu and Muslim traders as noted in the previous chapter. However, since the 1890s, two major developments affected the Indians, both of which were captured in fleeting scenes in two Hollywood movies, *The Ghost and the Darkness* (1996) and *The Last King of Scotland* (2006).

The ghost in particular referred to the Tsavo lion, a predator of such ferocity that it traumatized the workforce building the Uganda Railway in the 1890s, connecting Kampala in Uganda with Mombassa in Kenya. This workforce comprised nearly 40,000 Indians (represented by actor Om Puri in the movie), drawn mostly from Punjab on indenture contracts of three to five years.[22] The terrain was harsh, the lions were hungry and mortality rates were high during the construction of what the detractors called the 'lunatic line'. Once built, however, it transformed landscapes as towns and cities grew around it. While most of the workforce that built the railways went back to India, a few thousand stayed back and staffed the railways. Gujarati shopkeepers, called *dukka wallahs*, began setting up trading posts all along the railway line, moving towards the interiors of Africa for the first time.

Indian migration picked up during the inter-war period as British colonial rule consolidated in Tanganyika, now Tanzania, previously ruled by the Germans. East Africa attracted a large number of people from western India into a wide range of occupations in the services sector. Some Indian cotton ginning firms were also set up during this period. From roughly 50,000 in 1921, the Indian population doubled in size by 1939 and reached nearly 3,00,000 by 1969. However, after Independence in the 1960s, the East African states nationalized large parts of the economy and became openly hostile towards the immigrant Indian population. Just as Indian nationalists had blamed British capital for draining Indian wealth, African nationalists blamed Indian capitalists for draining African wealth.

The hostility reached its peak on 5 August 1972, when General Idi Amin, the then President of Uganda, delivered his 'Asian Farewell Speech'. In his view, the Indians had arrived to build the railways, and since the line was complete, they would have to go back. Asians, mainly Indians, were given an ultimatum to leave within ninety days. Within a few months, nearly the entire Indian population of 50,000 left, a scene vividly portrayed in *The Last King of Scotland,* the title of which referred to Amin's fetish for Scottish culture. A widespread fear gripped the Indian population of the wider region of East Africa, just as the Tsavo lions had instilled fear several decades earlier. As a result, a mass exodus took place as the 'twice migrants' moved to Britain, and to a lesser extent also to Canada and America.[23]

Since the 1980s, Indians have been wooed back to East Africa by subsequent political rulers, in appreciation of their economic contribution. Many have gone back. Currently, around 2,00,000 people of Indian origin live in East Africa. But many settled and succeeded abroad. In the USA, they can lock eyes again with the Tsavo lions of the Uganda Railway fame, as two of them are displayed at the Field Museum in Chicago.

Around 4000 km south of East Africa, Indians were a part of a very different landscape, creating a very different kind of history. Instead of predatory lions, there were discriminatory laws, and instead of Punjabis, there were Tamilians and Bhojpuris. What was common between East Africa and South Africa were the Gujarati traders, and it was in that context that a young Gujarati by the name of Mohandas Gandhi arrived as a qualified lawyer in Durban, Natal, aboard the *S.S. Admiral* on 24 May 1893. Apart from fighting court cases for traders, he immersed himself in the realities of South African discrimination and the fight for the rights of Indians. He would witness the plight of

indentured Indian labour first-hand because between 1860 and
1911, around 1,50,000 such migrant workers were brought to
Natal, along the east coast of South Africa, to work on sugar
plantations. Around half of them stayed back.[24] Most migrant
workers were male and drawn from the core zones of the Great
Indian Migration Wave—60 per cent were from the Tamil and
Telugu-speaking parts of south India and the rest were from the
Bhojpuri-speaking tracts of north India. In contrast with East
Africa, Gujarati traders followed the labour migration rather
than the other way round, but as in East Africa, they followed
the newly constructed railway lines to extend their trading posts
and drew the ire of the locals.

The prominence of a nascent Indian middle class in
Natal angered the White South Africans, who passed a raft of
legislations against the Indians after Natal achieved the status of
self-government in 1893. Racist legislations against the Indians
and Africans gained more currency in subsequent decades,
restricting settlement, migration and business. In response, the
Natal Indian Congress was founded in 1894, with Gandhi as its
first secretary. The political movement in South Africa shaped
Gandhi's thinking and methods of resistance, claimed successes
such as ending indentured emigration to Natal in 1911 and
abolishing a poll tax through the Indian Relief Act of 1914. The
next year, Gandhi returned to India to take part in the Indian
freedom movement.

The Indians who stayed behind in South Africa got caught
in the tension between the Africans and the Whites and suffered
from strong segregation polices enforced by the state. They
coalesced around their Indian identity in Natal and a few other
pockets of South Africa. By 1950, nearly fifty Indian organizations
served various requirements of the community from welfare
to entertainment. The political movement continued to
have links with India until 1947, but severed ties after India

attained independence. The Department of Indian Affairs was set up in 1961, which expanded educational opportunities and contributed to considerable economic mobility of the Indians as compared to the Africans. The children of the ex-indentured workers received better education, and in contrast with the Malaya world, average skill levels of the Indian community went up. More Indian women joined the workforce and a class of Indian industrialists also emerged. But all along, the apartheid regime that lasted till 1994 exacerbated racial tensions with conflicting support from the Indian side towards the Africans and ruling elites. In the post-apartheid era, the tensions have only partially subsided as the million-strong Indian-origin community that makes up 2 per cent of the South African population and 10 per cent of KwaZulu-Natal's population is now seen as an upwardly mobile class.

Outside East Africa and South Africa, Indians also made inroads into central and West Africa in the 20th century. The Chanrai Group, for instance, started as textile traders in Sindh and expanded through Malta in the 1870s to Nigeria in 1900. Since then, it has expanded all over the world. The Goan diaspora in Mozambique and Portuguese Africa has partially relocated to Portugal, and a small Indian trading diaspora also exists in Madagascar. Several countries now host tens of thousands of recent Indian immigrants, both in trade and business. Slowly but surely, Indians are waking up to the prospect of settling all over Africa.

Ponte all'Indiano: Bridging Europe and India

When sleepy Indians arrive in London's Heathrow airport and open their eyes to long immigration queues, they can barely identify which country they are in. At first sight, virtually all the attendants at the airport look like them. It's only when they

speak in a British-Indian accent that the Indian passengers are
jolted wide awake. Heathrow airport is located in west London,
around Southall, one of the densest South Asian tracts in Britain,
which explains why so many Indians work at the airport. But
how did so many people from South Asia manage to get there
in the first place? How did the United Kingdom get its nearly
2-million-strong population of Indian origin comprising over 2
per cent of its population?

Some of the first Indians in western Europe went there
as sailors and nannies, usually called lascars and ayahs, as part
of imperial connections. Since 1690, the East India Company
documents record the presence of Indians on ships heading
towards England.[25] Much later, the princes and maharajas of
India and their families spent lavish vacations in England as part
of the deals with imperial forces. In the 19th century, in addition
to lascars and ayahs, a greater variety of migrants went to Britain
including students, artists, jugglers and the proverbial snake-
charmers.[26]

Two Indians had little to do with snakes but still managed
to charm the political establishment in the 19th century.
Dadabhai Naoroji worked in Britain for decades and was the
first Indian to become a member of the British parliament in
the 1890s, winning the election by a narrow margin of five
votes and proceeding to champion causes favouring India. At
quite another level, Abdul Karim from Jhansi in British India,
working as a prison clerk in Agra, was shipped to England
in 1887 for a particular task during Queen Victoria's golden
jubilee celebrations. It was by chance that he caught the fancy
of the queen who made him her personal attendant amidst a
flourishing friendship, a remarkable story depicted in the 2017
British movie *Victoria & Abdul*.

From 1857, the number of lascars and ayahs circulating
between India and Britain rose to tens of thousands, and the

number of students studying in British universities grew from four in 1845 to around 700 in 1910.[27] Student migration to Britain began to account for the who's who of the Indian national movement as they were exposed to Western ideas and quickly recognized the mismatch between the theory and practice of democracy. In the early 20th century, some lascars began to 'jump ship' at ports and find jobs in cities like London, Manchester and Birmingham, and set a path of chain migration that populated these cities with many South Asians in the latter half of the century. The two world wars also brought thousands of Indians to Europe as soldiers, some of whom went to Britain for recuperation.

Post-Independence, many Indians decided to move to their 'imperial motherland' along with the returning British officers. Better wages was one driving force but more importantly, for many, it was a means to escape the horrors of Partition-related communal violence. Punjabis from the districts associated with the Great Indian Migration Wave dominated this migration due to their previous military links and settled in Southall. Mirpur district in present-day Pakistan and Sylhet in present-day Bangladesh emerged as major migrant-sending regions from South Asia, building on previous connections cultivated by the lascars. World War II also took a heavy toll on the male population of Britain and raised the demand for labour in many sectors, which was duly filled by South Asians in mining, mills, transport and even the National Health Service.

Stringent immigration laws in the 1960s restricted the flow of labour migrants from India and persuaded many circulatory migrants to settle in Britain permanently. A new wave of tens of thousands of East African-Indian migrants emerged in the late 60s and early 70s, dominated by Gujarati traders, who quickly set up shop in Britain. In subsequent decades, Gujaratis and Punjabis would draw in many more migrants from their states in India to realize their dreams and aspirations, travelling by airplanes rather than ships due to the revolution in transport. Strong migration networks also led to a clustering of residential choices as over three-fourths of the Indian diaspora settled along the M1 and M6 highways connecting London, Leicester, Coventry, Birmingham, Manchester, Leeds and finally Bradford, where that famous all-Patel cricket match took place.

Assimilation in British society was never going to be easy, especially with the colonial baggage of prejudices on both sides. Cricket itself became a litmus test of loyalty. The Tebbit test, named after Lord Tebbit, proposed that Indians could be considered to have successfully assimilated into British society only if they rooted for England during cricket matches against India. With a few exceptions like Madras-born Nasser Hussain, former captain of the England cricket team, most people of Indian origin would flunk this test even today, even though they have integrated on various other counts such as language and civic and political participation. Tensions rose high not so much with the British as against the Pakistani diaspora with occasional conflicts. Inter-generational conflict also occurred, best reflected in phrases such as British-Born Confused Desis (BBCDs) and Fresh off the Boats (FOBs) that clearly demarcated two different identities. Significantly, Britain was also shaped considerably by the Indian influx, developing a taste for the cuisine served in Indian (and Bangladeshi) restaurants that popularized chicken tikka masala and nightclubs that played bhangra music.

In the past two decades, Indian immigration has increased through the student–work migration route and was increasingly drawn towards high-skilled jobs in the finance and IT sectors, as the low-skill sectors were swamped by migrants from the European Union, who had preferential access to labour markets. As a result, the Indian community now has a much more positive image, marked by tremendous entrepreneurial energy.

Britain serves as a base for Lakshmi Mittal, steel tycoon and one of the richest magnates in the world, and numerous other Indian-origin business leaders. In 2010, one India-born businessman, Sanjiv Mehta, revived the East India Company by purchasing trademarks and assets associated with the firm that ceased to exist in 1874. The Company that had brought Britain to India and the Indians to Britain is now owned by a person of Indian origin, if only in name.

No other country in Europe, except Britain, hosts more than 3,00,000 Indians. Most others host only a few thousand. Belgium has around 20,000 Indians, mainly associated with the diamond business, as does Russia, in the education and high-skilled sector. Russia had mercantile links with India, as documented in the previous chapter, but post-Independence, it also attracted students and scientists, such as my grandfather, a mathematician who wanted to undertake cutting-edge theoretical research in harsh winters with an occasional glass of vodka on the side. Over a 1,00,000 Surinamese Hindustanis live in the Netherlands, and a similar number of Indian IT professionals live in eastern Europe, Germany and the Scandinavian countries combined. Germany, like Britain, attracted Indian students in the early 20th century, including Ram Manohar Lohia (1910–67), who later became a famous socialist leader in India, and Khwaja Abdul Hamied (1898–1972), whose studies in chemistry enabled him to set up the Chemical, Industrial and Pharmaceutical Laboratories in 1935, now known as CIPLA, a global giant in pharmaceuticals. Post-World War II, the migration of Christian Malayali nurses to Germany became prominent to meet shortages in the health sector, along with continued student migration due to the country's highly subsidized education system.

Similar to the British imperial connection, the French and the Portuguese also attracted migrants from their colonies in India. Initially, a few Parsis developed Parisian connections

in the early 20th century, reflected in the business houses of
both Tata and Godrej, but by the late 20th century, the major
segment of the 100-thousand-strong Indian diaspora in France
was the Tamilians, due to the link with Pondicherry. Unlike
the French, the Portuguese Empire in India ended by force in
1961, but many Goans who had migrated to Portugal earlier
for education moved to adopt Portuguese citizenship.[28] In the
1970s, they were joined by the 'twice migrant' people of Indian
origin in Portuguese Africa-Angola and Mozambique. The
Indian diaspora of over 60,000 in Portugal is thus complex with
multiple identities maintaining few economic or philanthropic
links with India.

Two other countries of Europe have notable Indian diasporas.
In Spain, the number exceeds 30,000, comprising many
Sindhis. But unlike most parts of the world, recent emigrants
to Barcelona are drawn from an ex-untouchable community of
India, the Ravidasias of Punjab, from the zones associated with
the Great Indian Migration Wave.[29] It represents a departure
from the standard Punjabi migration pattern to the English-
speaking world as immigration has not yet been capped only
for those who are highly skilled, thereby allowing entry, legal
and illegal, at different points into the labour market. But more
than Spain or any other country in continental Europe, it is Italy
which has attracted the maximum number of Indian migrants
in the past three decades. Punjabi Sikhs in the dairy sector of
northern Italy comprise the majority of the roughly 2,30,000
Indians that live in Italy today. The first wave of migration in the
1990s was male-dominated, but in recent years there has been
considerable family reunification, leading to new challenges of
isolation that women face while living in remote rural areas,
cut off from their large families in India.[30] In addition to the
Punjabis, there are several thousand Roman Catholic Keralites
working in the domestic service sector around Rome.[31] In Italy,

the production of milk and cheese, and the care of the aged, now have a significant Indian presence.

For centuries, Europeans had travelled to India, written about the Indians and got statues erected in the country. In the 19th and 20th centuries, Indians began travelling to Europe in greater numbers, wrote about the Europeans and, finally, were honoured with statues erected there. In central London, within a mile, stand a Gandhi statue in Tavistock Square garden, a Nehru statue outside the Indian embassy and an Ambedkar statue within the walls of his alma mater, the London School of Economics. But for sheer elegance and excitement, one has to walk along Arno river in Florence, all the way to Cascine Park, to see the white marble statue of the Maharaja of Kolhapur Rajaram II (1850–70). The young prince was sightseeing in Florence on his way back to India from Britain and died unexpectedly after an illness. He was cremated at night as existing rules did not permit such ceremonies, his ashes were scattered in the Arno, and a statue was soon erected.[32] Thus, in the city of the Renaissance and beautiful bridges like Ponte Vecchio and Ponte Santa Trinita, the bridge leading to Cascine Park was named Ponte all'Indiano. Along with eating gelato at Santa Trinita and sandwiches at All'Antico Vinaio, it is a part of Florence no visitor from India can afford to miss. It is literally a bridge between Europe and India.

Model Minorities: North America

In 1833, residents of Calcutta received a pleasant 100-ton surprise from a ship that had sailed for four months all the way from Boston. White and cold, packaged ice soon made waves among the Indian elite and transformed the idea of a dessert. This cool idea was the brainchild of Frederic Tudor (1783–1864), known as the Boston Ice King and founder of the Tudor Ice Company, whose mission was to ship manufactured ice from New England to the Tropics. He belonged to the 'Boston Brahmins', a term coined to describe the wealthy aristocracy of the New England area in the 19th century which emphasized core values of education, hard work, culture and thrift. In America, it was a time when the word 'Indians' referred to the native American Indians and not the residents of India. A century and a half later, it would be the Indian-Americans and the Brahmins in Boston that would make waves among the American elite.

Dubbed as 'the other 1 per cent' by political scientist Devesh Kapur and others, Indian migration to the United States in recent decades appears to be the most selective migration in human history, on account of 'triple selection'.[33] On the supply side, higher education in India was historically accessible only to the top-end of the social and economic hierarchy, while financing emigration for studies or work was feasible only for a few. On the demand side, the American immigration rules favoured workers in particular high-skilled sectors. As a consequence, Indian-Americans outperform every other sub-group in America in terms of income and education.

Migrant links between the USA and India were first fostered in the 19th century when missionaries and traders moved from the USA to India, and sailors or lascars landed on American soil. Some of the lascars settled in New York City's Harlem and other cities, starting families with women of different nationalities and races.[34] A more systematic migration stream developed in the early 20th century when the Punjabi Sikhs, serving in the British Indian army in East Asia, began to migrate to the west coast of America in the early 20th century, to work on the railway lines and lumber in the north and agriculture in the south. This was the migration that led to the growth of successful peach grower Didar Singh Bains in California, as noted in the previous chapter.

Student migration began in the late 19th century and attracted Anandibai Joshee, the first known Indian woman to receive an educational degree in the US, as early as in the 1880s. Massachusetts Institute of Technology (MIT) on the East Coast grew in prominence as a destination for science and engineering students from India, while Stanford and other universities on the west coast also began admitting Indian students. Even then, the total number of India-born immigrants in the US was less than 5000 in 1920.

The appearance of Indians as students and workers, all labelled Hindus irrespective of religion, was not well appreciated in early 20th century America. The mass migration of Europeans to America between 1850 and 1914 had acted as an important safety valve for their populations, but when other regions began aspiring to the American dream, there was a racial backlash and steep visa walls were erected to block Asians. According to an official report in 1910, Indians were 'the most undesirable of all Asiatics and the peoples of the Pacific states were unanimous in their desire for exclusion'.[35] In such a milieu, for five decades, immigration laws discriminated against most nationalities.

Amidst the civil rights movement and Cold War politics, these visa walls were torn down by the landmark Immigration and Nationality Act of 1965, opening the doors for millions around the world. But unlike in the past, the new immigration laws were biased towards skilled migrants. This did not matter much for neighbouring countries like Mexico as labour migrants could still slip in as undocumented workers, but for distant shores like India, the USA was an option only for those who had the means and the skills.

Indians migrated in three clearly discernible waves.[36] Between 1965 and the late 1970s, highly educated Indians, especially from the newly established Indian Institutes of Technology, moved to work in the science, engineering and medical fields. This was

followed by a phase of family reunification until the mid-90s
when the spouses and children joined the early emigrants. These
migrations were labelled the 'brain drain' in India, a concept
that will be discussed in the final chapter. Since the mid-90s,
the boom in the Information and Technology (IT) sector led
to the mass migration of computer engineers and students who
got jobs there. The major areas of Indian settlements have
been the New York–New Jersey cluster, Silicon Valley or San
Francisco Bay area, Washington D.C., Chicago, Houston and
Dallas. While Gujaratis and Punjabis dominated the earlier
waves of migration, the latter phase was dominated by south
Indians, especially Telugus and Tamilians, as private computer
training schools proliferated in the region since the 1980s.
Districts like Anand in Gujarat and Guntur in coastal Andhra
Pradesh thus became major sites of American emigration and
received large amount of remittances and diasporic philanthropy
in return. Similarly, Bengaluru and Hyderabad forged close
connections with American NRIs for entrepreneurial ventures
and investments in real estate.

The craze to go to the USA was, and is still, evident in
the numerous computer coaching centres that have sprung
up in India and the premium placed on 'America boys' in the
marriage market, much like what is was for 'Bombay boys' in
Ratnagiri district. In Andhra Pradesh, an engineering degree
and an American visa are considered to be rites of passage
towards upward mobility. The variety of visa acronyms such
as B-1, L-1, F-1 and H1B and the loopholes in the visa system
are also discussed threadbare. When the H1N1 pandemic broke
out in 2009, a popular refrain in India was that the queues at the
American embassy had grown longer as people thought it was a
new visa that the Americans were offering.

Despite mass migration in particular sectors, the USA was
not a destination in the Great Indian Migration Wave because

migration was more permanent and gender-balanced in nature. This led to the emergence of a large second-generation Indian-American population facing all the challenges of assimilation from choosing names to fitting in with society, as was eloquently described in Jhumpa Lahiri's *Namesake*, to earning sobriquets of being branded as American Born Confused Desis (ABCDs) by the Indians. It involves understanding baseball more than cricket and Hollywood more than Bollywood.

The people of Indian origin in America today are a diverse group in terms of language, class and religion, but not so much in terms of caste. They are Democrat-leaning in terms of political preferences and have diversified occupations through entrepreneurship.[37] They could be born in India, the USA or anywhere else in the world and collectively number over 3 million, forming 1 per cent of the US population. The USA, in fact, hosts the largest Indian diaspora as over a 1,00,000 Indians continue to emigrate there every year. India has also emerged as the second largest source of immigrants in the US, next only to Mexico. Poor and undocumented Indian workers do exist by the thousands, but their stories are rarely heard in the general narrative of Indian success. The Indians in the USA are known for the premium they place on education, hard work, culture and, perhaps more controversially, on thrift, like modern-day Boston Brahmins. The tag of being the 'most undesirable of all Asiatics' has been put to rest.

Like the Indian community in the USA, the million strong Indian community of Canada is also a model minority group—well-educated and entrepreneurial—representing around 4 per cent of the Canadian population. They mostly reside in Toronto in the east and Vancouver in the west. But the Indians in Canada are less likely to belong to Gujarat or Andhra Pradesh as in the USA and more likely to belong to a few districts of eastern Punjab that belong to the Great Indian Migration Wave.

The Punjabi link with Canada (pronounced as 'Kuhnedda' in Punjabi) stems from a variety of reasons that go back to the early 20th century. In 1902, Punjabi Sikhs of the British Indian army in Hong Kong sailed to British Columbia on Canada's west coast for the coronation celebrations of Edward VII.[38] They brought back stories of rich fertile lands. Between 1903 and 1908, as many as 5000 Punjabi Sikhs migrated to Canada to work in lumber mills, forestry and the railroads. Racist immigration rules were soon introduced to keep out the Punjabis to protect local jobs amidst an economic downturn, including one that barred immigrants from coming to Canada unless they made a continuous journey. Gurdit Singh, a Sikh leader, decided to test this rule by hiring a Japanese ship, the *Komagata Maru*, and sailed directly from Hong Kong to Vancouver in 1914 with nearly 400 'East Indians' on board. The Canadian authorities stalled the entry of the immigrants for two months before turning the ship away by force. As many as 102 years later, the wise Canadian Prime Minister Justin Trudeau apologized for this blatant act of racial discrimination.

The restrictive laws lasted till the 1950s, by when only 3000 Indo-Canadians remained. Since then, immigration from India has gone up steadily in every decade, as did the immigration of people of Indian origin from East Africa, Guyana and Fiji. In the past two decades, immigration has been dominated by highly skilled workers under a selective points-based visa system, with greater diversity among Indian sub-groups even though Punjabis continue to be the most dominant sub-group. As a result, the state of Punjab in India continues to receive large amounts of international remittances, as it did in the 1970s when remittances helped in financing the Green Revolution.

The Punjabi link with Canada has had two fallouts. First, the turmoil in Punjab in the 1980s that was associated with Sikh militancy, the Indian Army's storming of the Golden Temple

A portrait of Malik Ambar (1548–1626), painted in gold and opaque watercolour on paper, by Mughal artist Hashim circa 1620. Malik, who was born in Ethiopia and was brought to India as a slave, rose to become a powerful military commander in the Ahmadnagar kingdom and thwarted several attacks from the Mughals in north India. This folio is from a set of paintings called 'The Minto Album' that was purchased at an auction in 1925 and subsequently divided between the Victoria and Albert Museum in London and the Chester Beatty Library in Dublin.

HILL COOLIES LANDING AT THE MAURITIUS.

A report on hill coolies coming to work on sugar plantations in Mauritius, from the 6 August 1842 issue of the *Illustrated London News*. The abolition of slavery throughout the British Empire led to large-scale importation of indentured labour, dubbed as coolies.

The introduction of the railways in 1853 marked a distinct shift from horse power to horsepower, greatly increasing the speed of travel within the Indian subcontinent. Here, the *Illustrated London News* celebrates the arrival of the railways in its issue dated 19 September 1863.

LASCARS

BURMESE   BENGALI   MALAY   SIAMESE   SURATI

CHINESE

A group of lascars, or sailors, depicted in a sketch from 1873.
Lascars were among the first Asians to migrate to Western Europe.

An elephant being unloaded from a steamer on to the Andaman and
Nicobar Islands, circa 1900. Human beings were not the only ones moving
to distant shores during the wave of globalization in the late 19th century.

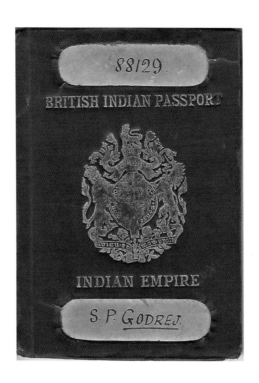

A representative passport of a citizen, S.P. Godrej, of British India issued in 1934.
He was the chairman of the Godrej company, a well-known Parsi enterprise.
In the early 20th century, passports were popularized as documents that
regulated international migration.

Source: British Library Images Online

Refugees flee Mandalay in Burma on foot and in bullock carts. The Burmese refugee crisis of 1942 led to the mass migration of nearly half a million Indians.

Photograph by Margaret Bourke-White, copyright © Getty Images

A boy sits on a mound overlooking a refugee camp in October 1947 in the aftermath of 'history's biggest refugee crisis' that was unleashed by Partition.

Refugees at a makeshift camp in Bongaon, West Bengal, in June 1971, during the Bangladesh Liberation War. As many as 10 million refugees had entered India at the time within a span of just eight months.

A migrant family from Rajapur taluk in Ratnagiri district inside a photo studio in Chembur, Bombay, sometime in the 1960s. The photograph was collected as part of the author's field research in Ratnagiri in 2015. Ratnagiri in western India is a core region in the Great Indian Migration Wave, witnessing mass migration since the 1870s.

Dr M. Ramaswamy creatively used the pressure cooker to warm a steam chamber at his Ayurveda centre in Ljubljana, Slovenia, to help the World War II veterans overcome anxiety and depression. Interestingly, Indian emigrants took their beloved pressure cookers to remote parts of the world they went to.

'That young professor wants a swivel-chair in his room—otherwise he threatens to emigrate to Canada!'

The cartoon above is from R.K. Laxman's book *Common Man Meets the Mantri* (Penguin Books).

'Remember the carpenter who lived there? He's an NRI now. He had emigrated to the Gulf and is back now.'

The cartoon above is from R.K. Laxman's *Common Man Goes to the Village* (Penguin Books).

A tribute to the late R.K. Laxman for his contribution to the nation.

and the anti-Sikh riots after Indira Gandhi's assassination by her Sikh bodyguards led to considerable support and funding for the Khalistani separatist movement from various sections of the diaspora in Canada. It led to the tragic bombing of Air India's Flight 182 from Toronto to Delhi in 1985, over the Atlantic Ocean near Ireland, claiming over 300 lives. It still stands as one of the largest mass murders in Canadian history. Second, Punjab is famously known in India for its agricultural might but also infamously known for its 'missing women' phenomenon. Sex ratios at birth are skewed starkly in favour of males due to a preference for sons and abortion of female foetuses. As it turns out, studies have shown that this cultural trait persists in Canada, even if it is under different material conditions.[39] Old habits often die hard in the diaspora.

Oil and Toil: West Asia

The demographic rise of the six Gulf Cooperation Council (GCC) countries—Saudi Arabia, United Arab Emirates, Oman, Bahrain, Qatar and Kuwait—from the 1970s is considered to be a major episode in global migration history. Immigrants now comprise half the population, more than three-fourths in some of the smaller states, in what has become the biggest destination for temporary migration in the world. Over seven million Indians work in the Gulf states, constituting a third of the foreign Asian workforce, a quarter of India's diaspora and half of India's current emigrant stock. Citizenship laws based on paternal jus sanguinis (right of blood) rule out permanent settlement and automatically create circulatory migration strategies that are male-dominated, even though Indian women, nurses in particular, dominate certain sectors. West Asia, or the Middle East, depending on your reference point, has therefore emerged as a major destination of the Great Indian Migration Wave.

The 'Gulf' is so strong in the Indian imagination that it is sometimes forgotten how and why India, and within India, the southern state of Kerala became an important part of its labour pipeline. Indian mercantile presence in the region, as recounted in earlier chapters, has a long history, as did the Haj pilgrimage routes, ferrying Muslims across the Arabian Sea, but labour migrations from India to the Gulf were relatively rarer. One exception to the rule was Aden in present-day Yemen, bordering the Gulf states, where the British ruled between 1839 and 1967. Until the 1930s, Aden was governed under the Bombay Presidency and hence hosted an Indian community estimated to be between 5000 and 10,000 people for a century.[40] Dhirubhai Ambani (1932–2002), founder of India's largest private company, Reliance Industries, associated usually with petrochemicals, worked in Aden from 1948 for a decade, learning the tricks of the trade as a gas station attendant.[41] But he returned to India, like many others, once British exit from Aden was imminent in the 1960s and the population of Indians in Aden or Yemen dwindled thereafter. Iraq was another West Asian country which attracted over a 1,00,000 Indian troops serving in the British army during World War I, and for a brief period flirted with proposals of Indian colonization, but to no further avail.[42]

It was oil that eventually took the Indians to the Gulf states in large numbers in the 1970s, but the trickle had already begun a few decades earlier. In the early part of the 20th century, British and American firms were scouting for oil along the Arabian shore of the Persian Gulf, after the Anglo-Persian Oil Company, or APOC (part of which became British Petroleum), had discovered a large oil field in Persia, or Iran, in 1908.[43] Significantly, the APOC's field manager, George Bernard Reynolds (1853–1925), an engineer, had worked with the Indian Public Works Department for two decades. After the firm's incorporation in 1909, he began recruiting Indian workers for APOC in Persia. One official commented that:[44]

> Local Arabs, like the Bakhtiari, are under no pressing necessity to look beyond their crops and flocks for employment, so nearly all artisans, labourers et cetera are being imported.

Within fifteen years, the number of Indians working with APOC in Iran rose to nearly 3000, with some of the recruits coming from the discharged army in Iraq. The abolition of the indentured system and the passing of the Emigration Act of 1922 meant that APOC had to open a formal recruiting office in Bombay, setting a template for others to follow. During the years of the Great Depression, APOC downsized its workforce and many Indians switched to the Bahrain Petroleum Company (BAPCO), an American firm founded in 1932 in Bahrain, which in turn opened its first recruiting office in Bombay in the late 1930s. This was followed by the Kuwait Oil Company (KOC) and the Arabian American Oil Company (ARAMCO), which placed a recruiting agent in Bombay in 1944.

All along, labour recruitment was intimately tied with protectionist policies. The concession treaties between the British and Arab rulers stipulated the employment of locals, or at most Arabs, but not foreign labour except in a few sectors such as clerical and managerial jobs. For a while, Hindus were banned in Qatar and Saudi Arabia.[45] These rules and the location of the recruitment office in Bombay meant that the recruits were mostly Muslims and Christians, belonging mainly to Kerala and Goa respectively, as those regions had exported a large number of educated youth looking for jobs to Bombay in the interwar years.[46] Migration networks slowly intensified and recruitment offices began to emerge in Kerala and Goa. From the 1950s, Malayali nurses also began to migrate to Kuwait and other places

which were setting up their health infrastructure. Thus began
the connection between the Gulf and India's west coast.

In 1950, over 6000 Indians were employed by oil companies
in the Persian Gulf, a number that steadily rose to 40,000 by
the early 1970s.[47] The trickle then turned into a torrent. Two
oil price hikes by the oil-cartel in 1973–74 and 1979 led to
windfall gains for oil companies and laid the path for a massive
push towards infrastructure creation, requiring huge amounts
of labour in all occupations. Between 1975 and 2010, the
population of the six Gulf states quadrupled from nearly 10
million to over 40 million.[48] Along with skyscrapers and malls,
the population of the United Arab Emirates (home to Dubai
and Abu Dhabi) rose spectacularly from around half a million to
over 8 million, while the population of the most populous Gulf
state, Saudi Arabia, rose from 7 million to 27 million. Other
Gulf states now have populations that exceed a million each.
Indian, and Keralite, immigration has been at the forefront of
this demographic boom.

Even though white-collar jobs and professionals make up
more than 30 per cent of the Indian emigrant workforce in the
Gulf, it is the labour class and its exploitation that routinely make
its way to newspaper headlines.[49] Labour right violations are
tied up with the infamous *kafala* system of sponsorship whereby
migrant workers become dependent on their employers for
entry to and exit from the Gulf. Living conditions for labourers
are not too great either and, from time to time, fraudulent
recruiters dupe prospective emigrants. Public-sector jobs are
often reserved for the locals because of which most Indian
immigrants work in the private sector, where abuse over terms
of employment is more rampant. In economic downturns, the
chorus against the migrant grows as nativist policies kick in. For
instance, in 2011, Saudi Arabia launched the *nitaqat* policy to
incentivize firms to hire more native workers. The Gulf states

have consistently followed a policy of 'separation' rather than 'assimilation'.[50]

Yet, the vast wage differential between India and the *Gelf*, as it is called in Kerala, is attractive enough for migrants to consider the option at least once in their lives. In the past decade, the locus of emigration to the Gulf shifted from south India to the north, and the Bhojpuri-speaking tracts of eastern Uttar Pradesh and western Bihar once again dominate annual labour flows outside India, much like they did a century and a half ago.[51] The billions of dollars of remittances from the Gulf that once touched the west coast of India has finally made its way to the Ganga. Reynolds could not have possibly anticipated the chain of events that he had helped trigger.

From Buddha Singh to Sucha Singh

Our tour of the overseas Indian world has three final stations: Oceania, East Asia and Latin America. In the early 19th century, a small trickle from India headed down under to Australia in Oceania as labourers and convicts. In the 1830s, as the first batch of 'hill coolie' indenture migrants were sent to Mauritius, a small batch of Dhangar labourers from Chhota Nagpur were also taken to New South Wales in Australia in 1837.[52] In the late 19th century, the camel trade between Australia and India opened up and Indian cameleers from the north-west were brought in to accompany expeditions and pastoral ventures in the deserts of Australia. The Indian population rose to nearly 5000 by the end of the 19th century, and this development along with other non-white immigration led to a major racial backlash. As in the USA and Canada, Australia passed an Immigration Restriction Act in 1901, known as the White Australia policy, effectively barring Indian migration for the next five decades. When the restrictions were slowly lifted in the 1950s and 60s, the India-born British citizens and Anglo-Indians arrived first, followed by a more sustained migration stream of professionals. From 15,000 in the 1960s, the Indian population went up to 80,000 in the 1990s and then shot up to over 4,00,000 in recent years to form 2 per cent of the Australian population, most of whom live in Sydney and Melbourne. A part of this surge was led by the Indo-Fijians moving out of Fiji, but more generally, student migration from India increased as Indian students found Australia to be a relatively low-cost high-quality market for higher education.[53] Like the racial backlash during the first phase of migration in the early 20th century, this surge also encountered racially motivated crimes and robberies against Indian students in the first decade of the 21st century. Nevertheless, Australia remains a major destination for Indians to pursue higher education and high-skilled work, replete with numerous Indian cultural associations and festival celebrations.

In New Zealand, the Indian diaspora traces its origin to Punjabi and Gujarati migration in the late 19th century, the former working in agriculture and the latter in trade.[54] Restrictive immigration laws, this time passed in 1899 through an English language test, thwarted the Indians' attempts to come in larger numbers until the 1980s. Since then, the Indian diaspora, including the Indo-Fijians, has steadily grown to nearly 2,00,000, representing 3 per cent of the population. The image of the Indian as a shopkeeper in New Zealand also changed as Indians diversified to managerial and professional roles. The broad similarity in the experiences of Indian migration to the English-speaking world of New Zealand, Australia, America, Canada and Britain is striking.

Hong Kong is yet another place where Indian professionals seek their fortunes. The Indian diaspora there traces its roots to traders and Punjabi Sikh soldiers on deployment in the 19th century. Indian soldiers in the British army fought the Opium

Wars that led to the colonization of Hong Kong and opening up of Chinese ports.[55] Those ports then received Parsi traders in the 19th century, as recounted in the earlier chapter and brilliantly described in Amitav Ghosh's *Ibis* trilogy. Mainland China, for long connected to India via the Silk Route, also attracted Indian soldiers employed by the British. In the early 20th century, Shanghai was a hotbed of nationalist fervour, not only for the Chinese but also for the Indians as the Ghadar Party, founded in America in 1913, had opened a branch there in 1914.[56] The Ghadar Party and the Chinese nationalists faced a common enemy, the British-run Shanghai Municipal Police (SMP), which happened to employ Punjabi Sikhs. The Indian and Chinese nationalists hatched a plan to instigate a strike among the serving police officers but this required the exit of one Buddha Singh, the highest ranking Indian officer of the SMP's Sikh branch. In a remarkable incident in 1927, Singh was assassinated in Shanghai by a nationalist Sikh from the Ghadar Party, all because of his intense loyalty to the British Empire.[57]

Most Indians in China were uprooted during the violent 1930s and 40s. Very little migration occurred in the second half of the 20th century due to the political standoff between the two countries. With liberalization of foreign trade, China grew to be a major trading partner of India in the 21st century. As a result, in the last two decades, tens of thousands of Indians have found trading jobs in China. Sindhi traders are commonly found in leading Chinese cities and Hong Kong today.

India's migrant ties with Japan go back to the 19th century, through the textile trade and education, centred in Yokohama and Kobe. For a brief while in the 1940s, it also served as a military training centre for Subhas Chandra Bose's Azad Hind movement, which was trying to overthrow the British. Recent decades have seen a more diverse migration stream taking the size of the Indian diaspora in Japan up to 30,000. South Korea today has a few thousand highly skilled Indians working mainly in multinational corporations, struggling with the language and winters but enjoying their dak galbi and soju.

In Latin America, there are few Indians outside the world of sugar plantations as noted earlier. They number less than 1000 in most countries, many of them those who migrated away from the plantations to countries such as Peru and Brazil. The Punjabi Sikhs, however, had links with Mexico during their sojourns to the East Coast farms of the USA in the early 20th century, leading to a small settlement there over time, and where Sucha Singh has become a Señor Sanchos.[58] These Punjabi links extended till Argentina as many chose new destinations to settle in after being blocked out by US immigration authorities. There is evidence of Sikh migration to Argentina as early as the 1890s. Even today, they dominate the Indian diaspora in Latin America.[59]

Indians now reside in every country of the world, barring perhaps North Korea and a few others. And with every new Indian adventure abroad, readers are greeted with a new book describing how Indians have made that particular part of the world their home. A recent addition to this documentation is Swarn Singh Kahlon's *Sikhs in Latin America*. The day is not far when a book is released on Indians in Antarctica. Penguin would be the ideal choice to publish it for more than one reason.

Videsi outside and within India: Sub-National Diasporas

There is an Indian diaspora and then there are sub-Indian diasporas. This is because migrations, even those outside the Great Indian Migration Wave, have been linked with specific communities, languages and regions within the country. These diasporas are in fact much larger as they also extend within the subcontinent. For instance, the Gujarati diaspora within India is much larger than its international counterpart. And so it is for the Marathi, Kannada, Telugu and Odia diasporas. The word *videsi* in Odisha, for instance, is used to refer to not only the overseas Indian but also the Odia migrant worker in Gujarat. The 'Emigration Act' used to apply to Assam in the late 19th century, even though it was within the geographic boundaries of British India and the Indian subcontinent. What constitutes inter-state internal migration in India can involve a cultural crossover that is similar to the one faced while moving abroad, especially because the states of India have mostly been drawn on linguistic lines. Thus, on first arrival, north Indians in south India or south Indians in north India can have a challenging time directing an autorickshaw, given the significant linguistic differences.

Using Census data on languages, I conservatively estimate the internal diasporas of ten major languages—Hindi, Bengali, Punjabi, Gujarati, Marathi, Odia, Kannada, Telugu, Malayalam and Tamil—that are spoken by over 90 per cent of the Indian population to collectively stand at over 60 million people, more than double the size of India's international diaspora.[60] These are people who have made a significant linguistic crossover. Their descendants who speak Hindi or one of its numerous variants outside the core Hindi heartland in north India and its immediate borders, comprise over 30 million people. This includes the labour diaspora of the Bhojpuris and the mercantile diaspora of the Marwaris concentrated mainly in Gujarat and Maharashtra. Both the diasporas extend towards south India and the North-east. The size of the internal Hindi diaspora is over four times that of what I estimate for the international Hindi diaspora, showing that Hindi or Hindi-variant speaking communities have crossed cultural boundaries within India more often than outside the subcontinent.

This is equally true of those who speak Telugu, Marathi, Bengali (Indian), Kannada, and Odiya. All have moved to

major metropolitan centres outside their linguistic zones, as
labourers and professionals or due to job transfers in public
and private sector enterprises. The Indian Bengalis have spread
westwards, but the language appears in large numbers in the
Northeast due to the east Bengal, or Bangladeshi, connection.
Clusters have also emerged, sometimes following the Great
Indian Migration Wave and sometimes outside it. There is thus
a Telugu community of over 2,00,000 people in West Bengal,
a Marathi-speaking community of over a 1,00,000 in Tamil
Nadu and Kerala in the south, and an equally strong Odiya
community in Gujarat.

The Gujaratis, as we have seen, have wide-ranging
transnational connections, but even they have a larger diaspora
within India than outside. The internal Gujarati diaspora is
roughly four million strong, in Mumbai and the southern states,
and exceeds its international counterpart. It is clearly reflected in
the spread of diasporic associations, the lifeblood of community
life in India's internal and international linguistic diasporas. There
is a Gujarati Samaj in Assam and Tamil Nadu, and there is also one
in St Louis in the US and one in Hong Kong. The government-
run Gujarat State Non-Resident Gujaratis' Foundation lists 176
such associations within India and 120 outside. In a rare case of
linguistic crossover, but perhaps it makes business sense, there is
also a Gujarati-Marwari Society of Thailand.

At over 2 million each, the internal and international
diaspora of the Indian Punjabis is roughly the same. But while
the international diaspora is closely linked with the eastern
Punjab cluster of the Great Indian Migration Wave, the internal
diaspora is more widely sourced and found in key industrial hubs
of the country. Of the ten major languages, it is the Tamilians
and Malayalis that have a wider international diaspora than
internal, although the internal diasporas are sizable—4 million
and 2 million respectively. One of the routes through which the

Tamilians migrated internally was through the civil services and government postings, sectors initially dominated in south India by the Tamil Brahmins, now popularly known as the Tam-Brahms. As a result, the Tamilian community in New Delhi and Mumbai runs into hundreds of thousands, where they are still sometimes referred to as the 'Madrasis', a word that originated in reference to the Madras Presidency, of which Tamil Nadu was a part. There is also a Tamil labour diaspora spread out across India, like its international counterpart. The Malayali diaspora, on the other hand, was formed by the outmigration of nurses, as well as clerks, secretaries and other administrative staff, all over India. Special training colleges for these sectors gave them an initial lead that still holds sway. In terms of the diaspora to population ratio, the Malayalis outdo all other linguistic groups of India, with a figure of over 10 per cent.

The internal diasporas of India are important to understand because they have also shaped international diasporas. Antwerp's diamond connection with Surat or West Asian oil firms' labour connection with Kerala were both channelized through Bombay because the city hosted a sizable Gujarati and Malayali diaspora. The internal diaspora also faces the same challenges of assimilation as Indians face when they move abroad. But because migration is heavily linked through social networks, assimilation need not even occur as migrants reproduce their customs and practices in their enclaves. Madhav Sadashiv Gore (1921–2010), an eminent sociologist, noted many of these issues in a book called *Immigrants and Neighbourhoods* in 1970, which studied the Marathi-, Hindi-and Tamil-speaking groups of Bombay. Writing about the most cosmopolitan city of India and the city of my birth, he observed that:[61]

> The path of migration is cleared and smoothened by friends
> and relatives. When our rural migrant moves from his home

into Bombay he need not experience the loneliness and uncertainty or even the anonymity of the big metropolis. He is only moving from the residential family unit to the extended family outpost in the city. This explains why the 'nearest' town or city is not always a preferred option.

Gore also studied friendships in the city and found that Brahmins were more likely to make friends belonging to their own caste than non-Brahmins across all three linguistic groups, with an extremely strong preference noted for the Tamilians.[62] In neighbourhoods, language was an important factor for developing acquaintances, even more than religion, and one third of the housewives in the sample reported no acquaintance of any kind outside the immediate family.

Since 1970, more immigrants from north India arrived in Mumbai, and Hindi emerged as the language to bind the masses, even more than Marathi which is spoken by roughly 40 per cent of the city's population. 'South Indians' make up around 10 per cent of Mumbai's population today while a fifth of the population speaks Gujarati. It has retained its multi-lingual character, and the enclaves and social exclusions described by Gore have weakened only partially through greater inter-linguistic marriage. Having married outside my linguistic group, just like my parents did much earlier, I am now party to bewildering household practices, super-spicy food, and tuned to learning aspects of Mumbai such as the social differences along the Western and Central Railways lines, something I could not have known earlier.

Each linguistic diaspora has its own style of celebrating religious festivals, cuisines and distinct music and dance classes attended by children. The spread of Ganesh Utsav celebrations is linked with the spread of the Marathi-speaking diaspora just like the attendance and craze for Durga Puja festival celebrations has risen with the growth of the Bengali diaspora. In such a milieu, the English language and Chinese food have emerged as two major attractions that bind ties as they keep everyone at a common disadvantage. Not only is English the language of the elite, it is the language of aspiration in the 21st century. And the distinctly Indian-Chinese food, remote from what the Chinese actually offer, has infiltrated menus across restaurants in India. Asked what they miss most when they go abroad, Indians are quite likely to say 'Chinese food', even in China.

Sub-national diasporas are also stereotyped in the same way as national diasporas are, as they tend to cluster in certain segments due to networks, strong peer pressures and demonstration effects. Odiya cooks and plumbers, Malayali nurses and secretaries and Bengali economists have all gained a reputation for excelling in what they do, across the country, if not the world. As an offshoot, economists in India often mull over learning a third language, Bengali, in addition to English and maths, to keep up with frenetic academic conversations.

A Matter of Water and Steam

Over the past century, the Indian international diaspora changed from a plantation (and not necessarily indenture) dominated diaspora in a few countries to a diverse diaspora spanning the world. In the erstwhile plantation world, caste dissolved into race or ethnicity as a marker of identity. The international diaspora that was once fairly representative of the Indian population is now a much more elite diaspora with miniscule representation of the lowest castes in recent waves of outmigration. There is religious diversity in the diaspora overall but with wide variations in selected migration corridors. Women's representation is low in the zones of the Great Indian Migration Wave, and autonomy is not always at par with men in other zones. The links established by the Punjabis, Gujaratis, Malayalis and Tamilians during the colonial period were critical in the extension of their internal and international diasporas. They were followed globally by the Telugus and Kannadigas, while the erstwhile dominant Bhojpuris lagged behind in relative terms. The march of the Bengalis within and outside India has also kept up pace, and the spread of the language was supplemented by outmigration from Bangladesh.[63]

If there is one striking cultural practice that unites Indians across all these identities and separates India from the places they usually migrate to, it is the use of water in toilets as opposed to tissue paper abroad. Indians' love for water is closely matched with their love for steam generated by the pressure cooker, a wonderful gift of humankind celebrating both rice and noise, amplified many times over in silent honk-less neighbourhoods abroad. It is no wonder then that a mug and a pressure cooker are important objects packed in the luggage of a first-time visitor or settler in new lands. Indian assimilation in host societies abroad not only involves learning the native language and celebrating their sporting teams but also, inevitably, wearing fewer saris and converting household practices towards using tissue paper and noiseless rice steamers, the last practice being the toughest to adapt to.

Assimilation was difficult for the first-generation migrant, despite Nehruvian advocacy for four decades after Independence. After the abolition of the indentured system, Indian nationalists and then the Indian government followed a hands-off policy on overseas Indians, turning away from the crises faced by Indians in East Africa in the 1970s for instance. 'When in Rome, do as the Romans do' was the unspoken official mantra. This began to change in the 1980s because the Chinese were successfully wooing their diaspora to invest in China, setting a template and opportunity for the Indian government to consider. Since the 1970s, concerns over the treatment of migrant workers in West Asia had already forced the governments of major sending states to set up services for emigrant welfare. During the Gulf War of 1990–91, the Indian government promptly evacuated 1,00,000 Indians stranded in Kuwait. In 2001, with the publication of an official report on the Indian diaspora, the engagement with the Indian diaspora began to fundamentally change. 'Diaspora' was no longer a phenomenon to be studied by sociologists, it would henceforth be considered a strategic asset used towards furthering gains in foreign policy and investment and sustaining Indian cultures.

An annual event called the Pravasi Bharatiya Divas was launched in 2003 to connect with overseas Indians. It is held on 9 January every year to commemorate the date of Gandhi's return from South Africa to India in 1915. During its first celebration, the then Prime Minister, Atal Behari Vajpayee, pleaded for ideas more than investment and the richness of experiences more than riches.[64] In practice though, the focus has been on investment and riches, and a proactive concern about the welfare of overseas Indians. In 2004, the ministry of overseas Indian affairs was created though this was later submerged within the ministry of external affairs in 2016. And while dual citizenship is still not permitted, a new category called the Overseas Indian Citizen was created with the major benefit of not requiring an Indian visa to travel to India even after giving up Indian citizenship. Dual identities however remained, and the world 'transnational' came into vogue to reflect the many connections that migrants continued to have with their homeland, facilitated by easier transport, communication and satellite television. For the Indian diasporas, dreams were first about aspiration and return and only much later about assimilation. Diaspora conflicts were first with the natives and only then inter-generational. This was equally true of immigrant diasporas based in India—Sri Lankan, Tibetan, Afghan and others—even though most of them emerged from involuntary migration, the subject of the next chapter.

Table 1[65]

Indian Diaspora and Emigrants (% of Total), 1910–2010

Destination	Diaspora					Emigrants	
	1910	1930	1980	2000	2010	1910	2010
North America	0	0	7	16	19	1	21
United States	0	0	4	11	13	0	16
Canada	0	0	3	4	5	0	5
Asia	64	70	44	48	50	74	64
West Asia	1	0	7	21	26	1	50
Sri Lanka	24	26	10	6	4	30	0
Nepal	4	3	3	4	3	5	6
Myanmar	22	21	5	3	2	22	0
Malaysia	11	17	15	11	9	13	1
Singapore	1	1	2	2	3	1	3
Oceania	2	2	5	4	4	2	4
Australia	0	0	1	1	2	0	3
New Zealand	0	0	0	0	1	0	1
Fiji	2	2	4	2	1	2	0
Europe	0	0	10	10	10	0	10
United Kingdom	0	0	8	7	7	0	6
Italy	0	0	0	0	1	0	1
Africa	21	17	22	15	12	10	2
South Africa	7	5	10	7	6	5	0
Mauritius	11	8	8	5	4	2	0
Réunion	1	1	2	1	1	0	0
East Africa	1	3	1	1	1	2	0
Latin America & Caribbean	13	10	12	7	5	12	0
Trinidad & Tobago	5	4	5	3	2	3	0
Guyana	6	4	5	2	1	6	0
Suriname	1	1	1	1	1	2	0
World total (%)	100	100	100	100	100	100	100
World total (million)	2.3	3.4	8.2	15.1	21.7	1.6	11.0
World stock as % of total Indian population	0.9	1.2	1.2	1.5	1.8	0.6	0.9

Major Hotspots of the Indian Diaspora

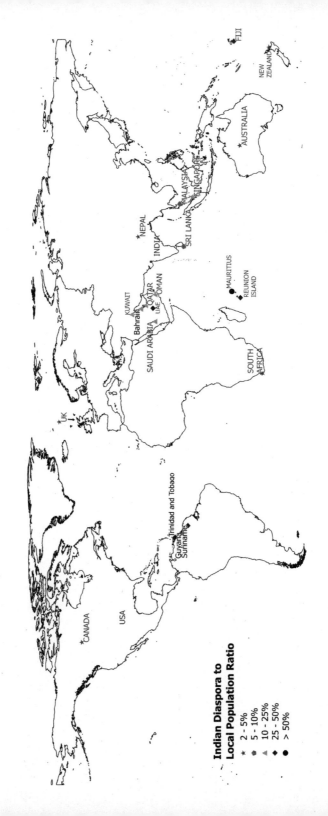

5

Partitions and Displacements

'Two or three years after the 1947 Partition, it occurred to the
governments of India and Pakistan to exchange their lunatics
in the same manner as they had exchanged their criminals.
The Muslim lunatics in India were to be sent over to Pakistan
and the Hindu and Sikh lunatics in Pakistan asylums were to
be handed over to India. It was difficult to say whether the
proposal made any sense or not.'

—Opening lines of 'Toba Tek Singh', a short story by
Saadat Hasan Manto (1955)

Madness. In hindsight, this word best sums up the decision to
hurriedly partition the Indian subcontinent based on religious
lines in 1947. Amidst horrific bloodshed, over 17 million people
were pushed out, making the Partition 'one of the largest and
most rapid migrations in human history'.[1] The Partition, which
led to the creation of India and Pakistan as two independent
countries, was a landmark event of the 20th century but it was
only one among many partitions linked with the decolonization
of the British Empire after World War II. Indians were affected
not only within the country but also in Burma, Sri Lanka,

East Africa and the other parts of the world that they had migrated to. It was with great dismay that Indians found out that they were perceived as foreigners, just like the colonial rulers, and were not welcome to stay on after Independence.

The Partition of Pakistan in 1971 and the creation of Bangladesh were associated with another refugee crisis in eastern India, involving a staggering 10 million people at its peak.[2] Mass migrations due to the partitions are etched in public memory in India's border-states as their ramifications persist even now. On a smaller scale, Tibet and Kashmir also witnessed intimidation, persecution and exodus. Yet, these events and other partitions are dwarfed by the fact that more than 40 million people have been displaced *within* India due to development-related projects since Independence.[3] Collectively, all these events shaped the contours of involuntary migration with words like 'refugee', 'relief', 'rehabilitation', and 'DPs' or 'Displaced Persons' entering the common vocabulary.

The Partition of 1937: Burma

The first major partition of British India took place in 1937, when Burma was constitutionally separated amidst strong native voices calling for political representation and restrictions on the flow of Indian migrants. Ever since its integration with British India in 1886, people of the Indian subcontinent had full access to the Burmese labour market across multiple sectors and occupations, riding on the Great Indian Migration Wave. By the 1930s, there were around 1 million people of Indian origin in Burma, constituting 7 per cent of the total population and over half the population of Rangoon city.[4] During the Great Depression, the Burmese economy sank as rice exports shrank, jobs dried up and allegations of Indian usurpation sprang forth. In addition to the interests of Chettiar capital, as noted in a previous chapter, even labour migrants were targeted by locals. In 1930, racial riots broke out near the Rangoon docks between Indian and Burmese labourers, killing dozens and injuring hundreds. What began as a quarrel over jobs and wages spiralled into a rallying cry for restrictive immigration policies by nationalists. Anti-migrant sentiment and a weak economy dampened migration flows from the Indian subcontinent to Burma over the next decade.

On 23 December 1941, Rangoon was bombed by Japan amidst World War II hostilities.[5] The attack was sudden and caught the British off guard. As the British army retreated, civilians of non-Burmese origin, mostly from India, began to flee by sailing to Madras, Calcutta or Chittagong from the port of Rangoon. However, the port's closure in February 1942 and subsequent closure of different sea routes prompted most evacuees to trek almost 1000 km north towards the Indian border. One route via the Arakan led to Chittagong, another via the Chindwin valley led to Manipur and a third route via the northern passes led to Ledo in north Assam.[6] The journey was undertaken by people across social strata, along congested roads plied by laden ox carts and lorries moving slowly in one direction at difficult altitudes. Estimates suggest that this hurried and unplanned process of evacuation cost anywhere between 10,000 and 50,000 lives due to starvation, exhaustion, diseases, war-related injuries and other reasons. By May 1942, the Japanese military campaign was over and exit routes were sealed even though refugees continued to trickle into India for another two months. A refugee camp survey by the Indians Overseas Department of the Government of India counted close to 4,00,000 people, even though the actual number was likely to be upward of half a million as many evacuees had left the camps for their homes in India. Essentially, India already had a full-blown refugee crisis at hand a good five years before the Partition of 1947.

The refugee crisis occurred a few months before the Quit India Movement was launched by Indian freedom fighters in August 1942. Jawaharlal Nehru latched on to the issue while touring Assam in April 1942, pointing out serious shortcomings in arrangements for the evacuation, including racial discrimination against the Indians.[7] Europeans often had access to safer exit routes and were covered by insurance policies that were not available to the Indians.[8] The lack of adequate resources and frequent mistakes in the evacuation process prompted even British officials to call it 'a horrid mess' and a 'first class disaster'.[9] Problems were complicated further because of harassment, at times, at the hands of the native Burmese nurturing anti-Indian sentiments. Nevertheless, the government built refugee camps with medical facilities along with non-official charitable bodies and organized transport and civil supplies that gradually brought the situation under control. Many evacuees departed for their ancestral homes in India, while many awaited a return to Burma as they had left all aspects of their lives back there.

Between 1942 and 1945, policies and legislative debates over resettlement of the Burma refugees took place even though major Indian political leaders were behind bars for their activities during the Quit India Movement. Refugees had also arrived in India from other parts of South East Asia that Japan had attacked, but Burma was clearly the special case as was reflected in the formation of a dedicated Burmese Refugee Association. Provincial governments opened employment bureaus for those who had returned from Burma, subsistence allowance was provided for and university fees were waived for students. In early 1945, Burma was re-occupied by the British and the refugees could return following an agreement between the governments of India and Burma later that year. However, only a fourth of the evacuees went back.[10] Shamshad Begum's *Mere Piya Gaye Rangoon* was sung against the backdrop of this upheaval.

Following Burmese Independence in 1948, new citizenship, immigration and land nationalization laws were introduced that hurt the interests of Indian labour and capital. With the advent of military dictatorship in 1962 and nationalization of various sectors, people of Indian origin began leaving by the thousands over the next two decades. Unresolved claims on assets and business properties implied that the returnees often came back empty-handed. Most headed for their provinces or states of origin while some relocated to other countries. Until 2001, Tamil Nadu, an important source of Indian settlers in Burma, had rehabilitated nearly 1,50,000 returnees.[11] Rehabilitation measures included land grants and loan facilities for housing the returnees after they spent time in temporary transit camps. Major 'Burma Colonies' sprung up in New Delhi, Jaipur, Bhopal, Patna, Kolkata, Moreh (Manipur), Vishakapatnam, Vellore, Chennai, Trichy and Madurai as families of the returnees reassimilated into Indian society.[12]

Just as the repatriation policies regarding Indian settlers in Burma were winding down in the 1980s, a new refugee problem arose. Hundreds of native Burmese students crossed over into India in 1988 to escape the backlash against their pro-democracy protests. Over the next decade, the annual flow of Burmese refugees rose to several hundred, and they were based in two refugee camps set up by the Indian government in Leikun (Manipur) and Champhai (Mizoram). Some of these migrants were 'Chins', Christian tribals claiming to have escaped religious persecution in Buddhist-majority Burma. Another community which consistently faced the brunt of religious persecution in Burma were the Muslim Rohingyas, who had moved several generations ago from Chittagong in present-day Bangladesh to settle in new agricultural frontiers in the Arakan. They sought refugee status sporadically in Bangladesh since the 1970s and suffered heavily in 2016–17 under state-sponsored persecution in Myanmar. Over a half a million Rohingyas now live in Bangladesh while another 40,000 are estimated to be in India.

The Partition of 1937 and the traumatic ordeal of 1942 were pivotal events that marked the end of an era of active Indo-Burmese migrant links. The first Burmese refugee crisis pre-dated the 1947 Partition crisis by a few years and gave valuable lessons to political leaders and members of the Indian Civil Services in relief and rehabilitation work. This would prove to be of immense value in tackling the next crisis, more gigantic in scale and viciousness than anything in the past.

The Partition of 1947: India and Pakistan

The word 'prepone', as opposed to postpone, is widely used in India but was added to the Oxford English dictionary only in 2010.[13] Its historic use in India could be related with the fact that the country was formed by an act of 'preponement' in a land accustomed to postponement. On June 3 1947, Louis Mountbatten (1900–79), the last Viceroy of India, brought forward the departure date of British exit by nearly a year to 15 August 1947, leaving little time for administrative preparation in a region with over 300 million people. By then, Partition seemed inevitable after a seven-year-long political agitation by the Muslim League, skilfully led by Muhammad Ali Jinnah (1876–1948). In the absence of Partition, it was argued that Muslims would suffer under Hindu dominance in undivided India, a point bitterly opposed by Gandhi and the Indian National Congress for long. Frequent communal clashes in the 1940s re-enforced the stance of the Muslim League. The case for Partition was debated at length and dissected from multiple angles in the 1940s but the modus operandi of the final decision was remarkably absent from these discussions. The freedom fighters and British policymakers were likely to have been well aware of the ghastly population exchange of nearly two million people between Greece and Turkey on religious lines in the early 1920s, but in that case a formal exchange was agreed upon *after* a refugee crisis and not before. With the benefit of hindsight, the lack of consideration on the physical movement of people at the policy level appears to have been striking. To a question on the foresight of mass transfer of population at a press conference on 4 June 1947, Mountbatten replied:[14]

> Personally, I don't see it. There are many physical and practical difficulties involved. Some measure of transfer will come about in a natural way. That is to say I have a feeling that people who have just crossed the boundary will transfer themselves. Perhaps Governments will take steps to transfer populations. Once more, this is a matter not so much for the main parties as for the local authorities living in the border areas to decide.

In June 1947, British exit and Partition were imminent within two months but the exact contours of the new boundaries were yet to be finalized. Worse, the decision of the Boundary Commission, chaired by Cyril Radcliffe (1899–1977) during his first and only visit to India, on the bifurcation of Punjab in the west and Bengal in the east was delayed and released two days after the formal transfer of power on August 17. Independent India was thus born prematurely, without definite borders, waiting for its umbilical cord in the wings to be cartographically clipped after two days.

The Western Front

When the Boundary Commission awards were finally announced, officials of newly formed Pakistan condemned it calling it 'disgusting', 'extremely unfair and unjust', 'based on no principles', and found it violating the 'democratic principles of contiguity of majority areas'.[15] The grouse was against the partitioning of Punjab, or the districts of Gurdaspur and Lahore to be more specific, where some Muslim-majority sub-districts contiguous to West Punjab were retained in India. The border stayed put but people did not. On the western side, over 6 million people poured into Pakistan, and close to 5 million moved to the Indian side, along with an estimated 2 million casualties.[16] Undivided Punjab had half the population of undivided Bengal but the displacements and casualties were more than double on the western frontier than in the east. This is why, in public memory, the Partition of 1947 is more closely associated with Punjab than Bengal.

Punjab differed from Bengal in two important aspects. First, it housed three numerically significant religions rather than two. Muslims, Hindu and Sikhs made up roughly a half, third and sixth of the population of undivided Punjab respectively. Many districts had thin majorities, and in some no religion enjoyed an absolute majority. Geographically and emotionally, Sikhs got the rawest deal because the Radcliffe line ran right through the centre of their homeland, with important shrines on both sides. The demographic case to move was thus felt stronger in Punjab than in Bengal. In addition, undivided Punjab was home to a large number of the 2.5 million-strong British Indian army that had served a few years earlier in World War II. As one research study has shown, war veterans had exposure to combat experience that fostered particular organizational skills useful for co-ethnic immigration and minority ethnic cleansing.[17] Building on the communal clashes of 1946–47, the level of violence unleashed by this potent mix of hatred and organizational skill was truly horrific as blood-stained trains rolled across the borders, vividly captured in Khushwant Singh's novel *A Train to Pakistan*.

People ran for their life, and at least one such escapee, Milkha Singh, would continue running long after, representing India in professional athletics at the highest levels. As news of mass murder and rape filtered through at each end, more minority families were convinced of the need to migrate, even if they did not intend to do so. They were gripped by a kind of fear that was poignantly described by novelist Amitav Ghosh in *The Shadow Lines:*[18]

> It is a fear that comes of the knowledge that normalcy is utterly contingent, that the spaces that surround one, the streets that one inhabits, can become, suddenly and without warning, as hostile as a desert in a flash flood. It is this that sets apart the thousand million people who inhabit the subcontinent from the rest of the world—not language, not food, not music—it is the special quality of loneliness that grows out of the fear of the war between oneself and one's image in the mirror.

This fear had set in many months before Partition and refugee camps had already been set up due to violent communal riots in some places. The wealthy elites, money lenders and landlords were the first to depart, by motor and air transport to the other sides, whereas the relatively poor were huddled into refugee camps waiting for clarity over the exact boundary.[19] After the notification of the boundary, between August and October 1947, the displacement was spontaneous, violent and exhausting. The transportation routes were chock-a-bloc with people and carts. Week-long journeys were much shorter than those endured by Indians fleeing Burma in 1942 but were more complicated as it was a crisis with two-way traffic. The rural masses dominated the foot columns while the urban folk dominated the refugee trains known as 'India Specials' and 'Pakistan Specials', carrying 2000 or more passengers each, without ticket charges. While trains were a faster way to get across the border, they were also potential death traps.

The scale of the crisis finally dawned after two million people had already moved to each side, and in mid-October 1947, the Military Evacuee Organization (MEO) of India and Pakistan formulated a Joint Evacuation Movement. The detailed plan covered strategies on evacuation, relief and transport to move people from transit camps to refugee camps across the border. Thousands of military and civilian trucks were pressed into service. Schedules were drawn to avoid clashes of caravans moving in opposite directions. Government employees were given preference during evacuation and many were airlifted out of crisis zones with flights between Lahore, Quetta, Rawalpindi, Peshawar, Karachi, Bombay and Delhi. The MEO was updated by the District Liaison Officers about 'stranded refugees, abduction of women and children and forcible conversions taking place in their areas' after which police and army rescue missions were coordinated.[20] The organized nature of evacuation had one flipside: it also led to organized violence with easier identification of the refugee movements for the attackers.

The refugee camps that the displaced encountered after their 'last journey' across the border were run by an assortment of charitable organizations. The radio broadcast in the camps every night was a significant event as it would relay news on the people missing, dead or found elsewhere.[21] With people huddled into refugee camps or homes of their friends and relatives, an even more daunting task of rehabilitation awaited the policymakers. India's first Union government had set up a dedicated ministry of relief and rehabilitation to tackle these challenges. The nature of the challenges can be surmised by the fact that the ministry was disbanded only four decades later in 1984.[22] K.C. Neogy (1888– 1970) from West Bengal headed the first ministry and outlined a vision of rehabilitation closely tied up with broader goals of national development. Rehabilitation work included the building of new townships from scratch, repatriation of movable property, re-use or disposal of vacant immovable property, and much more, for millions of people. Official categories of the displaced included agriculturists and townspeople, traders and artisans, orphaned or unclaimed children, widows, or abducted or destitute women, and each had their own requirements. A series of legislations, agreements, treaties and financial assistance measures were passed to cater to people's needs, culminating in the Displaced Persons (Compensation and Rehabilitation) Act of 1954.

The most spectacular success in rehabilitation was achieved in agricultural resettlement. Two decades before Punjab's much-touted Green Revolution of the late 1960s and 1970s, vast lands lay uncultivated with no clear titles due to Partition-related displacement. Tarlok Singh (1913–2005), an economist trained at the London School of Economics and member of the Indian Civil Services (ICS), was the director-general of rehabilitation in east Punjab and rose to the occasion along with thousands of revenue officials in resolving a complicated problem.[23] The first step of resettlement involved group-based relocation of refugees and allotment of land in groups to owners and tenants. This was possible because the great displacement during Partition had occurred at the community level, along particular district to district corridors. Village level allotments were undertaken to ensure that close relatives didn't live too far off. Using a system of the graded cut of a 'standard acre', the displaced were allocated land to compensate for what they had lost to the best extent possible, taking into account criteria such as land size, yield, revenue assessment, value of gross produce, profit value and lease value. Land allotment coincided with financial assistance given towards the purchase of agricultural inputs. As a result, over half a million families could resume agricultural activities in Punjab in quick time. Tarlok Singh was rewarded for his efforts by a promotion to the powerful Planning Commission where he worked for nearly two decades. Later, he served as the deputy executive director of the United Nations Children's Fund (UNICEF) between 1970 and 1974.

Urban rehabilitation proved to be trickier as vacant properties could not simply be re-occupied by incoming migrants. As A.P. Jain (1902–77), minister for relief and rehabilitation would find out, the economic status of outgoing urban Muslims was lower than those of incoming urban non-Muslims.[24] In 'history's biggest refugee crisis', as he described it, differing occupational profiles in the population exchange mattered greatly when it came to effective rehabilitation. Half a million families from West Pakistan had to be accommodated in towns, and by 1952 over 80 per cent had found a place in 'evacuee houses, houses and tenements newly constructed by the rehabilitation ministry and in houses constructed by the displaced persons'.[25] More than ten new townships were also developed. However, in housing arrangements, caste would inevitably be a source for segregation as 'Harijan refugees' were physically separated from upper castes in government resettlement policies.[26] According to one nasty upper-caste parody, 'untouchable' sweepers did not care about the violent chaos surrounding them during Partition, as nobody was going to 'touch' them in any case.[27]

The recovery of abducted persons and rehabilitation of widows proved to be another challenge. Tens of thousands of women were abducted during Partition, and after an inter-dominion treaty was signed, the Central Recovery Operation was launched, lasting nearly a decade.[28] Kamlaben Patel and Mridula Sarabhai (1911–74) played stellar roles in locating, repatriating and rehabilitating abducted women. In one of the more remarkable titles in Indian legal history, The Abducted Persons Recovery and Restoration Act was passed in 1949. Another issue related to women was widowhood, which was traditionally stigmatized in Indian society. The sheer scale of the phenomenon jolted the government into action by creating a separate women's section in the ministry of rehabilitation headed by Rameshwari Nehru (1886–1966), the founding member of the All India Women's Conference. The women's section provided care homes and hired the services of numerous charitable organizations, women's welfare groups and academic institutions engaged in social work such as the Tata Institute of Social Sciences.

While Punjab was the epicentre of mass migrations, there were migrations and incidents in other places too along the western frontier. Extreme violence against Muslims and displacements were observed in Hindu-dominated Alwar and Bharatpur of present-day Rajasthan as well as in Jammu, near Kashmir.[29] Many Muslims from present-day Maharashtra, Uttar Pradesh and other states migrated to West Punjab and Sindh. These Urdu-speaking migrants, called muhajirs, were influential members of the Muslim League and played an important role in defining Pakistani politics in the initial years. The situation of Hindus and other non-Muslims in Sindh, the other large province of Pakistan, was uncertain for quite some time but the influx of muhajirs and escalating levels of violence led to the evacuation of over half a million people by air, road and sea.[30] Hindus dominated four of the five major cities of Sindh— Hyderabad, Shikarpur, Larkana and Sukkur—and were almost as dominant as the Muslims in Karachi. This changed soon after Partition, though a much larger share of Hindus stayed back in Sindh than in West Punjab. A large number of the Sindhis who moved to India settled in present-day Maharashtra and Gujarat.

The Eastern Front

Bengal had already faced a short-lived partition in 1905, supposedly on administrative grounds, but that measure did not trigger major population movements. The Partition of Bengal in 1947, however, was a different matter altogether. Compared to the western frontier, which witnessed larger displacements and casualties, the displacement along the eastern frontier was more unbalanced and prolonged. By 1951, India had sent 7,00,000 migrants across the new eastern border and received 2.5 million migrants, mainly in West Bengal and parts of present-day Assam and Tripura.[31] India later received close to 2 million more migrants in the 1950s and '60s with virtually no flow in the reverse direction.[32] Casualties along the eastern front are difficult to estimate because the Bengal Famine of 1943 had already taken a huge toll, but recent research is converging on an estimate of around one million people, in contrast with a figure of over two million along the western front.[33] A breakup of casualties in terms of those killed by violence as opposed to disease, exhaustion and other factors is not available, but the casualty to displacement ratio appears to be much higher along the eastern front than in the west. Serious riots in several districts, especially Noakhali and Tippera in Chittagong division of East Bengal, had broken out in late 1946, moving thousands of people, mostly Hindus, into shelter camps well before Independence.[34] The madness continued in eastern India, and on the eve of Independence, Gandhi was praying for peace in Calcutta, far away from all the political action in Delhi. Post-Partition, the violence continued sporadically until major riots broke out again in early 1950, prompting more inflows of Hindus from East Bengal into India. Migration from East Bengal was therefore a more 'fluid' problem for policymakers, 'the pace being determined from time to time by political events in Pakistan'.[35] Many did not migrate to India in the initial years, echoing perhaps the views of the old man in the novel *The Shadow Lines:*[36]

> Once you start moving, you never stop. That's what I told
> my sons when they took the trains. I said: I don't believe in

this India-Shindia. It's all very well, you're going away now, but suppose when you get there they decide to draw another line somewhere? What will you do then? Where will you move to? No one will have you anywhere. As for me, I was born here, and I'll die here.

In order to heal the wounds of Partition, the Liaquat-Nehru pact was signed in April 1950 between India and Pakistan, which among other things proposed to set up minority commissions and allow the displaced to return unharmed to dispose of their property. Migrations on the eastern front were unbalanced towards India and evacuee land was inadequate to settle the incoming migrants. By 1951, only half the number of displaced families had been resettled.[37] Two townships at Habra-Baigachi and Fulia in West Bengal were being built and numerous extensions were built to existing towns. Close to 40,000 'unattached' women and children were being looked after as the state's responsibility.[38] Government officials were providing relief work but had kept rehabilitation plans on hold in the expectation that a large number of migrants would go back across the border. They never did. In fact, many of the Muslim evacuees returned to West Bengal.

Three years later, in June 1953, a detailed survey-based report by West Bengal government officials, on the conditions of the displaced, was published. It argued that permanent rehabilitation had to be top priority to 'avoid forced idleness' in the transit camps, which was demoralizing.[39] The report recommended the dispersal of people from transit camps to rehabilitation centres and work sites. Among new initiatives, the Dandakaranya project was the most ambitious as it entailed starting a resettlement zone in the wilderness bordering western Orissa and Chhattisgarh.[40] The project was marred with a lot of problems as the migrants sent there, mostly low-caste, would return to West Bengal in

the absence of good facilities and employment opportunities.
The Andaman and Nicobar Islands was another site where a
few thousand migrants were sent. But by and large, Assam,
West Bengal and the region surrounding Calcutta in particular
continued to be the mainstay of the migrants.

Along with picking up a new life, East Bengali migrants
in West Bengal also picked up a new moniker. They were
the Bangalis as opposed to the local population, known as
Ghotis, with legendary stereotyping on both sides. Bangalis
were depicted as being coarse, loud and lacking in refined taste
and dialect. Ghotis, on the other hand, were depicted as being
arrogant and selfish. One second-generation Bangali, whose
family moved from Faridpur in East Bengal to West Bengal by
train in 1948, recounted:[41]

> Ghotis still claim West Bengal to be theirs only; they still
> treat us like foreigners, like refugees. They are selfish, self-
> centred. Bangalis, by contrast, are *dil-doriya* [loving], easy-
> going, with the ability to bring people closer . . . If you come
> to my house at 2 p.m., you will have to have lunch with us
> because it is lunchtime. If you got to a Ghoti house, you
> won't get any food.

The Bengali penchant for food was matched only with that
of football, where the Bangali–Ghoti divide would be on full
display, in the iconic battles between East Bengal and Mohan
Bagan football clubs of Calcutta.

The Consequences of Partition

The Census of 1951 revealed that 7.5 million people, or 2 per
cent of the Indian population, were uprooted from regions in
Pakistan due to Partition; around 5 million from the west and

2.5 million from the east.[42] In Delhi, every third person had been uprooted from across the border, in Punjab and West Pakistan every fifth person, in West Bengal, every twelfth person and in East Bengal or East Pakistan, every fiftieth person.[43] Partition also led to internal displacement as migrants moved in to newly vacated territories, and undertook international emigration to Britain and other distant shores. Partition-related displacement had placed a fiscal burden on the newly formed Indian republic to the tune of Rs 1.4 billion up to March 1952, nearly half of which was spent on evacuation, relief and rehabilitation grants, a third spent on housing and a fifth spent on resettlement loans.[44]

The economic consequences of Partition were significant in the long run too, as vibrant trade across lands marked without borders shrunk after the demarcation of strict boundaries. The tea plantations of Assam lost direct routes to the sea ports. The jute industry in eastern India was crippled because the jute fields lay in East Bengal and the mills were in Calcutta in West Bengal. This was compensated for India to some extent as the migration of jute cultivators from East Bengal to West Bengal brought in significant expertise and boosted agricultural yields in the new lands they cultivated.[45] The migration of entrepreneurs led to the creation of new industries but also the division of partnerships. Mahindra and Mohammed was a firm formed in 1945, but after Ghulam Mohammed (1895–1956) left to become Pakistan's first finance minister, the firm's name was changed to Mahindra & Mahindra. It later grew to become a large Indian firm producing utility vehicles and tractors.

Three key leaders of India and Pakistan between 2004 and 2007 were born on the other side of the border, with memories about their ancestral places hogging national headlines: Pakistani President Pervez Musharaff was a Delhi-born muhajir; former Indian prime minister Manmohan Singh is a West-Punjab born Sikh; and former leader of the Opposition in India, L.K. Advani, is a Karachi-born Sindhi. Memories of Partition continue to haunt families and their descendants in the 21st century as erstwhile immigrants are sometimes portrayed as 'outsiders'. In some communities, such as the Sindhis in India, this may have crystallized stronger religious identities in a bid to assimilate with their adopted countries.[46]

If the Partition of 1947 was supposed to be the solution to the perceived dominance of Hindus over Muslims, two decades later it was clear that even Muslims and Muslims could not hold peace in events leading up to the Partition of 1971. Religion could never be the sole identity of importance in the Indian subcontinent where diverse identities had been shaped through historical migrations.

The Partition of 1971: Bangladesh

In the 1960s, Pakistan's economy considerably outperformed India's under two military general presidents, Ayub Khan until March 1969 and Yahya Khan thereafter.[47] Yet, beneath the surface, the turmoil within Pakistan was far greater than in India, as non-democratic rule was taking its toll, especially in East Pakistan which was more populous than West Pakistan. When general elections were finally conducted in December 1970, Mujibur Rahman's Awami League won an absolute majority, winning nearly every seat in East Pakistan. Zulfikar Ali Bhutto's Pakistan People's Party was dominant in West Pakistan and came in second place.[48] The transfer of power, however, dithered as the demand for provincial autonomy by the Awami League caused much consternation among political leaders in West Pakistan. After negotiations broke down in Dhaka in March 1971, Yahya Khan flew back to West Pakistan. On 26 March 1971, he launched a brutal military crackdown on the separatist movement in East Pakistan. In what is often described as 'genocide', tens, if not hundreds of thousands of civilians were killed and raped over the next eight months.[49] On 16 December 1971, the 'Liberation War' of Bangladesh finally ended with the unconditional surrender of Pakistan to the Indian army. India was dragged into the war because during those eight months, the country faced the world's largest refugee crisis ever to have been confronted by a modern sovereign state, a record unsurpassed till the present day.

In April 1971, India received about 60,000 refugees on an average on a *daily* basis.[50] In May, the daily average exceeded a 1,00,000. In June, it was a little under 70,000. Over 6 million refugees had crossed over in just three months. Nearly 4 million more refugees would arrive in the next four months, taking the peak tally to 10 million in November. Of this, West Bengal took in 7 million, while the three eastern regions of Tripura, Meghalaya and Assam received approximately one, half and a third of a million respectively. In some districts, the influx exceeded the district's pre-influx population. Of the 10 million, nearly 7 million lived in refugee camps and the others lived on their own, on the streets or with friends and relatives. This was an extraordinary refugee crisis that required an extraordinary response, involving not only the government but other organizations, not only Indian but from the wider global community.

The Indian government pursued an open-door policy on the influx of refugees on humanitarian grounds. Refugees were first registered at border crossings and provided ration for four days before receiving renewed assistance in camps.[51] Before makeshift camps came up, public schools and educational institutions served as stopgap arrangements as they were closed for the summer vacations in April and May. In West Bengal, the Central Relief Office of Calcutta provided the tarpaulin and plastic sheets while locally available bamboo was used to erect camps. Numerous welfare groups in India joined in the effort, buoyed by a call towards national duty. The Marwari Relief Society, based in Calcutta, had over fifty years of experience in relief work, including significant roles during the Burmese crisis and the 1947 Partition. The 'parasites', as Bengali nationalist P.C. Ray had once mockingly called them, ran ten relief camps in Basirhat with over 3,00,000 Bengali-speaking refugees.

A pressing concern in the camps was the procurement of adequate supplies of essential commodities. By one estimate, 5,80,000 tonnes of rice were required to feed 6 million refugees for six months. India's refugee problem was larger than that. Existing stocks were depleted and replenished by food aid from other countries. New depots of the Food Corporation of India (FCI) were set up to distribute food rations. This helped curtail the rising pressure on prices of essential commodities along India's eastern border. Similarly, medical store depots were regularly stocked and re-stocked, and public health personnel were moved to the border areas to contain potential epidemics that may have broken out from the camps. Cholera had claimed the lives of over 5000 refugees until September 1971, and the danger of a public health disaster loomed large. Water tankers were arranged for distributing water, tubewells were sunk and thousands of latrines were constructed. Volunteer groups conducted educational lectures for children in the camps, while separate women's homes and orphanages were also set up. The central government financed refugee assistance and sought aid from outside. As the refugee influx overwhelmed India's districts along the borders, the Indian legislature discussed ways to move the refugees to other states. The uncertainty over the period of stay and the size of the influx led to heated debates. In the end, a few of the 800-odd camps that were set up in 1971 appeared in states away from the eastern border, in Bihar, Madhya Pradesh and Uttar Pradesh.

The international engagement for relief work in 1971 was extensive. The Red Cross, Oxfam, Care, Caritas pitched in, as did the UNICEF, where Tarlok Singh was on deputation. American reluctance to support India due to its traditional support towards Pakistan complicated international affairs as India aggressively reached out to other countries to highlight the East Pakistan issue and the scale of the refugee crisis. One outcome was the constant stream of visits by foreign dignitaries to the refugee camps to see the problems first-hand. Another was India's appeal to the United Nations High Commissioner for Refugees (UNHCR) in April 1971 for assistance. The assistance finally provided was less than what India asked for but still extensive as it comprised important material for relief work, collected from around the world. Thousands of vehicles, tonnes of rice, polythene sheeting and blankets for three million people were provided at short notice. In one long airlift mission, 700 tons of medical supplies were flown over to India.

The refugee crisis could have lingered on for much longer if decisive action had not been ordered by India's then prime minister, Indira Gandhi (1917–84). In what remains her moment of crowning glory, the Indian army won a quick victory in December 1971 after months of resistance offered by Bengali separatists to the Pakistani army. Within a few weeks, ten million people returned to their land—Bangladesh. Camps were disbanded and nearly everywhere, officers noted that repatriation was 100 per cent complete. Within Bangladesh itself, the erstwhile migrants from India, or the muhajirs, found themselves stranded as they had lent support to the Pakistani army. Known even today as the 'stranded Pakistanis', they had succumbed to the fears expressed by the old man in *The Shadow Lines:* 'Where will you move to? No one will have you anywhere.'

India had played a stellar role in providing temporary shelter to 10 million people, managing world opinion to its advantage and opening a new relationship with its eastern neighbour that had seemed unfeasible before. But this also opened up new challenges. In his memoirs, former Reserve Bank of India governor and economic diplomat, I.G. Patel (1924–2005), recounted his efforts at spreading awareness about the Bangladeshi refugee crisis around the world in 1971 and a memorable remark made by a labour economist at a dinner at Harvard in 1972:[52]

> Dr Patel, now that you are friendly with Bangladesh, I suppose the historical migration of Bengali Muslims into Assam and India's North-east will be resumed.' This had never occurred to me and I asked him what he meant. He told me about natural population and economic dynamics and how, under the British, a large-scale migration had taken place and this was interrupted by Partition . . . How little attention do we pay in India to history and to the understanding of geopolitical realities!

The observation was spot on. The 'displaced' of 1947 and 'refugees' of 1971 would give way to 'migrants' or more accurately 'illegal migrants' as the key phrase used to characterize human flows between Bangladesh and India in subsequent decades, a theme we will return to in the final chapter.

Tibet

On the road between Mysore and Madikeri in south India lies a settlement so removed in appearance from its neighbours that it can stun the lay traveller. Bylakuppe is a place replete with prayer flags, momos, pagodas and men in deep red robes. It is home to around 10,000 people and is the largest Tibetan settlement in India with schools, health facilities and a monastery called Namdroling. It also proudly displays posters of Tenzin Gyatso, better known as the fourteenth Dalai Lama, the spiritual leader of Buddhist Tibetans. The Dalai Lama himself lives 3000 kilometres north, in picturesque Dharamsala in Himachal Pradesh, the headquarters of the Central Tibetan Administration (CTA), a parliament-in-exile. Some 3000 kilometres to the east lies its inspiration—Lhasa—across the Himalayas, nestled within the 'roof of the world', the Tibetan Plateau, governed by China.

When the roof began to splinter in the 1950s with Chinese occupation, it was not evident to the Tibetans that their young spiritual leader would spend his life in exile. A failed uprising in March 1959 led the twenty-three-year-old Dalai Lama to make a dramatic escape from Lhasa, disguised as a soldier. His whereabouts were unknown to the international media for two weeks until he resurfaced in Tawang, in present-day Arunachal Pradesh in north-east India, riding a yak and accompanied by close officials, attendants, guards and his brother, sister and mother. He sought refuge in India. Nehru's government treated him as a guest of honour in the land of the Buddha, a treatment maintained by every government since then.

The Chinese crackdown after the Tibetan uprising of 1959 was severe, and by 1961, close to tens of thousands of Tibetan refugees had poured into India and Bhutan by foot, following their spiritual leader.[53] Refugee camps were set up at Missamari (Assam) and at Buxa in Coochbehar (West Bengal), from where they were dispersed to other settlement sites.[54] As security along the Indo-China border tightened after the 1962 war, escape and return became more difficult. The refugee flow slowed down to a trickle, but it continues even today. Presently, the Tibetan exile population is estimated to be 1,40,000 worldwide, of which around 1,00,000 are based in India in thirty-plus settlements in Himachal Pradesh, Uttar Pradesh, Sikkim, Arunachal Pradesh, Odisha, Madhya Pradesh, West Bengal, Karnataka and

Maharashtra.[55] These settlements, like Bylakuppe, are tucked away from the gaze of the public such that most Indians are not aware of them, apart from Dharamsala. The settlements themselves are mostly self-sufficient, carefully preserve the Tibetan Buddhist culture and, barring rare skirmishes, live in harmony with their neighbours. Overall direction is provided by the CTA, first set up in the hill station of Mussoorie in 1959 and later moved to Dharamsala in May 1960. Since its inception, the CTA has been associated with rehabilitation work through education and advocacy for democracy and self-reliance within the Tibetan community.

As refugees, Tibetans don't enjoy the same rights as Indian citizens.[56] India has not been a signatory to the 1951 Geneva Convention Relating to the Status of Refugees and 1967 Protocol (Refugee Convention and Protocol). It did, however, accept the important principle of refugee law called non-refoulement, which forbids returning asylum seekers to a country in which they would face persecution, by adopting the 1966 Bangkok Principles on the Status and Treatment of Refugees. Tibetans and their children born in India have to have registration certificates renewed on an annual basis. Those who entered India between 1959 and 2003 belong to an administrative category called 'long term stay'. Since 2003, when India formally accepted Tibet to be a part of the People's Republic of China, Tibetans are allowed to enter India through fewer checkpoints on a 'special entry permit' issued by the Indian embassy in Kathmandu in Nepal.

Tibetan refugees in India enjoy a large number of benefits, especially after the Tibetan Rehabilitation Policy of 2014. The economic success enjoyed by Tibetan settlements in agriculture, handicrafts, infrastructure and industry has been exceptional relative to other refugee groups in India. Obtaining Indian citizenship is not a high priority for many, unless they want to purchase land or property. An Indian court ruling in 2016 allowed Tibetans to apply for the Indian passport, but subsequent guidelines made this conditional on giving up refugee status and departure from the Tibetan settlements. Tibetans in India argue that this would make them settlement-less for the second time and, for the time being, it remains an unsettled issue.

Economic success and a strong sense of social cohesion did not mean that the 'Little Tibets' were untouched by Indian influences. Along with the daily prayers and traditional tasks, cable television slowly penetrated Tibetan settlements in the 1990s, bringing the hustle and bustle of Bollywood and television serials, and ideals of romance and love-marriage.[57] Second-generation Tibetans encounter all the issues associated with a diaspora, mainly a continuous negotiation with family and the larger society they live in. In northern Indian settlements, Hindi is spoken fluently, and young Tibetans increasingly consider themselves a 'remix of Tibetan, Indian and Western'.[58]

In a surreal triangle connecting Lhasa, Dharamsala and Bylakuppe, over 1,00,000 Tibetans are dispersed away from their homeland. While 'Free Tibet' slogans still resonate, the official line is more subdued, accepting that Chinese rule is inevitable in the near future. This has eased Indo-China foreign relations to some extent. If the Tibetan cause shaped India's foreign relations with its northern neighbour, then the Tamilian cause shaped India's foreign relations with its neighbour in the south.

Sri Lanka

Tamil Nadu in south India is home to the majority of the Tamil-speaking population. But there is another important Tamil world in the little island nation facing Tamil Nadu across the Palk Straits. It, in fact, houses more than one variant of Tamil. Since 1911, the Census of Sri Lanka, then Ceylon, began to classify the Tamilians as either Sri Lankan or Indian to distinguish between two different migrations. The Sri Lankan Tamilians are the descendants of early settlers from south India who originally arrived for the purpose of conquest, and are found in the northern and eastern parts of Sri Lanka.[59] The Indian Tamilians refer to the plantation labour migrants who began arriving since the 19th century and their descendants. They are also called the Hill Country Tamils and live mainly in the central highlands. In 1911, the Tamilians comprised a quarter of the population, equally split between the Indian and Sri Lankan Tamilians. This figure only marginally declined until the 1950s. By then, in absolute terms, they were about a million each. Over the next fifty years, the absolute magnitudes and population shares dipped substantially due to violence and mass exodus.

The Sinhalese (Buddhist) were the dominant ethnic group comprising two-thirds of the island's population in the middle of the 20th century. After gaining independence from British rule in 1948, they began to assert their dominance, making Sinhala the official language in 1956 and enforcing policies in education, employment and investment that led to widespread cries of discrimination from the Tamilians. The Indian Tamilians or estate labour were the first casualties as most of them were considered to be 'Indian nationals' according to the newly drawn Sri Lankan citizenship laws. But at the same time they were seen as 'stateless' in India due to their long stay in Sri Lanka.[60] The Indo-Ceylon pact of 1964, or the Sirima-Shastri Pact, attempted to resolve this issue by agreeing on a formula of repatriation and non-repatriation. Some 3,00,000 Tamilians would receive Sri Lankan citizenship, half a million would be repatriated to India and the situation for the 1,50,000 remaining would be decided later. The programme was phased over fifteen years, but in the end not everyone was repatriated as planned.

The Sri Lankan Tamils, on the other hand, resisted Sinhalese power. In 1976, a militant organization called Liberation Tigers of Tamil Eelam (LTTE) was formed in north-eastern Sri Lanka, demanding a separate state for the Tamilians. Since 1983, a serious armed conflict began against the government. Just as the Bangladeshi separatist movement appealed to Indian Bengalis, the LTTE found support among many Tamilians and influential political parties in Tamil Nadu, but the similarity and support base ended there. India's complex involvement in Sri Lankan affairs in the late 1980s, from relief to peacekeeping missions to demobilization of militant groups led to a fierce backlash culminating in the assassination of former prime minister Rajiv Gandhi in 1991 by LTTE operatives. The LTTE was finally decimated by the Sri Lankan army in 2009, ending a twenty-six-year civil war that was waged in different phases, each prompting an exodus of refugees to Tamil Nadu.

The Sri Lankan civil war prompted mass displacement among the Tamilians, both internally, towards India and around the world. The first Ealam War (1983–88) brought in over a 1,00,000 refugees into Tamil Nadu.[61] Most of these refugees went back to Sri Lanka but another 1,00,000 came in 1990–91 with the outbreak of the second Ealam War (1990–94). These included many who were making their second trip to India as refugees within a decade. After Rajiv Gandhi's assassination, the refugee exodus was blocked by the Indian navy for a brief period, and the Tamil Nadu government began to cut down on the number of refugee camps. The next violent uprising in Sri Lanka in the late 1990s, and again between 2006 and 2009, witnessed a relatively smaller refugee influx.

While fleeing to India, almost all the refugees ended up at Dhanushkodi Island in Ramanathapuram district of Tamil Nadu. After due inspection and registration, they were dispatched to the Mandapam transit camp, and from thereon to one of the numerous refugee camps scattered across Tamil Nadu. In 2009, there were a little over a 1,00,000 refugees in Tamil Nadu, and 70 per cent were living in 115 government-run camps across twenty-six districts. The camps have strict surveillance, few government benefits, temporary houses and rationed provisions. Movements out of the camps are closely watched, restricting the scope for meaningful employment. There is, therefore, a desire to escape camp life and India, to greener and freer pastures abroad. This is sometimes facilitated by strong social networks that have been cultivated by the global Sri Lankan diaspora. Another way out is by marrying locals and attaining Indian citizenship that provides a range of benefits. But until the camps are finally shut down, the Sri Lankan refugee issue will continue to be India's biggest refugee problem, as it has been for the past three decades.

Kashmir

Kalhana's 12th century CE Sanskrit classic on Kashmir, *Rajatarangini,* marks one of the first systematic efforts at history-writing in India. At one point, it alludes to trading interactions between Kashmiri kings and mlecchas or foreigners, interpreted by historians as a reference to Muslims.[62] Some eight centuries later, after invasions, conversions and assimilation, Muslims formed over 90 per cent of the population of the Kashmir valley and in a role reversal, Kalhana's community, most likely Kashmiri Hindus, were perceived by some as *mlecchas* of the Kashmir valley.

The exodus of over 2,00,000 Kashmiris in 1989–90 due to intimidation and violence within their own country defies belief.[63] The fearsome atmosphere that led to the exodus is best recounted by Jagmohan, who was then the governor of Jammu and Kashmir:[64]

The ruthless Kalashnikov, the 350 bomb explosions in the second half of 1989, the hysterical exhortations of 'Jihad' from hundreds of loudspeakers fitted on mosques, the 'Tirana-e-Kashmir' of having the Quran in one hand and a rifle in the other, the sinister design of 'killing one and frightening one thousand' . . . impelled the Kashmiris to abandon their homes and hearths in the Valley and move to the inhospitable camps of Jammu.

The people who left were mostly Kashmiri Pandits or Brahmins who had a historic connection with the Kashmir Valley, but it also included others, including a few Muslims who wanted to escape the suspicions cast by militants on one side and the Indian armed forces on the other.[65] Hundreds died, before and after 1990, in planned encounters. At the peak of the crisis in 1990, there were also accounts of women being raped. The lack of convictions in hundreds of cases in subsequent decades did little to assuage the feeling of injustice felt by the Kashmiri Pandits.[66] After 1990, some Kashmiri Pandits did go back but most of them remained outside. Hindus' share of population in Kashmir declined from 4 per cent in 1981 to 1.8 per cent in 2001, even though their share of the population in Jammu and Kashmir overall remained the same as in 1961, around 29 percent.[67] Between 1981 and 2001, around 1,20,000 Hindus are estimated to have left the Kashmir valley, on a net-basis.[68]

There are no simple explanations as to how one of the most beautiful places of the world became such a cesspool of hatred and violence in 1990. Kashmir's position as being the key bone of contention between India and Pakistan, leading to conflict and wars, was certainly a driving factor. Suspicions of rigged elections in 1987 and police crackdowns alienated the people to a point where chants of *azadi* (freedom) rang loudly in the late 1980s. Across the border, Pakistan sensed an opportunity to avenge the loss of Bangladesh and began training and arming the Kashmiri youth to fight for freedom, just as India had done with the Bangladeshi youth in 1971. The key difference was that India had responded to a major refugee crisis in 1971, whereas in Pakistan the response was linked closely with elements spreading nascent ideas of global jihad. It was not entirely a coincidence that in the winter of January 1990, when minority Hindus were being killed in Kashmir in cold blood amidst chants of azadi, a similar fate befell the minority Armenian Christians in Baku, the capital of Muslim-majority Azerbaijan, with calls for independence from the USSR. The Kashmir insurgency that took off in 1989 had the blessings of radical mujahideen that were promoted across the border in a bid to counter the USSR's march on Afghanistan in the 1980s. Caught in the crosshairs of international and domestic politics and religion, Kashmiri Pandits were targeted as being the 'others' who did not support the freedom movement or, worse, were informers of the Indian armed forces. Militant groups placed advertisements in Urdu newspapers with a deadline to leave the Valley and hit-list notices were stuck on people's gates. The army was called in and curfews were put in place, but the hostile sentiment in the Valley overwhelmed both, the law-keeping forces and the Kashmiri Pandits. In his memoir about the exodus, Rahul Pandita describes his feelings as a young child in 1990:[69]

I can't fathom why all this is happening. If the Kashmiris are demanding Azadi, why do the Pandits have to be killed? Why do we have to leave our house, where I play freely, and ride my cycle, and exchange comics with my friends? How is the burning of a temple or molesting a Pandit lady on the road going to help in the cause of Azadi?

In early 1990, thousands of Kashmiris left their homes for Jammu through the only link road—the Jawahar Tunnel—ironically named after the first prime minister of India and arguably the most famous Kashmiri Pandit. The poorest and those from rural areas filled the refugee camps while the better-off stayed in hotels, houses of relatives, rented rooms or moved to Delhi and beyond.[70] As per the relief commissioner, there were over 20,000 people in sixteen migrant camps in Jammu.[71] The migrant camps initially comprised cloth tents and later transformed into one-room tenements that housed four to five members.[72] They were locally referred to as *kabutarkhana*s (pigeon-cages). Some people in the refugee camps remained unemployed for a long time, supported by salaries and pensions that were promised before the exodus. Since the migrants had not sold their Kashmiri houses, expecting to return eventually, a large number of properties were kept in the care of trusted Muslim friends and neighbours. But the security situation in Kashmir remained fragile for the next two decades with heavy militarization, as a result of which most Kashmiri Pandits did not return home. In fact, many Kashmiri Muslims also began migrating seeking jobs and education outside the Valley. Some Kashmiris moved on to build new lives, but always carried the burden of loss and longing. A study conducted in Delhi found Kashmiri Pandits reported lower life satisfaction levels than the Tibetan Buddhists.[73] The Manmohan Singh government offered a financial package for the return and rehabilitation of Kashmiri Pandits in 2008, but the amount per family was too low to evoke serious interest. The saga of the Kashmiri exodus remains an unresolved matter with vacant properties in Kashmir and migrant camps in Jammu.

The Kashmiri exodus is whipped up routinely by Hindu fundamentalists in 21st century India to show how Muslims can dominate Hindus within 'their' own country. The real lesson of the episode, however, is to note the toxic cocktail

of hyper-religiosity, hyper-nationalism and hyper-masculinity
that marked the events of 1989–90. It is a heady cocktail that
unfortunately continues to re-surface every now and then, both
in India and the world.

Internal Displacement

The multiple partitions of the Indian subcontinent and various
refugee crises led to significant displacements across political
borders. And yet, it was internal displacement within India,
like the Kashmiri exodus, that was of far greater magnitude and
reach. Natural disasters, floods and storms pushed hundreds of
thousands of people out of their comfort zones for brief periods
every year. The history of communal riots in India provides a
painful litany of displacements towards shelter camps and slums,
most infamously in Delhi and Punjab during the Hindu-Sikh
conflict in the 1980s and in Gujarat during the Hindu-Muslim
riots over several decades, especially in 2002. More generally, war
and famine, two major sources of internal displacement in India
throughout history, waned in significance over the 20th century.
They were replaced by ethnic conflict and development projects
as the key factors stimulating involuntary movement. What was
common to both was the disproportionate and adverse impact
on the indigenous population, or the STs.

The unique demography of India's north-eastern region and
the special political status conferred on it via the Sixth Schedule of
the Indian Constitution precipitated several inter-tribal and tribal-
migrant conflicts.[74] What began as one or two demands for separate
homelands and autonomous councils eventually engulfed the
entire region, leading to violent protests, fights and displacements.
Arunachal Pradesh, Nagaland, Mizoram and Meghalaya are thinly
populated states, with less than 10 million people in total, but STs
make up over two-thirds of the population in each state. Further,

over 90 per cent of legislative seats in the state governments are reserved for members of the STs. As a result, dominant tribes or groups have tried to enforce their power by calling for the physical relocation of less dominant groups from their areas, or have demanded exclusive protected enclaves. As a result, the Reangs were displaced in Mizoram, just as the Kukis, Paites and Nagas were displaced in Manipur. Throughout the Northeast, migrants from Nepal, Bangladesh and the rest of India added fuel to the simmering fires of ethnic division and found themselves in shelter camps after multiple rounds of displacement. In central India, the violence erupted from the Naxalite movement determined to overthrow the Indian state, rather than migrants or other tribes. The end result was similar as shelter camps emerged for villagers, mostly tribals, escaping the crossfires between the Naxals and the Indian security forces. In 2015, there were over 6,00,000 internally displaced people in India on account of armed conflict and communal violence, concentrated in central India and in the Northeast.[75]

An even more potent means of internal displacement arose in the form of development projects. The pursuit of modernity required dams and electricity, highways and railways, ports and plantations, cities and canals. All these activities required land for construction, cultivation and submergence. In India, one of the first sectors where land was acquired on a vast scale was for construction of the railways in the middle of the 19th century.[76] Inevitably, there were protests, court cases and arbitration leading to realignment of routes and changes in plans. Unlike Radcliffe's lines, there was more flexibility and give and take in this process as the close attachment to homesteads and ancestral lands came in the way of neatly demarcated railway lines on maps. According to some tribal notions, forest clearance would anger their buried ancestors and lead to rains of fire balls rather than water.[77] With such heated arguments, even colonial officials had to backtrack and reconsider their designs, bending straight lines into curves.

From such rudimentary beginnings, the state's power to acquire land and immovable property was extended considerably in 1850 to cover the railways, made uniform across regions in 1857, referred disputes to courts in 1870 and eventually culminated in the Land Acquisition Act of 1894.[78] Despite a few amendments, the basic spirit of this legislation survived till 2013 when India finally passed the Right to Fair Compensation and Transparency in Land Acquisition, Rehabilitation and Resettlement Act. The difference in nomenclature reflected what had gone terribly wrong in the century between the two Acts, with land acquisition mired in serious issues of poor compensation, lack of transparency, lack of rehabilitation and, at times, even lack of resettlement.

Since 1894 and especially post-1947, large-scale development programmes acquired land on the principle of 'eminent domain' for the public good. Dams and irrigation projects accounted for the largest component of development-induced displacement with the submergence of vast tracts of land and thousands of villages. Resettlement and rehabilitation were after-thoughts. It was only after protracted social movements in the late 20th century that the government and donor agencies began to pay some attention to the severity of the issue. In one extreme example near the Alamatti dam in Karnataka in 1996–97, the dam construction schedule was not synchronized with people's relocation, catching them unawares of rising waters.[79] An emergency evacuation operation involving boats and helicopters had to be arranged as people were literally flooded out of their homes.

If resettlement was an issue in most projects, marked by delays and incomplete and poor housing sites, rehabilitation was not on the policy agenda for a long period of time. It was assumed that cash, land and houses were enough to tide over the problem. In reality, resettlement and involuntary displacement led to impoverishment risks of 'landlessness, joblessness, homelessness, marginalization, food insecurity, increased morbidity and mortality, loss of common property assets and social disarticulation'.[80] Estimates suggest that over 40 million people were displaced due to development projects in India since Independence and over 40 per cent of those displaced belonged to the STs, even though they comprised only 8 per cent of the Indian population.[81] Women and children were even more vulnerable, thrust into new and alien environments. In some cases, people were displaced multiple times, from forests to the city's slums and then again to the fringes after slum demolition drives.

Among thousands of projects ranging from mines and roads to industries, the big dams received the most sustained protests. The Narmada Bachao Andolan, formed in the 1980s, ultimately failed in its quest to limit the displacement of over a 1,00,000 'project affected persons' caused by the Sardar Sarovar Project on the Narmada in western India but succeeded in galvanizing global opinion against massive displacement caused by large development projects. The acceptance of rehabilitation as an important aspect of land acquisition policies, and the need to spread the benefits of the development project to the people displaced by it, are only now well entrenched in policy debates. And yet, even today, urban renewal projects, special economic zones and numerous other projects routinely fall short of basic expectations, providing benefits to select groups and imposing high costs on those who have been forced to move.

Refugees and the Displaced

The word 'refugee' connotes an element of involuntary or forced international migration to escape natural disasters, war or persecution, and is nested within the larger concept of 'displacement' associated with both international and internal movements. The Partition of 1947 technically created 'displaced persons' and not refugees though both words were used frequently throughout the episode. In the 20th century, India witnessed some of the largest refugee crises and displacements, across political boundaries and within. Three partitions of regions that were once part of British India led to the creation of four independent countries and millions of refugees and displacements. In addition to the Partition-related displacements and Sri Lankan and Tibetan refugees noted earlier, India also hosted tens of thousands of Hajongs and Chakmas from Mymensingh district in present-day Bangladesh and the Chittagong Hill Tracts. They were settled in Arunachal Pradesh and some other north-eastern states as refugees fleeing persecution in East Pakistan in the 1960s.[82] Another 10,000 Afghan refugees arrived in and around Delhi, mostly Hindus and Sikhs, fleeing the Soviet-Afghan War in the 1980s.[83] Overall, some 2,00,000 refugees live in sites and camps across India today.[84] In contrast, the number of refugees from India has been negligible though Sikh asylum seekers, fleeing violence in the 1980s, have been documented in border crossings in the Americas. A few people were also forced to leave because of intolerance towards their work, such as the writer Salman Rushdie, or intolerance towards their sexuality as Indian laws criminalize homosexuality.

India can boast of a reasonably successful record in refugee management and assimilation, even though it is not a signatory to key UN protocols on refugee issues. Given enough time, healing and compassion, some if not most are able to move out of their refugee status to build new lives and contribute to their host society. The historic acceptance of the Parsis and Baghdadi Jews in India, who fled persecution, led to flourishing contributions from those communities. India's most famous military victory in 1971, after all, was in no small measure led by a Parsi (Sam Manekshaw) and a Baghdadi Jew (J.F.R. Jacob). Indian nationalist leaders who favour the deportation of Rohingya Muslims to a regime that persecutes them would be well advised to recollect this rich Indian history in engaging with injustice and displacement. Indeed, the distinct communal bias in attitudes to refugee acceptance in recent decades when comparing the Tibetan, Sri Lankan and Burmese Rohingya cases is a matter of deep concern and a departure from the much hallowed philosophy of *atithi devo bhava*, which means 'a guest is the equivalent of God' practised in India since time immemorial.

What is paradoxical in the Indian context is that until recently international refugees or non-citizens have often got better treatment, and even rights, than the internally displaced citizens of the country. The phrase 'R & R', linked with relief and rehabilitation in India since the 1940s, became associated with resettlement and rehabilitation for the internally displaced only at a much later stage, by when millions of Indian citizens had already been resettled but left to fend for their own. After having become victims of natural disasters, ethnic violence, or development projects they were slotted into shelter camps in desolate areas or city slums with precarious means of existence. It was proposed that the projects would help the nation, but the proposal of development rarely worked for these migrants in Indian history. Like the exchange of lunatics in Manto's story, it was difficult to say whether the proposals made any sense or not.

6

Migration and Development

'An ideal society should be mobile, should be full of channels for conveying a change taking place in one part to other parts.'

—Bhimrao Ramji Ambedkar[1]

Ambedkar's view on migration was deeply conditioned by his own experience, of breaking away from the traditional shackles of caste in India, earning respect and dignity while studying at Columbia University and London School of Economics, and his numerous travels. For him, migration was intimately linked with his personal development and aspirations. He famously called the Indian village a 'sink of localism, a den of ignorance, narrow-mindedness and communalism'.[2] In contrast, Gandhi, who had lived outside India for over two decades, celebrated village life and shunned modern cities. He considered the 'growth of cities as an evil thing, unfortunate for mankind and the world'.[3] A third character in 20th century Indian politics—Bal Thackeray (1926–2012)—viewed migration as a potential source of conflict with native interests. While he was born in Pune, it is significant that he spent nearly his entire life in Mumbai, a city whose name he got changed.

Ambedkar and Thackeray reflect two ends of the spectrum between cosmopolitanism and nativism. The widely-travelled cosmopolitan considers migration to be the norm while the rarely-travelled nativist sees it as an aberration. Gandhi added a third dimension, that of the cosmopolitan recommending fixity. These three views summarize the range of views towards migration across the world and they are intrinsically linked with the process of 'development' or the general rise in living standards. For the question each is asking is: *whose* living standards are being raised by migration?

Migration in Five Transitions

'Development', used here as a term to reflect rising per capita incomes and human capital in education and health, has been associated with the scientific, political, economic, urban and demographic revolutions or transitions of the modern world. The scientific revolution led to the creation of technologies that transformed the scale of production, transportation and communication. The political transition refers to the transition from autocracy to democracy, often via the status of being a colonizing or colonized state. The economic transition manifested itself in the dramatic diversification of economic activity away from agriculture—in capitalist, socialist and communist systems. Economic development was also closely linked with urbanization or a spatial shift away from villages to cities as the global share of population living in urban areas crossed 50 per cent in the first decade of the 21st century. Finally, every society underwent, or is undergoing, the demographic transition from high death and birth rates to low death and birth rates.

It was once thought that a similar 'mobility transition' accompanied this process of development, from low rates to high rates and from nomadic to settler and finally circulatory streams of migration.[4] Careful historical research has shown that mobility rates in the Eurasian world before 1800 CE were not as low as was previously thought and that mobility rates fell from the highs of the late 19th and early 20th century in many 'developed' societies.[5] Circular migration for work and military migration have also been documented as a major driving force of migration in those societies in recent centuries. What has been noted for sure is the distinct phase of urbanization and demographic transition whereby natural growth rates—the difference between birth and death rates—tend to increase and place pressure on available agricultural land leading to a movement away from villages. For many countries in western and southern Europe, this movement took place in the cities and settlements in the Americas and colonies around the world. As these societies have completed their demographic transitions and face low or even negative natural growth rates, they tend to attract immigrants, especially in the low-end jobs vacated by the natives. Wage differentials form an important part of this narrative as they signal opportunities for people to move. Thus, relatively more developed countries and major cities tend to have net immigration or inmigration rather than net emigration or outmigration as they offer higher wages.

The historical experience of migration in India follows some of these broad patterns, but with interesting twists. As the previous chapters have documented, migration has been highly circulatory and clustered in nature. Certain parts of India have experienced mass migration histories for centuries while other regions have been bypassed or have only recently witnessed signs of rising spatial mobility. Science and technology mattered in terms of the railways, steamboats and communications services that propelled spatial mobility in the late 19th century. Mobility in India—internal and international—also closely followed the logic of globalization, rising in the late 19th and early 20th century and then again towards the end of the 20th century. In this, the colonial experience was critical in shaping the initial surge in outmigration and the choice of destinations, with persistent legacies. Patterns of migration broadly followed economic development, with the more developed and fast-growing states or provinces experiencing net inmigration rather than outmigration.[6]

Democracy in independent India continued the earlier ideas of unrestricted spatial movement, with a few caveats, in stark contrast to communist China which regulated rural–urban migration through an internal permit system known as the *hukou*. And yet, over the past four decades, the relatively higher pace of economic growth in China propelled a much larger volume of internal migration than in India, taking Chinese urbanization rates past 50 per cent. In comparison, India's urbanization rate rose gradually to a little over 30 per cent. At first glance, this may reflect low rates of spatial mobility but this artefact has more to do with definitions and rural–urban divergence in natural growth rates.[7] India's demographic transition began slowly in the first half of the 20th century and natural growth rates peaked in the 1980s but, curiously, since the 1970s, rural natural growth rates outstripped urban natural growth rates and dampened the process of urbanization. Even then, India is unique in having a large economic diversification taking place from agricultural to non-agricultural activities within rural areas themselves as cities have not been able to provide enough jobs for the rural poor.

The most remarkable aspect of Indian migration concerns itself with international migration. Standard development theory would predict India to be a country of net emigration and yet, since Independence, emigration has been balanced by immigration from the relatively poorer neighbouring countries of Nepal and Bangladesh. In every decade between 1971 and 2011, India was, in fact, a country of net immigration.[8] India's position in the global migration map is therefore fairly unique as it sustains considerable volumes of internal migration, emigration and immigration, alongside involuntary migration generated as a reaction to developmental activities.

Rags to Riches or Rages?

Bihar and Kerala stand poles apart on the ladder of development. Bihar is one of the poorest states of India, while Kerala is among the richest. On many indicators, Bihar fares worse than sub-Saharan Africa whereas Kerala mirrors countries in Europe. And yet, both states experience similar rates of outmigration, defying simplistic assumptions that poverty is the main driver of migration, especially from rural to urban areas. What unites Bihar and Kerala is an extremely high rate of rural population density that simply cannot support enough livelihoods in the agricultural sector. Both these states have therefore been a part of the Great Indian Migration Wave, latching on to circulatory networks that extend far and wide. How did migration shape poverty and inequality in these regions? Did migration convert rags to riches or did it fail and fuel rages?

One of the principal ways migration alleviates poverty in the source region is through financial remittances, closely linked with the corridors of the Great Indian Migration Wave. Whether sent through postal money orders or electronic media, the remittance market of India is enormous, equivalent to over $20 billion for internal migration and close to $70 billion for international migration.[9] Nearly 40 per cent of the international remittance flows are concentrated in Kerala, Punjab and Goa, which are among the leading remittance-dependent economies of the world.[10] Likewise, domestic remittance dependency was high in Uttar Pradesh, Bihar, Rajasthan and Odisha. In 2008, over 60 per cent of the domestic remittance market

comprised inter-state transfers and 80 per cent was directed
to rural households. Domestic remittances also financed over
30 per cent of household consumption expenditure in remittance-
receiving households that comprised nearly 10 per cent of rural
India. The empirical evidence on remittances and poverty in
India is clear. Remittances reduce poverty and the impact is
stronger for international remittances, even after accounting for
selection bias.[11]

While source region poverty can be dented through outmigration, an equally important question to ask is if migration
improves the condition of the migrants in places they move to,
or whether rural poverty is being replaced by urban poverty
and the creation of slums. Here, the evidence in India is more
conflicted. At one level, the nature of urban poverty is less harsh
than that of rural poverty, with less pressures of empty stomachs
and greater access to educational and health facilities. One study
on urban centres noted that the probability of being poor in
India was lower among migrants than the natives, and that
migration was a 'definite instrument of improving economic
well-being and escaping from poverty'.[12] On the downside, the
health risks of migration have been documented to be quite
severe. First, there is the 'caloric cost of culture' whereby
migrants end up consuming fewer calories per rupee, because
they bring along food preferences from their places of origin
and end up paying higher values for them.[13] More importantly,
maternal health is affected as migrants often don't have access
to public services that they have back home and migrants avoid
paying for health care due to exorbitant costs.[14] This can have
an inter-generational impact on the health of children and their
cognitive development. These health risks are compounded by
the fact that 'footloose labour' in informal jobs in the urban
sector faces a high degree of income volatility and a very real
prospect of downward mobility.[15] Nevertheless, the idea that

urban poverty is an extension of rural poverty is incorrect and, on most dimensions, the average slum-dweller in India is better off than counterparts of the same social group in villages.[16]

The relationship between spatial and economic mobility in India is highly contingent on the nature of migration by duration. In short-term seasonal migration streams dominated by the poorer segments of the Indian population towards harvesting operations and construction work, remittances are scarce, savings are limited, debts are high and the economic returns of migration are low. According to Priya Deshingkar, a pioneering researcher on Indian migration, these migrations are for survival or 'coping' mechanisms, whereas semi-permanent circular migrations through social networks are instances of 'accumulative' migration.[17] Based on extensive field work across many parts of India, her research showed that on balance, migration was an important route out of poverty through livelihood diversification. The historical evidence of the Great Indian Migration Wave also points to a similar conclusion and shows a clear pattern where 'coping' types of migration transformed into 'accumulative' migrations in the long run.

The selective nature of migration for work in India affects not only poverty, but also inequality. International remittances are directed to the relatively more developed states, contributing to widening inter-state inequalities. Remittances are also sent primarily by semi-permanent and permanent migrants, who are drawn from the relatively richer segments of the Indian population. The top 25 per cent of households, for instance, corner 50 per cent of the domestic remittance intake, as a result of which remittances lead to greater consumption inequality.[18] Nowhere is this more evident than in Kerala, which is one of the most unequal states of India in terms of consumption expenditure. The Gulf outside Kerala has led to a gulf within, despite long political rule by communist ideals. But because efforts to improve education and healthcare in Kerala have far exceeded those in Bihar, its return on migration in the long run has been more substantive. The migratory path from rags to riches in India, therefore, depends on the duration of stay and investment in education.

Caste Away

The potential of migration to narrow down social inequalities is clearest in the case of caste. Untouchability is impossible to entertain in a jam-packed Mumbai local train, and notions of caste purity are watered down in dense urban settlements. This does not mean that caste has no role to play in migration as job recruitment in India is strongly mediated through caste- or region-based social networks.[19] Nor does it mean that caste-based residential segregation does not exist in urban centres. But compared to rural settings, the freedom to try out different jobs and live in different places is substantially enhanced.

The historical evidence on migration as a means to escape caste oppression is also overwhelming, as witnessed in the earlier account of the Great Indian Migration Wave and Ambedkar's numerous exhortations. In her work on land and caste in south India, economic historian Dharma Kumar noted the possibilities opened up by emigration in the 19th century for social mobility including 'greater knowledge of agricultural techniques and less willingness to abide by caste restrictions'.[20] Similarly, the Census of 1931 observed that emigration from southern India was 'a great teacher of self-respect' and had 'contributed most to the growth of consciousness among the depressed classes'.[21] Several personal memoirs such as Narendra Jadhav's *Untouchables* or Daya Pawar's *Baluta* or Sujatha Gidla's *Ants among Elephants*, have recounted how the act of internal or international migration was inevitably linked with the beginning of social emancipation.[22]

Migration has also been noted to be an important pathway to upward mobility through entrepreneurship. According to a study on twenty-one Dalit entrepreneurs:[23]

> the path to social mobility offered by entrepreneurship began with spatial mobility, most of all escaping rural India. Seemingly placid from the outside, its rigid hierarchies can suffocate those at its receiving end. The chaos and squalor of urban India provides at least a cloak of anonymity that keeps the possibility of individual initiative alive. Anonymity increases risk taking since failure has less social costs. Dalit entrepreneurs do not mind failing in places where their kith and kin are not around to mock their failed attempts, even though this might mean a weaker social network.

The puzzle then is why the low-ranking castes of India exhibit the lowest rates of semi-permanent or permanent migration, both in internal and international migration streams, when they have the most to gain by moving for long durations. One answer lies in the limited stock of physical capital that permits only short-duration migration strategies. Another theory argues that caste serves as a mechanism of rural insurance such that permanent departure from the village is costlier for the lowest-ranking castes that face greater income risk.[24] A more potent reason is limited informational networks that restrict access to new jobs and destinations. As previous chapters have shown, the migration networks fostered by priests, warriors and merchants over centuries gave their descendants a major informational advantage over the SCs and STs that is as important as the economic advantages in grabbing new opportunities. This is why, as per Census 2011, even though the all-India urbanization rate stood at 31 per cent, it was only 24 per cent among the SCs and 10 per cent among the STs.

The possibility of a 'Great Migration', as in the case of African-Americans in 20th century America, is remote as members of the lowest-ranking castes are far more evenly spread out over the countryside in India than the clustered location of African-Americans in the American South in the 19th century. In the USA, as Isabel Wilkerson noted in *The Warmth of Other Suns,* 'they did what human beings looking for freedom, throughout history, have often done. They left.'[25] Over six decades, nearly six million black Southerners, mostly from rural areas, left their lands and spread out across the wide expanse of America, settling mainly in urban centres. In India, on the other hand, Gandhian prescriptions against city life hold importance in certain policy circles such that rural to urban migration is still considered to be a 'problem' that needs to be checked.[26] But despite Gandhi's love for the village, it should be remembered that even he was sympathetic to the question of caste and migration as he noted that:[27]

> If Harijans are physically ill-treated in a place and if they cannot get redress in any other way, they should leave that village and we should encourage them to do so . . . what is the harm if the Harijans, all or some of them, leave the place after serving notice on the caste Hindus?

Brain Drain

Britain, and to a lesser extent the United States of America, began attracting Indian students for higher studies from the late 19th century. Almost all the stalwarts of the Indian freedom movement pursued higher studies abroad and returned to India to work. In 1888, in one of his first recorded speeches as a teenager about to depart for higher studies in England, Gandhi told his friends, 'I hope that some of you will follow in my footsteps, and after you return from England you will work wholeheartedly for big reforms in India.'[28] By 1946, on the eve of Independence, his view on foreign education was slightly different. Asked if independent India should continue sending people abroad for studies, he replied:[29]

> No, not just now. I would advise her to send them there only after, say, 40 years . . . I repeat that they should go there only after they have reached maturity. Because, it is only when they have learnt to understand the good that is in their own culture that they will be able to truly appreciate and assimilate the best that England or America has to give them. Imagine a boy of seventeen, like myself, going to England—he will simply be submerged.

Gandhi could not have anticipated the developments in international migration and education in the second half of the 20th century. The steady trickle of circulating Indian students gave way to more permanent migration as both Britain and the USA loosened immigration restrictions placed on Indians. More significantly, doctors, nurses, engineers and scientists trained at leading higher education institutions in India, especially the newly set up Indian Institutes of Technology (IITs), and began to migrate to the USA for further studies or work. In the 1960s and 70s, the cumulative stock of these emigrants stood at less than a 1,00,000 people. Four decades later, the annual flow figure had risen well over this number. This phenomenon of high-skilled emigration was dubbed the 'brain drain' and received close attention in the public discourse.[30] Three centuries after a potential 'brain drain' was detected from Persia to India during the Mughal era, as noted in the first chapter, it would be India's turn to supply brains to other parts of the world.

There were two aspects of the brain drain, linked with patriotism and public finances. The move abroad was seen by the elite, who didn't move as an abdication of responsibility, as a step towards undertaking the 'big reforms' that India required and young Gandhi had talked about. For those who did move, the prospect of working in the best laboratories of the world and living in large homes, or enjoying a vastly improved standard of living overturned any patriotic sentiment that they may have harboured. The classic 2004 Indian movie, *Swades*, about an Indian project manager at NASA returning to produce electricity in villages, reflected the possibilities and the outliers, but not the general norm. What the Indian elite in America and Britain often missed was not the lack of involvement in India's politics and development, but the absence of domestic help that they were routinely used to employing in India. 'In America, we have to do everything on our own,' is a common phrase heard even today in conversations of transnational families.

'Brain drain' was a major rallying cry in the 1970s and 80s because Indian students who went abroad did so after receiving subsidized education. It appeared as if India and many other countries were investing in training highly skilled professionals so that the USA could benefit from their talent. In the 1970s, Jagdish Bhagwati, a leading Indian economist, argued for 'taxing the brain drain' whereby emigrants paid income taxes into a fund that would be routed back to their home countries via the United Nations.[31] Bhagwati himself had initially returned to India after his education abroad to teach in the 1960s but subsequently spent his career in the USA. His taxation proposal would go unheeded not because of operational complexities alone but also because the notion of 'brain drain' eventually gave way to that of brain circulation, brain bank and even brain gain by the first decade of the 21st century.

This turn of events occurred due to the tremendous success of highly skilled Indian emigrants and also because their continued links with India through economic and social remittances limited the negative fallouts of the brain drain. Economic remittances from these emigrants filled the foreign exchange coffers and grew to comprise an amount representing nearly 2 per cent of India's GDP.[32] The rapid growth of India's IT and health sector enterprises was facilitated by close contacts with the latest developments occurring in the rich world via the high-skilled Indian diaspora. And most importantly, the very same educational institutions that sent their best and brightest outside India, successfully reached out to their overseas alumni for money, ideas and inspiration. Sundar Pichai, CEO of Google, is today a source of great inspiration for the students of IIT Kharagpur, his alma mater, just as Indra Nooyi, CEO of PepsiCo, is for the students of IIM Calcutta and economists Raghuram Rajan and Arvind Subramanian are for the students of IIM Ahmedabad.

Public institutions and discourses have therefore moved away from 'brain drain' to addressing the best ways to connect with and leverage the success of the highly skilled Indian diaspora. This applies equally for the lesser known 'brain drain' that occurs within the borders of India. When educated Bihari civil servants and professionals work outside Bihar, they contribute not only towards other economies but also in inspiring others within Bihar to seek education so that they may themselves improve their lives. Any compulsions on them to serve Bihar exclusively would inevitably backfire. Indeed, as education levels improve in India, one can expect more high-skilled internal migration for higher studies and work, concentrated in a few urban centres. Restrictions on the migration of the highly skilled would be counter-productive and also reduce overall human welfare. As per one study, the ratio of patents filed by

Indians in North America to that by Indians in India stood at a staggering 28,000:1.[33] Clearly, the productivity of Indians is highly dependent on enabling environments, whose provision would reduce the outflow of brains or even lead to a return of brains. Until then, there is considerable truth in an adage attributed to a member of India's Planning Commission that 'a brain drain is better than a brain in a drain.'[34]

There is, however, an alternative brain drain that is rarely talked about. This refers to the migration of high-skilled spouses, almost always women, who accompany the high-skilled migrant workers, but do not end up working for remuneration due to restrictions placed by families or visa regulations. Within India, this leads to a colossal under-utilization of talent as millions of female graduates forgo active professional careers upon their move to a new state or city, to look after children or the family. Outside India, visa restrictions on work for dependents can kill aspirations and dull the brains. In the USA, over a 1,00,000 Indian dependents live on the less-known H4 visa, known as the depression visa. Studies have shown how this brings about a loss of self-confidence and discomfort because of financial dependence on the spouse, even for remittances, and overall, retards professional careers due to the erosion of skills.[35] In such cases, the American sitcom *Desperate Housewives* offers only partial relief to the brain pain.

Trafficking and Female Flight

The gendered nature of the brain drain is only one of the many ways in which migration and gender are interlinked. The Great Indian Migration Wave was fundamentally a male-dominated mass migration stream with mixed implications for the women left behind. It did lead to greater female autonomy in nuclear families but did not change much in joint families. It also contributed to the feminization of the agricultural workforce with men taking up the relatively better paying jobs outside farms. In recent years, female migration rates—for marriage and work—within India have surged, but with little evidence of diversifications in occupations.[36] Outside India, the share of women among Indians is well below 50 per cent in nearly all countries where data is available, and in the Persian Gulf, it is less than 30 per cent. Initial waves of merchant migrants did not include women whereas Partition and involuntary displacements negatively impacted women. Women, like the lowest-ranking castes, have also been outside many circuits of migration characterized by better pay and upward mobility.

The ultimate form of exploitation of women was, of course, slavery. In ancient and medieval India, slavery targeted women in particular occupations like prostitution which continued through the colonial period. The male ghettoes of the cities in the Great Indian Migration Wave such as Calcutta and Bombay comprising both Indian and European labour and the elite had raised the demand for prostitution in the 19th century. The labour was provided by homeless or abandoned children and women, usually brought to the city by deception or force. In one official record in the late 19th century, a cultivator's girl was made to swap with a prostitute's boy because apparently neither was of any use to their natural parents.[37] Girls were trafficked to Indian settlements abroad, such as Fiji, by mercenary parents.[38]

Other female occupations of service to patrons also underwent a change in nature and perception. The courtesan tawaifs of Awadh moved to Calcutta after Awadh was annexed by the British in the 19th century, where they sought new patronage from the British and Bengali elite. However, their artistic contributions were devalued over time and replaced by sexual services. The nautch girls in music and dance at parties and functions were stigmatized for their 'immoral acts' and dubbed prostitutes. There was also a demand for 'white prostitutes' to serve the needs of the British soldiers. When anti-trafficking movements against the 'white slave trade' began in the early 20th century, colonial officials were careful to punish or deport prostitute Englishwomen, and replace them with women from eastern Europe. In the 1930s, by one estimate, there were over 50,000 prostitutes in Calcutta alone. Only with the nationalist movement and international campaigns in the 1940s did endorsement and encouragement of military prostitution decline, though much earlier, an early Indian feminist movement had already abhorred the practice.

Independent India passed an anti-trafficking law, the Immoral Traffic Prevention Act in 1956, but it did not curtail trafficking. The law has been criticized for victimizing the victim rather than the trafficker and customer. In 2016, the National Crime Records Bureau recorded nearly 20,000 people who were trafficked that year alone—half of whom were children and the other half women.[39] These were only the reported cases and conceal the real magnitude of flows. West Bengal was party to one-third of those cases, followed by Rajasthan and Maharashtra. Mumbai's red light area, Kamathipura, had an old connection with the Kamathi workers from the region in present-day Telangana in south India, which continues to be a source of trafficking. One study in the Rayalaseema region of Andhra Pradesh, the same region where centuries before Afghani immigrants had controlled the traffic in horses, found trafficking to be high among the erstwhile Banjara-Lambada groups.[40] The stories of the survivors or return migrants revealed the role of poverty in sex trafficking, the deception involved and regret. Not all trafficking is for sex work as it can also include domestic helps, work in dangerous settings and even marriage, within India and outside. Neither is all of it entirely by coercion. Yet it places a large number of women and children in highly vulnerable positions.

Trafficking represents one end of the spectrum of female migration in India. At the other end, women have also moved by their own volition for work and become successful. Cornelia Sorabji, a pioneer lawyer, was the first woman to study law at Oxford in the late 19th century. She moved to different places in her life championing the cause of women. Of her, it was said:[41]

> She travelled up and down the country like some knight-errant of old, rescuing distressed damsels, and . . . bringing justice and succour to lonely women who had no other reliable helper. She travelled [by] every kind of conveyance—boat, train, elephant and palanquin. She crossed flooded rivers or camped under the stars in sandy wastes. Always she must be on the move, even when fever or weariness demand rest.

Ignoring fever and weariness, millions of migrant women who work as domestic maids in contemporary India positively contribute to their own households.[42] Female migration from east India to garment factories in south India is now a feasible option to earn decent wages.[43] Many Muslim women in Delhi have migrated from small-town prejudices and the tight gaze of their families to lead more fulfilling lives.[44] Women from specific regions are also occupying niche sectors in Delhi: Rajasthani construction workers, tribal women from Bihar, Jharkhand, Odisha and Chhattisgarh as live-in maids, educated English-speaking women from the Northeast in tourism, airlines and beauty and health parlours, and nurses from Kerala.[45] The phenomenon of nursing ambitions in particular is remarkable because it is dominated by Christian Malayalis, who work all over India and the world.[46] Christians were first movers in this field because of fewer taboos on working in this profession compared to other religions, though their success has now paved the way for others to join in. The nursing ambition is one of step-migration, first within Indian states, then to the Gulf and finally the rich countries of the West. All through, they send back considerable amounts of remittances to support their families. It is a rare case of all-women migration networks spanning the world. It has led to the mushrooming of private nursing schools in Kerala, mirroring the rise of private computer training centres in Karnataka, Tamil Nadu and Andhra Pradesh for (mostly male) software engineers. And just as the America boys are valued in the marriage market, so are the Malayali nurses. So much so that matrimonial columns which used to first advertise for nurses working in the Gulf have now switched to simply seeking women who have cleared the examinations that test proficiency in English and nursing, knowing very well the value attached to the profession. From Marie Rozette in 18th century Mauritius to Anandibai Joshee and Cornelia Sorabji in the 19th century, and Malayali nurses in the 20th century, migration has offered prospects of upward mobility to women, even in the most trying conditions.

Identity, Politics and Citizenship

Indians outside India often cry out about charges of discrimination, real or perceived. The racist immigration policies of the anglophone world in the early 20th century certainly set the tone in those parts of the world for the rest of the century. In West Asia today, the demands are about social justice, even as migrants accept the reality that there can never be any permanent settlement in that region. But the fault-lines of migration and identity are more clearly witnessed back home in India, in the major metropolitan cities and along national and provincial borders. The much hallowed Indian diversity is routinely tested by claims on ethnicity, region and language, pitting the insiders or 'sons of the soil' (and presumably daughters) versus the proverbial mlecchas or outsiders.

One of the earliest instances of the 'sons of the soil' movement was under the Nizam rule of Hyderabad state in the late 19th century. The state was founded by Asaf Jah in 1724 after the collapse of Mughal power. His subjects were known as the *mulki*s (the word 'mulk' meaning country).[47] Non-mulkis were referred to as the *ghair*-mulkis, and they began to enter the government services in large numbers under Salar Jung's administration in the late 19th century. Jung had inherited an administration in chaos and was trying to rope in the best talent from outside. The immigrants were Muslims from the Bombay, Madras and Bengal Presidencies and the United Provinces (Uttar Pradesh). Through their kith and kin many more arrived to serve the Hyderabad administration. The mulkis, especially the Muslim mulkis, became hostile to this influx from outside and under pressure, in 1868, Jung instituted a policy to recruit only mulkis in government administration. This laid the foundation of the principle of promoting native interests over the migrants in government employment. Further steps were taken in subsequent decades such as changing the official language of the government from Persian to Urdu, the language of local Muslims, and the establishment of the Osmania University in Hyderabad, primarily for the locals. The mulki rules gave preference to those born in Hyderabad or residents who had lived there for at least fifteen years. After Independence, these rules were enshrined in political agreements between the elite of different regions of the newly formed state of Andhra Pradesh, but continued to create tensions between those in Telangana of erstwhile Hyderabad and coastal Andhra of the erstwhile Madras Presidency. The latter was beginning its ascendance in government employment in the capital city of Hyderabad and became the new ghair–mulkis for the old mulkis. The tension would continue to fester until the state of Telangana was created in 2014.

The mulki rules inspired the milking of political capital in other parts of independent India. After the linguistic reorganization of states in 1956, there was first an agitation in western India for a separate state of Maharashtra on the linguistic principle. Once that was achieved in 1960, the attention shifted to the ghair-mulkis in the city of Bombay, the *lungiwala*s. South Indians, especially Tamilians, among whom the lungi is a popular form of attire for men, drew flak from the Shiv Sena, a political party founded in 1966 by Bal Thackeray, a political cartoonist. The cartoons themselves were crisp, depicting the middle-class south Indian as an 'ugly, grotesque figure' with taglines such as 'S.I. vultures' and the complaint was against them stealing jobs from the locals.[48] The anti-migrant theme sold well politically and also effected policy changes in recruitment for government employment. But this had little impact on the demography of the island city in subsequent decades as migrants from all parts of India continued to pour in. Later on, the ire shifted against the relatively poor *bhaiya*s from Uttar Pradesh and Bihar. South Indians were forgotten and north Indians became the new enemies, given the Shiv Sena's sway in the city's politics. But for all the grandstanding, there was little evidence provided on the alleged stolen nature of jobs. And because the labour market of Mumbai was strongly segmented along regional lines, the migrants rarely entered the occupations of the native Marathi-speakers, who in any case did not constitute an absolute majority in the city. In the 1960s, a similar anti-migrant movement was started by the Kannada Chaluvaligars in Bangalore against the other south Indian migrants in the city. Today, a similar mantle is donned by the Karnataka Rakshana Vedike. A few other states witnessed agitations at different levels and intensities, and they would also be characterized by demands for the protection of jobs for locals, changes in the language of signboards and occasional violence.

In Assam, however, the 'sons of the soil' movement was literally an SOS agitation, leading to violence at a heightened level. As forewarned by I.G. Patel's friend in the previous chapter, the historic migration of Bengali Muslims towards Assam in the Northeast continued after the liberation of Bangladesh in 1971, leading to tensions on the basis of region, religion, language and nationality, all rolled together. To understand the special case of anti-migrant sentiments in Assam, one needs to go back to the 19th century.

Assam in 19th century colonial India was a part of the Bengal Presidency and included most of the north-east area of the Indian subcontinent. The British conquered the Ahom kingdoms in the 1820s, ending six centuries of their rule that had earlier held out even against the rampaging Mughals. Since then, Assam became a frontier area for massive settlement, to occupy land, work in tea gardens and oil fields, start new businesses and initiate modern professions and the bureaucracy. Since the second half of the 19th century, it witnessed a migration-led demographic boom that lasted for nearly a century. Between 1901 and 1971, it was the fastest growing area of the subcontinent, growing from around 3 million to nearly 15 million.[49] Assam was earlier an important part of the Great Indian Migration Wave but, over time, migrations became more gender-balanced and permanent. Tribals from central India migrated to the tea gardens, Bengali Hindus occupied the bureaucracy and urban centres, Bengali Muslims from Mymensingh settled as peasants after clearing forest lands, Biharis and Nepalis worked as labourers in assorted jobs, and the Marwaris and Punjabis went as traders. In the early 20th century, over a fifth of Assam's population was born outside, but the share of migrants fell to around 10 per cent in the next five decades. In 1971, nearly a third of the population spoke languages other than Assamese—mainly Bengali, but also Hindi, Nepali, Oraon, Santali and Munda, the last three being tribal languages from eastern India.

Mass migration would be a major force for political, social, cultural and economic change, often resisted by the indigenous Assamese. Their sense of alienation was further attenuated by the fact that Bengali was the official language of the government when they were part of the Bengal Presidency. Between 1912 and 1947, Assam was a separate chief commissioner's province that included Sylhet district, dominated by Bengali-Muslims. The 1937 elections threw up a minority Muslim League government, stoking Hindu–Muslim tensions on account of proposals to incorporate Assam within Pakistan after Independence. However, the Congress won the elections in 1946 and ensured that Assam was kept out of Pakistan though Sylhet was transferred to Pakistan after a referendum. Since then, the Assamese Hindus in political power passed a raft of regulations in favour of the 'sons of the soil'. For about two decades, the Bengali Muslims were an unspoken coalition partner of the Assamese, even adopting the local language. Collectively, they ran up against the Bengali Hindus over the language options for examinations in educational institutions, an issue that generated a large student-based political movement.

This political understanding was shattered in the late 1970s when a sizable immigration influx was detected from Bangladesh, evidenced by the inflated numbers on the revised electoral roll during elections. Close to 2 million Bengalis from Bangladesh were estimated to have entered Assam between 1971 and 1981.[50] These migrations were partly triggered by the Bangladeshi refugee crisis but, more importantly, were built on social networks laid down in the colonial era, mainly directed towards agricultural settlements. To protest, the dominant political parties led a civil disobedience movement and triggered violent agitations. In February 1983, in what would later be dubbed as the Nellie massacre, hundreds, if not thousands, of Bengali Muslims in villages close to Guwahati were killed and thousands fled to temporary refugee camps. The Nellie massacre remains Independent India's worst episode of anti-migrant violence.

The chief demand of the Assamese movement was the detection and deportation of illegal Bangladeshi immigrants. Under the Foreigner's Act of 1946, the burden fell on the accused to prove Indian nationality.[51] In 1983, in response to the agitation, a new law for Assam called the Illegal Migrants (Determination by Tribunals) Act or IMDT Act was passed, defining foreigners as those who settled in Assam after 25 March 1971, the day Pakistan began its crackdown on Bangladeshi separatists. However, the law was considered to be ineffective as the burden of proof fell on the denouncer to show someone's illegal incursion. In subsequent decades, under different political regimes, only a few thousand migrants were deported before the Act was struck down as being unconstitutional in 2005. Migration from the Hindi heartland and Bangladesh continued to persist over decades because the migrants mostly occupied low-skilled jobs which the locals didn't perform. The most recent development of the saga is the creation of the National Register of Citizens for Assam in 2017, again aimed to identify and deport illegal migrants. In a way, the Assamese experience resembles the US–Mexico immigration debate, with anti-migrant political rhetoric mixed with little on-the-ground action on immigration controls. And if the growing influence of the Spanish language is a matter of concern for the Americans, in India, the issue is communally charged because the share of the Muslim population in Assam has steadily increased from 24 per cent in 1971 to 34 per cent in 2011. To be sure, not all immigration occurs from Bangladesh, and Bihari migrants have also been caught in the crossfire of anti-migrant agitations, invoking retaliation against the Assamese travelling in trains passing through Bihar.

South of Bihar is the state of Jharkhand with a large tribal population covering the Chhota Nagpur plateau. It was created in 2001 after a long regional movement that, like Assam, traces its roots to migration in the 19th century. British colonization not only led to the mass migration of many Chhota Nagpur tribes—Munda, Oraon, Hos and others—towards the east as part of the Great Indian Migration Wave, but also brought in Bengali and Bihari labourers, administrators and professionals. With the development of coal mining, and then several mineral-based industries, there was a steady influx of outsiders or what the local tribals or adivasis called the *dikku*s. Commenting on the Hos tribe near Kolhan in 1914, one official observed that:[52]

> The Hos want to be left to themselves and the Kolhan to become fully a Ho reserve. Their hatred of the *dikku*s is as great as it was before. They will prefer a system that will exclude the *dikku*s from the Kolhan and they would appreciate much, if it were possible, to drive out the *dikku*s already settled there.

The dikkus, Bengalis, lungiwalas and ghair-mulkis were the 'outsiders' who caused deep resentment in the places they settled in even though their settings and contexts were quite different. But interestingly enough, migrants did not cause resentment everywhere they went in India. Why did nativist movements start in some parts of India and not others?

There are several reasons that appear to explain the emergence of nativist movements in India. In many places, the demographic impact of migration from outside a cultural region was quite severe and rapid, invoking local anxieties. Cultural differences were usually highlighted for only those migrant groups that commanded a higher social status than the locals, and especially during bouts of economic stagnation or when there was competition for limited resources. According to political scientist Myron Weiner (1931–99), who studied India's nativist movements in great detail, 'nativist movements convert cultural differences into cultural conflicts'.[53] These conflicts were particularly stark when cross-cultural mobility was relatively unknown to the locals. Nativist movements rarely occurred in regions which themselves experienced outmigration, such as Gujarat or Punjab, which also received a large number of internal migrants.

Not all anti-migrant policies need to be nativist as they can be formulated on considerations of the resources at hand, fiscal or ecological. Nativism arises when there is a conflict between the social mobility of the native population and the spatial mobility of the migrants. But nativism more often than not is a convenient ruse for political gain, based on little or faulty evidence. To ignore the contribution of migrants is to forgo a tremendous opportunity cost in obtaining valuable skills. As one sarcastic letter to a newspaper editor in 1973 pointed out:[54]

> There is much talk these days about the 'Sons of the Soil' . . .
> Only those born in the alluvial soil can work in the alluvian region. They may call themselves 'alluvians' . . . People may be given identity cards with the name of the soil clearly printed on it. To solve the problems of babies born in the air (planes), they should be employed as pilots and air hostesses. Nobody except the sons and daughters of the air should get these air jobs. They should be allowed to stay on earth in a non-classified soil region when they are off-duty.

Cultural differences in India that spark nativism and discrimination manifest from various identities, usually language and religion, but increasingly, race. In recent decades, people from the eight states of the Northeast have been moving to major metropolitan centres such as Delhi, Bengaluru and Mumbai for education and jobs in the services sector where their English-speaking skills are highly valued. In those cities, they face discrimination not because of fears of a demographic somersault but due to racial differences as many have Mongoloid features.[55] In one outrageous episode in Bengaluru in 2012, north-easterners began to flee the city because of rumours about revenge attacks by Muslims protesting Muslims being killed in distant Burma. Women from the Northeast, many who work in the beauty and care sector, and have a relatively higher degree of autonomy, are stereotyped by the locals as being 'easy' or pliable for sexual favours. As a result, obtaining rental accommodation can be a nightmarish ordeal for them. The word 'chinki', meaning Chinese, was earlier used as a derogatory word but using it now is a punishable offence. However, Indian-Chinese restaurants do staff a large number of people from the Northeast, a phenomenon that has little logic but accords well with the idea that Indian consumers are supposed to assume that people with Mongoloid features ought to serve in Chinese restaurants. Racial tensions against migrants are also played out these days against Africans, many of whom come to India for higher education. Today's stereotype of the African in India is that of a drug dealer, far removed from the medieval era when Habshi freed-slaves were part of the Deccan nobility and noted for their integrity.

Migration, identity formation and political movements have played a pivotal role in transforming the idea of citizenship in India.[56] The Indian Citizenship Act was first formulated in 1955, a good eight years after Independence because Partition-related migration flows delayed and complicated the deliberations. Citizenship was premised on the principle of jus solis, or citizenship by birth, and the Republic Day on

26 January 1950 was chosen as the baseline. Those who were born in India after that date were citizens of India, with minor exceptions. Naturalization was also permissible after a specified duration of stay in India. The most famous naturalized citizen of independent India, Sonia Gandhi, was born in Italy and faced tremendous political agitation over her 'foreignness' in the 1990s, which persisted even after she became the president of the Indian National Congress in 1998.

The first amendment to the Citizenship Act came in 1986 to provide special provisions for the state of Assam, including new cut-off dates to legitimize or delegitimize Bangladeshi migrants. The second amendment to the Act came in 2003 to define Overseas Indian Citizen (OCIs), indicating a shift to the jus sanguinis principle of citizenship by blood ties. In the initial discussions, OCIs were restricted to the countries of the richer world, but later it was widened to more countries, albeit with a cut-off date of emigration. Such cut-offs are now routine even for domestic citizenship clauses that permit access to state-domiciled services or for that matter urban citizenship clauses that 'regularize' slum-dwellers occupying public land only if they can show documents that prove that they moved to the city before a specified date. Migration from rural to urban areas and across state and national borders have and will continue to redefine the meaning of citizenship in India, one cut-off date at a time.

Migration in the 21st Century

The past two decades have witnessed a surge in internal and international mobility in India and attracted attention from various stakeholders. The 2001 government report on the Indian diaspora has led to several important measures that bridged the gap between India and the diaspora. In 2017, the report of the working group on migration was released by the ministry of housing and urban poverty alleviation, which analysed the policy gaps associated with internal migration. It observed that while in theory, freedom of movement was guaranteed by the Constitution of India under Article 19, in practice, there were considerable bottle necks that restricted mobility. The major problem identified was that public welfare services were tied to local or domiciled areas and did not move with the migrant. It therefore argued for greater portability of public services to facilitate easier and safer migration, marking a big shift from earlier policies that were explicitly designed to curtail migration. The report also argued for migrant helplines, more options for rental housing, dormitories for female migrants in cities and inter-state coordination of migrant welfare services to provide food security and better health and education. It also pointed out the need for better data on migration so that policy debates are informed by evidence and not empty rhetoric. The *Economic Survey of India 2016–17*, published by the ministry of finance, ran a full chapter on internal migration for the first time in its history, highlighting the scale and extent of the phenomenon.

Outside the government, firms especially those working in the field of financial inclusion, began to provide customized solutions for migrant workers. Non-Governmental Organizations (NGOs) also pitched in with innovative ideas. The Aajeevika Bureau in western India, for instance, is an NGO solely devoted to the welfare of migrant workers, in the source and destination region. Among other services, it provides identity cards for migrant workers that enable access to various other services in cities, skill training and legal education and aid. There is therefore a perceptible shift in attitudes to both internal and international migration taking place currently in India. But what does the future hold in store? If humankind survives till the 22nd century and the map of internal and international economic inequalities gets redrawn, would there be political parties in Bihar that shun Maharashtrian migrants or Indian A1 visas rationed out to the Americans? Such a possibility is not as far-fetched as it may seem after all, Bihar once did attract students from far and wide.

There are at least three major developments that I foresee in the 21st century. First, the Great Indian Migration Wave will veer southwards as high north–south wage differentials outweigh previous linguistic barriers. Since south India will also age faster than north India, it will precipitate the migration of a large number of people to work in the care economy, similar to migrations taking place towards Europe. Southward migration can potentially generate strong anti-migrant sentiments and nativist movements. The Bhojpuri-speaking belt will continue to send out migrants, as it has for centuries, and in many other regions there will be a transition from seasonal to semi-permanent, and then to permanent migrations. Autonomous female migration will also increase significantly due to better education and there will be concerns about internal brain drains, similar to the concern over the international brain drain from India in the 1960s and 70s.

In addition, there is a real risk of climate change and erratic weather triggering mass migrations in old and new corridors. Since Bangladesh is a low-lying area that is highly prone to the downside of climate change, it will lead to more migration to India, causing even more consternation than what is observed today. India will have to be prepared to deal with climate-change-induced internal and international migration.

Finally, as India's economy grows, it will also become a country of immigration, attracting people in large numbers beyond Bangladesh and Nepal. The stock of migrant workers from North America and Europe, also called expatriates, can potentially increase from thousands to hundreds of thousands, giving a very different texture to India's leading metropolitan centres.

As a matter of principle, India should embrace the tide of rising mobility that would add to its diversity. The leading personalities of Indian history were almost always migrants, who spent over half their life outside their place of birth, exposed to new and different ideas precisely because they moved.[57] As a migrant, the least one should be able to do is respect the cultures and sensibilities of the society one enters, maybe even learn the local language. As natives, a tolerance to peaceful outsiders without violence is the best way to enrich one's society.

If the major ideological battle of the 20th century was between capitalism and communism, in the 21st century it is likely to be between cosmopolitanism and nativism. On this ground, I hope that the views of Gandhi and Thackeray yield to those of Ambedkar. This, of course, reflects my own cosmopolitan moorings, but I do think that by accepting this wisdom, we would only reinforce that age-old Indian belief, engraved in the entrance hall of the parliament of the world's largest democracy: *Vasudhaiva Kutumbakam*—the world is one family.

Notes

In a previous monograph, the *India Migration Bibliography,* freely accessible online, I had listed over 3000 academic publications on the subject of internal and international migration linked with India. This book has benefited by consulting this extensive body of research. Migration before the 19th century has only recently attracted the attention of researchers and this remains an exciting field of discovery for historians and migration scholars alike. The references below provide a quick snapshot of important works on Indian migration, and I use abbreviations of some of these works in the citations for chapters from edited books.

General References

Globalising Migration History: The Eurasian Experience (16th-21st Centuries), ed. Jan Lucassen and Leo Lucassen (Leiden: Brill, 2014).

Migrations in Medieval and Early Colonial India, ed. Vijaya Ramaswamy (Delhi: Routledge, 2016).

Slavery and South Asian History, ed. Indrani Chatterjee and Richard M. Eaton (Bloomington: Indiana University Press, 2006).

Society and Circulation: Mobile People and Itinerant Cultures in South Asia, 1750-1950, ed. Claude Markovits, Jacques Pouchepadass and Sanjay Subrahmanyam (Delhi: Permanent Black, 2003).

Tirthankar Roy, *India and the World Economy: From Antiquity to the Present* (Delhi: Cambridge University Press, 2012).

Sunil Amrith, *Migration and Diaspora in Modern Asia* (Cambridge: Cambridge University Press, 2011).

The Encylopedia of the Indian Diaspora, ed. Brij V. Lal (Singapore: Editions Didier Millet, 2006).

Devesh Kapur, *Diaspora, Development and Democracy: The Domestic Impact of International Migration from India* (Delhi: Oxford University Press, 2010).

India Migration Report, ed. S. Irudaya Rajan, Annual Series 2010–17 (Delhi: Routledge).

Circular Migration and Multilocational Livelihood Strategies in Rural India, ed. Priya Deshingkar and John Farrington (Delhi: Oxford University Press, 2009).

Refugees and the State: Practices of Asylum and Care in India, 1947–2000, ed. Ranabir Samaddar (Delhi: Sage, 2003).

Special Issues on Indian Migration, *International Review of Social History*, Supplement 14, On Labour History (2006); South Asian Studies Issue 1, On Indenture (2017); *Indian Journal of Labour Economics* (2011); *Journal of Interdisciplinary Economics*, On Change and Continuity (2018).

Chapter 1: Indian Diversity and Global Migrations

1. Jawaharlal Nehru, *The Discovery of India* (Oxford University Press, 1946) p. 562.

2. According to the website of *Ethnologue: Languages of the World*, an authoritative source on language data, Papua New Guinea had 840 living languages, the most in the world, followed by Indonesia, Nigeria and then India at 454. On a scale from 0–1,

India scores 0.91 on the language diversity index, the highest among countries with a population size of over five million people. China's score on this index was 0.52.

3.   Tarasankar Banerjee, *Internal Market of India [1834–1900]* (Academic Publishers, 1966) p. xiv.

4.   Nina G. Jablonski and George Chaplin, 'The Evolution of Human Skin Coloration', *Journal of Human Evolution* 39 (1) (2000): 57-106.

5.   Charles Darwin, *The Descent of Man, and Selection in Relation to Sex* (John Murray, 1871) pp. 192–93.

6.   Nina G. Jablonski and George Chaplin, 'Human Skin Pigmentation, Migration and Disease Susceptibility', *Philosophical Transactions of the Royal Society B: Biological Sciences* 367 (1590) (2012): 785–92.

7.   N.J. Shaw and B.R. Pal, 'Vitamin D Deficiency in UK Asian Families: Activating a New Concern', *Archives of Disease in Childhood* 86 (3) (2002): 147–49.

8.   Alice Roberts, *The Incredible Human Journey* (Bloomsbury, 2010).

9.   David Reich, Kumarasamy Thangaraj, Nick Patterson, Alkes L. Price and Lalji Singh, 'Reconstructing Indian Population History', *Nature* 461 (7263) (2009): 489–94.

10. Edwin Bryant, *The Quest for the Origins of Vedic Culture: The Indo-Aryan Migration Debate* (Oxford University Press, 2001).

11. Analabha Basu, Neeta Sarkar-Roy and Partha P. Majumder, 'Genomic Reconstruction of the History of Extant Populations of India Reveals Five Distinct Ancestral Components and a Complex Structure', *Proceedings of the National Academy of Sciences of the United States of America* 113 (6) (2016): 1594–99.

12. Romila Thapar, *The Penguin History of Early India: From the Origins to 1300 AD* (Penguin, 2002), p. 77.

13. As cited in G. Findlay Shirras, 'Indian Migration', *International Migrations, Vol. II: Interpretations,* ed. Walter F. Willcox (National Bureau of Economic Research, 1931), p. 594.

14. Thapar, *The Penguin History of Early India,* p. 77.

15. Himanshu Prabha Ray, *Colonial Archaeology in South Asia* (Oxford University Press, 2007), p. 153.

16. Thapar, *The Penguin History of Early India*, pp. 112–15.

17. Murali Kumar Jha, 'Migration, Settlement and State Formation in the Ganga Plain: A Historical Geographic Perspective', *Journal of the Economic and Social History of the Orient* 57 (4) (2014), p. 608.

18. Priya Moorjani et al., 'Genetic Evidence for Recent Population Mixture in India', *American Journal of Human Genetics* 93 (3) (2013): 422–38.

19. Rukmini S., 'Just 5% of Indian Marriages are Inter-caste: Survey', *The Hindu,* November 13, 2014, based on the India Human Development Survey of 2011–12.

20. Morris E. Opler, 'The Extensions of an Indian Village', *Journal of Asian Studies* 16 (1) (1956): 5–10.

21. D.E.U. Baker, 'Patterns of Migration, Settlement and Integration: Bagelkhand, Madhya Pradesh, c. 1000 BC–1300 AD', *Indian Historical Review* 34 (1) (2007): pp. 125–51, notes the settlement of Bagelkhand from the west.

22. Jha, 'Migration, Settlement and State Formation in the Ganga Plain', pp. 587–627.

23. Though Buddha was born in Lumbini in Nepal, he spent considerable time travelling in Bihar.

24. Kautilya, *The Arthashastra*, ed. L.N. Rangarajan (Penguin, 1987), pp. 47–63 and pp. 71–2 on travel and mlecchas, p. 130 on famines, p. 293 on travelling allowance, pp. 357–60 on movement control officials, pp. 392–412 on marital life, pp. 503–07 on the secret service, p. 797 on mudradhyaksha.

25. Romila Thapar, *A History of India: Volume 1* (Penguin, 1966), p. 76.

26. Ibid.

27. Thapar, *The Penguin History of Early India*, p. 49.

28. Swati Datta, *Migrant Brahmanas in Northern India: Their Settlement and General Impact, c. A.D. 475-1030* (Motilal Banarasidass, 1989); Subrata Kumar Acharya, 'Kings, Brahmanas and Collective Land Grants in Early Medieval Odisha', *Indian Historical Review*, 45 (1) (2018): 24–57.

29. Luca Pagani, Sarmila Bose, Qasim Ayub and Chris Taylor-Smith, 'Kayasthas of Bengal: Legends, Genealogies and Genetics', *Economic & Political Weekly*, 52 (47) (2017), pp. 44–52.

30. Datta, *Migrant Brahmanas in Northern India*, p. 224.

31. Ryosuke Furui, 'Brahmanas in Early Medieval Bengal: Construction of their Identity, Networks and Authority', *Indian Historical Review*, 40 (2) (2013): 223–48.

32. Ibid., pp. 159–60.

33. Aloka Parasher, *Mlecchas in Early India: A Study in Attitudes towards Outsiders up to AD 600* (Munshiram Manoharlal, 1991).

34. Suchandra Ghosh, 'Migration of the Gana-samghas of Punjab: The Underlying Factors', *Journal of the Asiatic Society*, LIV (1) (2012), 45-54.

35. Thapar, *The Penguin History of Early India* p. 301.

36. R. Champakalakshmi, *Trade, Ideology and Urbanization: South India, 300 BC to AD 1300* (Oxford University Press, 1996).

37. Monica L. Smith, '"Indianization" from the Indian Point of View: Trade and Cultural Contacts with Southeast Asia in the Early First Millennium', *Journal of the Economic and Social History of the Orient* 42 (1) (1999), 1–26.

38. *A Concise History of South India*, ed. Noboru Karashima (Oxford University Press, 2014), p. 133.

39. B.R. Grover, 'Contribution of Indian Immigrants in the Socio-Economic and Cultural Life of West Asia and Central Europe', *Indian Historical Review* 28 (1–2) (2001): 50–67.

40. Naira Mkrtchyan, 'Indian Settlement in Armenia and Armenian Settlements in India and South Asia', *Indian Historical Review* 32 (2) (2005): 64–87.

41. John Keay, *India: A History* (Harper Press, 2000), p. 114 and p. 124.

42. Ibid., p. 146.

43. Grover, 'Contribution of Indian Immigrants', p. 52.

44. Ibid., p. 54.

45. Ibid., pp. 54–5.

46. Ibid., p. 50–67 for linguistic connections. For genetic links, see Niraj Rai, et al., 'The Phylogeography of Y-Chromosome Haplogroup H1a1a-M82 Reveals the Likely Indian Origin of the European Romani Populations', PLOS ONE 7 (11) (2012).

47. Kalidasa, *Meghadutam: The Cloud Messenger,* Trans. Srinivas Reddy (Delhi: Penguin, 2017).

48. Jos Gommans, 'The Silent Frontier of South Asia, c. A. D. 1100–1800', *Journal of World History,* 9 (1) (1998): 1–23.

49. Dirk Kolff, *Naukar, Rajput and Sepoy: The Ethnohistory of the Military Labour Market in Hindustan, 1450–1850* (Cambridge University Press, 1990).

50. Irfan Habib, 'Population', *Cambridge Economic History of India, Vol. 1, c.1200-c.1750,* ed. Tapan Raychaudhuri and Irfan Habib (Cambridge University Press, 1982), p. 166.

51. Gommans, 'The Silent Frontier of South Asia', 13–6.

52. Tirthankar Roy, *India and the World Economy: From Antiquity to the Present* (Cambridge University Press, 2012) p. 13.

53. Gagan D. Sood, *India and the Islamic Heartlands: An Eighteenth Century World of Circulation and Exchange* (Cambridge University Press, 2016).

54. Antje Fluechter, 'Handling of Diversity in Early Modern India? Perception and Evaluation in German Discourses', *Medieval History Journal,* 16 (2) (2013): 297–334.

55. See notes of Chapter 4 on lascars and ayahs. On Tamil teachers in Germany, see Knut A. Jacobsen, 'Scandinavia', *Encyclopedia of the Indian Diaspora,* ed. Brij Lal (Editions Didier Millet, 2006), p. 361.

56. Sanjay Subrahmanyam, *Three Ways to be Alien: Travails and Encounters in the Early Modern World* (Permanent Black, 2011) on the identity of the Italian chronicler of the Mughal Empire, Nicolo Manuzzi, in India, p. 177.

57. Tapan Raychaudhuri, 'Inland Trade', *Cambridge Economic History of India, Vol. 1, c.1200-c.1750,* ed. Raychaudhuri and Habib (Cambridge University Press, 1982), p. 325.

58. Burton Stein, 'South India', *Cambridge Economic History of India, Vol. 1, c.1200-c.1750,* ed. Raychaudhuri and Habib, p. 39.

59. On Muslims: see Richard M. Eaton, 'Shrines, Cultivators and Muslim "Conversion" in Punjab and Bengal, 1300-1700', *Medieval History Journal* 12 (2) (2009): 191–220. On the Conversion of Christians in 16th Century Goa: see Sanjay Subrahmanyam, *Three Ways to be Alien: Travails and Encounters in the Early Modern World*, pp. 27–8.

60. Irfan Habib, 'Population', *Cambridge Economic History of India, Vol. 1, c.1200-c.1750,* ed. Raychaudhuri and Habib, p. 171.

61. Gavin Hambly, 'Towns and Cities: Mughal India', *Cambridge Economic History of India, Vol. 1, c.1200–c.1750,* ed. by Raychaudhuri and Habib, p. 444.

62. Keay, *India: A History*, p. 270.

63. Muzaffar Alam and Sanjay Subrahmanyam, *Indo-Persian Travels in the Age of Discoveries, 1400-1800* (Cambridge University Press, 2007), p. 177.

64. Surajbhan Bharadwaj, 'Migration, Mobility and Memories: Meos in the Processes of Peasantisation and Islamisation in the Medieval Period', *Migrations in Medieval and Early Colonial India,* ed. Vijaya Ramaswamy (2016), 87–126; Gagan D. Sood, 'The Informational Fabric of Eighteenth-Century India and the Middle East: Couriers, Intermediaries and Postal Communication', *Modern Asian Studies,* 43 (4) (2009): 1085–116.

65. Shireen Moosvi, 'Skilled Labour Migration in Pre-Colonial India from 16th to 18th Centuries', *Historical Diversities: Society, Politics and Culture,* ed. K.L. Tuteja and Sunita Pathania (Manohar, 2008), pp. 125–39.

66. Vijaya Ramaswamy, 'Mapping Migrations of South Indian Weavers Before, During and After the Vijayanagar Period: Thirteenth to Eighteenth Centuries', *Globalising Migration History,* ed. Jan Lucassen and Leo Lucassen (Brill, 2014), pp. 91–121.

67. Ibid, p. 111.

68. The Trans-Atlantic Slave Trade Database, http://www.slavevoyages.org/.

69. Kautilya, *The Arthashastra*, ed. L.N. Rangarajan, pp. 446–55.

70. *Slavery and South Asian History,* ed. Indrani Chatterjee and Richard M. Eaton (Indiana University Press, 2006).

71. Richard M. Eaton, 'Introduction', *Slavery and South Asian History,* ed. Chatterjee and Eaton, p. 2.

72. Daud Ali, 'War, Servitude and the Imperial Household: A Study of Palace Women in the Chola Empire', *Slavery and South Asian History* (2006), pp. 44–58.

73. Thapar, *The Penguin History of Early India,* p. 358.

74. Ramya Sreenivasan, 'Drudges, Dancing Girls, Concubines: Female Slaves in Rajput Polity, 1500-1850', *Slavery and South Asian History* (2006), pp. 136–61.

75. Rila Mukherjee, 'Mobility in the Bay of Bengal World: Medieval Raiders, Traders, States and the Slaves', *Indian Historical Review* 36 (1) (2009): 109–29.

76. Sunil Kumar, 'Service, Status, and Military Slavery in the Delhi Sultanate: Thirteenth and Fourteenth Centuries', *Slavery and South Asian History* (2006), pp. 83–114.

77. Saying of Nizam al-Mulk (d. 1092) as cited in Richard M. Eaton, 'The Rise and Fall of Military Slavery in the Deccan, 1450-1650', *Slavery and South Asian History* (2006), p. 115.

78. Kolff, *Naukar, Rajput and Sepoy,* p. 11.

79. Samuel Lee, trans., *The Travels of Ibn Battuta: In the Near East, Asia and Africa* (New York: Cosimo Classics), pp. 97–98.

80. Eaton, 'The Rise and Fall of Military Slavery in the Deccan, 1450-1650', *Slavery and South Asian History* (2006), pp. 115–35.

81. David Ludden, 'Caste Society and Units of Production in Early Modern South India', *Institutions and Economic Change in South Asia,* ed. Burton Stein and Sanjay Subrahmanyam (Delhi, 1996), p. 108.

82. Ian Kerr, 'On the Move: Circulating Labour in Pre-Colonial, Colonial, and Post-Colonial India', *International Review of Social History,* 51 (S14) (2006), 85–109.

83. Bhangya Bhukya, *Subjugated Nomads: The Lambadas under the Rule of the Nizams* (Orient BlackSwan, 2010).

84. Tanuja Kothiyal, *Nomadic Narratives: A History of Mobility and Identity in the Great Indian Desert* (Cambridge University Press, 2016).

85. Jan Lucassen, 'Working at the Ichapur Gunpowder Factory in the 1790s (Part II)', *Indian Historical Review* 39 (2) (2012), 251–71; Nitin Sinha, 'Contract, Work, and Resistance: Boatmen in Early Colonial Eastern India, 1760s-1850s', *International Review of Social History* 59 (Supplement) (2014), 11–43.

86. Ravi Ahuja, 'On Roads', *Pathways of Empire: Circulation, 'Public Works' and Social Space in Colonial Orissa, c. 1780-1914* (Orient BlackSwan, 2009).

87. Douglas Haynes, *Small Town Capitalism in Western India: Artisans, Merchants and the Making of the Informal Economy, 1870-1960* (Cambridge University Press, 2012).

88. Santosh Kumar Rai, 'Many Madanpuras: Memories and Histories of Migrant Weavers of Northern India during the Nineteenth and Twentieth Centuries', *Migrations in Medieval and Early Colonial India*, ed. Vijaya Ramaswamy (2016), pp. 225–58.

89. Jean Deloche, *Transport and Communication in India prior to Steam Locomotion, Vol. 1: Land Transport* (Oxford University Press, 1993), p. 3; Tirthankar Roy, *India in the World Economy*, p. 161.

90. Moosvi, 'Skilled Labour Migration in Pre-Colonial India from 16th to 18th Centuries', p. 125–26.

91. Kingsley Davis, *The Population of India and Pakistan* (Princeton University Press, 1951), p. 99.

92. *Society and Circulation: Mobile People and Itinerant Cultures in South Asia, 1750–1950*, ed. Claude Markovits, Jacques Pouchepadass and Sanjay Subrahmanyam (Delhi: Permanent Black, 2003), p. 3.

93. Chinmay Tumbe, 'India and Global Migrations', forthcoming research, provides estimates on cross-cultural migrations over the past few centuries.

94. Chinmay Tumbe, *Migration and Remittances in India: Historical, Regional, Social and Economic Dimensions,* doctoral thesis, Indian Institute of Management Bangalore.

95. Ravinder Kaur, 'Bengali Bridal Diaspora: Marriage as a Livelihood Strategy', *Economic & Political Weekly* 45 (5) (2010), 16–8.

96. Census of 2011, D-5 Provisional Migration Tables.

97. Chinmay Tumbe, 'Remittances in India: Facts and Issues', *Indian Journal of Labour Economics* 54 (3) (2011), 479–501.

98. *Economic Survey of India 2016-17*, Government of India, p. 267.

99. S. Chandrasekhar, 'Workers commuting between the rural and urban: Estimates from NSSO data', *Economic and Political Weekly* 46(46) (2011), 22–5.

100. Chinmay Tumbe, 'Missing Men, Migration and Labour Markets: Evidence from India', *Indian Journal of Labour Economics* 58 (2) (2015), 245–67.

101. R.B. Bhagat and Kunal Keshri, 'Temporary and Seasonal Migration: Regional Pattern, Characteristics and Associated Factors', *Economic and Political Weekly* 47 (4) (2012), 81–8.

102. Tumbe, *Migration and Remittances in India*, p. 19, based on NSS 2007–08 data.

103. Seid Gholam Hussein Khan, *The Seir Mutaqherin*, Calcutta (Printed for the Translator), 1789, p. 590.

Chapter 2: The Great Indian Migration Wave

1. Regions are identified based on three indicators—outmigrant to population ratio, sex selectivity of outmigration and remittance receiving propensity—calculated from the 64th National Sample Survey of 2007–08. For historic data, inference is made using age-adjusted sex ratios. About the link between migration and sex ratios in India, see Chinmay Tumbe, 'The Missing Men: Migration and Sex Ratios', *India Migration Report 2015: Migration and Gender,* ed. S. Irudaya Rajan (Routledge, 2015), pp. 221–39. The benchmark of 5 per cent for 'mass migration' is close to that used by Timothy Hatton and Jeffrey Williamson, *The Age of Mass Migration* (Oxford University Press, 1998), p. 9.

2. Chinmay Tumbe, 'Migration Persistence across Twentieth Century India', 87–112.

3. Rajnarayan Chandavarkar, *The Origins of Industrial Capitalism in India* (Cambridge University Press, 1994), p. 131.

4. Ibid., p. 131.

5. 'Mahar and Non-Brahman Movements of Nineteenth Century', *Encyclopaedia of Dalits in India: Vol. 3, Movements*, ed. Sanjay Paswan and Paramanshi Jaideva (Kalpaz Publications, 2002), pp. 89–128. The exact birth year of many personalities in Dalit history is often not well-documented. The surname 'Ambedkar' was apparently changed from 'Ambadawekar', referring to a village called Ambadawe in Mandangad taluka of Ratnagiri district. As per the Census of 1941, the Scheduled Caste population of this village was 36 per cent, double that of the taluka average.

6. G.M. Yamin, *The Causes and Consequences of Rural–Urban Migration in 19th and Early 20th Century India: The Case of Ratnagiri District,* doctoral thesis, University of Salford (1991), p. 13.

7. Kalyani Vartak, Chinmay Tumbe and Amita Bhide, 'Mass Migration from Rural India: A Restudy of Kunkeri Village in Konkan Maharashtra, 1961–1987–2017', *Journal of Interdisciplinary Economics*, forthcoming.

8. The list includes Karve, Ambedkar, Sanskrit scholar P.V. Kane (1880–1972), Lata Mangeshkar and Sachin Tendulkar. The latter two are associated with Konkan Goa.

9. 'Ferry Passenger's Grievances: Ousted by Mango Parcels', *Times of India*, 27 September 1935, p. 12.

10. *Statistical Appendix, Together with a Supplement to the Two District Manuals for South Kanara District*, Madras District Gazetteers, Government of India, 1938.

11. The share of 'Brahmans' in the Madras Presidency was 3.1 per cent in 1901 and 9.7 per cent in south Canara district, of which Udupi was one taluka, Census of India-1901, Vol. 15A, Part 2, pp. 158–205. Bunts (10 per cent), Billavas (13 per cent) and Holeyas (10 per cent) were the other numerically significant castes of south Canara.

12. Stig Toft Madsen and Geoffrey Gardella, 'Udupi Hotels: Entrepreneurship, Reform and Revival', *Curried Cultures,*

Globalization, Food, and South Asia, ed. Krishnendu Ray and Tulasi Srinivas (University of California Press, 2012), pp. 91–109.

13. 'South Canara Floods', *Times of India*, 7 August 1923.

14. Vegard Iversen and Yashodhan Ghorpade, 'Misfortune, Misfits and What the City Gave and Took: The Stories of South-Indian Child Labour Migrants, 1935-2005', *Modern Asian Studies* 45 (5) (2011), 1177–226.

15. Iversen and P.S. Raghavendra, 'What the Signboard Hides: Food, Caste and Employability in Small South-Indian Eating Places', *Contributions to Indian Sociology* 40 (3) (2006), 311–41.

16. *Karnataka Human Development Report 2005,* Government of Karnataka (2006).

17. According to data from the Census of India-1901, Saran and Muzaffarpur had densities of over 900 people per square mile, placing them above all other predominantly rural districts of British India.

18. Kolff, *Naukar, Rajput and Sepoy*, p. 160.

19. Anand Yang, 'Peasants on the Move: A Study of Internal Migration in India', *Journal of Interdisciplinary History* 10 (1) (1979), p. 43.

20. Yang, *The Limited Raj: Agrarian Relations in Colonial India, Saran District, 1793-1920* (Oxford University Press, 1989), pp. 182–85.

21. Ibid., p. 42.

22. Ibid., p. 48.

23. Ibid., p. 53.

24. Arjan de Haan, *Unsettled Settlers: Migrant Workers and Industrial Capitalism in Calcutta* (Verloren, 1994).

25. Samita Sen, *Women and Labour in Late Colonial India: The Bengal Jute Industry* (Cambridge University Press, 1999).

26. Nitin Sinha, 'When Women Sang in the Age of Steam', the Wire, 31 July 2016.

27. Yang, 'Peasants on the Move', p. 55.

28. Sunil Amrith, *Crossing the Bay of Bengal: The Furies of Nature and Fortunes of Migrants* (Harvard University Press, 2013), p. 11 and p. 21.

29. These years are selected based on various reports in the *Times of India* on cyclones affecting Ganjam. Among those mentioned, 1866 and 1987 were intense drought years in the district.

30. Adapa Satyanarayana, 'Birds of Passage: Migration of South Indian Labourers to Southeast Asia', *Critical Asian Studies* 34 (1) 2002: p. 92. The location of 'suvarna bhumi', noted in historical texts, is still contested and could refer to the broader southeast Asian peninsular region, including Thailand and Malaysia.

31. James Baxter, *Report on Indian Immigration*, Rangoon (1941), Appendix 15 (c).

32. Ibid., p. 86.

33. Satyanarayana, 'Birds of Passage: Migration': p. 95.

34. Ibid., p. 96, and Baxter, *Report on Indian Immigration*, p. 105.

35. Bidyut Mohanty, 'Migration, Famines and Sex Ratios in Orissa Division between 1881 and 1921', *Indian Economic and Social History Review (IESHR)* 29 (4) (1992): 516. The inference on remittances is applied to Ganjam as it lay just below Cuttack.

36. Gagan B. Sahu and Biswaroop Das, *Income, Remittances and Urban Labour Markets: Oriya Migrant Workers in Surat City* (Adhikar, 2008), p. 26.

37. Ibid., p. 63, and Baxter, *Report on Indian Immigration*, Rangoon (1941), p. 54.

38. Remy A.D. Dias, 'Emigration: Goa's Transformation from an Agrarian to a Remittance based Economy', *Migration in South India,* ed. K.S. Mathew, M. Singh and J. Varkey (Shipra Publications, 2005), pp. 24–54.

39. Goa Migration Study, Department of Non-Resident Indian Affairs, Government of Goa (2008), p. 25.

40. Ibid, p. 25 and 48.

41. K.C. Zachariah, E.T. Mathew and S. Irudaya Rajan, *Dynamics of Migration in Kerala: Dimensions, Differentials and Consequences* (Orient Longman, 2003), Migration from Kerala: A Historical

Review, pp. 12–73. Some migration to Ceylon was also noted in the 19th century because of which the word 'Malabars' was used to denote all overseas south Indians; Hugh Tinker, *A New System of Slavery: The Export of Indian Labour Overseas, 1830-1920* (Oxford University Press, 1974), p. 55.

42. Zachariah, *Migrants in Greater Bombay* (Asia Publishing House, 1968).

43. Zachariah, Mathew and Rajan, 'Impact of Migration on Kerala's Economy and Society', *International Migration* 39 (1) (2001), 63–87.

44. Tumbe, 'Remittances in India: Facts and Issues', *Indian Journal of Labour Economics* 54 (3) (2011), 479–501.

45. Christophe Z. Guilmoto, 'The Tamil Migration Cycle, 1830–1950', *Economic & Political Weekly,* 28 (3–4) (1993), 111–20; Dharma Kumar, *Land and Caste in South India* (Cambridge University Press, 1965) p. 129.

46. See Table 1 at the end of Chapter 4.

47. Tinker, *A New System of Slavery,* p. 59.

48. Tumbe, 'Migration Persistence across Twentieth Century India', 100.

49. Tumbe, *Migration and Remittances in India: Historical, Regional, Social and Economic Dimensions,* doctoral thesis, p. 58.

50. Satyanarayana, 'Birds of Passage', p. 111.

51. Ibid, p. 99 and 109.

52. Tumbe, 'Migration Persistence across Twentieth Century India', p. 100.

53. Tinker, *A New System of Slavery: The Export of Indian Labour Overseas 1830–1920,* pp. 52–53.

54. As cited in Panchanan Saha, *Emigration of Indian Labour, 1834–1900* (People's Publishing House, 1970), p. 74.

55. Tumbe, 'Migration Persistence across Twentieth Century India', p. 104. For the full scale of inter-provincial movements, see K.C. Zachariah, *A Historical Study of Internal Migration in the Indian Sub-Continent, 1901–1931* (Asia Publishing House, 1964).

56. Douglas Haynes and Tirthankar Roy, 'Conceiving Mobility: Weavers' Migrations in Pre-colonial and Colonial India', *IESHR* 36(1) (1999): p. 35.

57. Tirthankar Roy, 'Sardars, Jobbers, Kanganies: The Labour Contractor and Indian Economic History', *Modern Asian Studies,* 42 (5) (2008), 971–98.

58. Prabhu P. Mohapatra, 'Coolies and Colliers: A Study of the Agrarian Context of Labour Migration from Chotanagpur, 1880–1920', *Studies in History* 1(2) (1985), 247–303.

59. Crispin Bates, 'Regional Dependence and Rural Development in Central India: The Pivotal Role of Migrant Labour', *Modern Asian Studies*, 19 (3) (1985), 573–92.

60. K.L. Gillion, 'The Sources of Indian Emigration to Fiji', *Population Studies*, 10 (2) (1956): 155.

61. Tumbe, 'Migration Persistence across Twentieth Century India', p. 102.

62. As cited by Tinker, *A New System of Slavery: The Export of Indian Labour Overseas 1830–1920,* pp. 45–6.

63. Ibid., p. 45.

64. David Northrup, *Indentured Labour in the Age of Imperialism, 1834–1922* (Cambridge University Press, 1995), Table A.1.

65. Tinker, *A New System of Slavery,* p. 58.

66. Amarjit Kaur, 'Indian Labour, Labour Standards, and Worker's Health in Burma and Malaya,' *Modern Asian Studies* 40 (2) (2006), p. 445, cites the figure of 13 per cent as the share of indentured migration towards Malaya from 1844 to 1938. In Sri Lanka, the figure would be less as alternative modes of recruitment started even earlier.

67. Rana P. Behal, *One Hundred Years of Servitude: Political Economy of Tea Plantations in Colonial Assam* (Tulika, 2014).

68. Northrup, *Indentured Labour in the Age of Imperialism,* p. 75.

69. Tinker, *A New System of Slavery,* pp. 41–2. The Turkish reference comes from literature on the Slave Dynasties.

70. Ibid., p. 69.

71. J. Geoghegan, *Note on Emigration from India* (Calcutta, 1873), p. 14.

72. Marina Carter, *Servants, Sirdars and Settlers: Indians in Mauritius, 1834–1874* (Oxford University Press, 1995); Ashutosh Kumar, 'Naukari, Networks and Knowledge: Views of Indenture in Nineteenth Century North India', *South Asian Studies* 33 (1) (2017): 52–67. In Assam, indenture would last longer until legislative change.

73. Northrup, *Indentured Labour in the Age of Imperialism*, p. 67, considered inter-continental migrations. Personal estimates tally with this assessment since indenture during this period was a small portion of overseas migration to Ceylon, Malaya and Burma— the three key overseas destinations. Indentured migration to Assam was also less than 10 per cent of overall internal migration for work during this period.

74. Tinker, *A New System of Slavery*, cites John Russel in 1840 for the phrase.

75. Roy, 'Sardars, Jobbers, Kanganies', pp. 971–98.

76. Daniel Thorner, *Investment in Empire* (University of Pennsylvania Press, 1950), p. 58.

77. Morris D. Morris and Clyde B. Dudley, 'Selected Railway Statistics for the Indian Subcontinent (India, Pakistan and Bangladesh), 1853–1946–47', *Artha Vijnana* 17 (3) (1975), 187–298.

78. Ibid.

79. Ritika Prasad, *Tracks of Change: Railways and Everyday Life in Colonial India* (Cambridge University Press, 2015), p. 30.

80. Ibid., p. 35.

81. Ibid., p. 26.

82. Ibid., p. 47.

83. Ibid., pp. 51–2.

84. Ibid., p. 54.

85. Lisa Mitchell, 'To Stop Train, Pull Chain: Writing Histories of Contemporary Political Practice', *IESHR* 48 (4) (2011): 469–95.

86. *Railways in Modern India*, ed. Ian Kerr (Oxford University Press, 2001), p. 25.

87. Ibid., p. 71, and an editorial in *Bombay Times* and *Journal of Commerce*, 17 December 1856, for the daily figures.

88. Annual Report of the Indian Railways, 2014–15, Statistical Summary Sheet.

89. On Gandhi's opposition, see his piece re-printed as Chapter 3, 'The Condition of India-Railways', in *Railways in Modern India*, ed. Ian Kerr (Oxford University Press, 2001); on Gandhi's quote, see Prasad, *Tracks of Change: Railways and Everyday Life in Colonial India*, p. 97.

90. Ibid., p. 97.

91. The section on the post office draws from Chinmay Tumbe, 'Towards Financial Inclusion: The Post Office of India as a Financial Institution, 1880–2010', *IESHR* 52 (4) (2015): 409–37.

92. Shahid Amin, *Event, Metaphor, Memory: Chauri Chaura, 1922–92* (University of California Press, 1995), p. 37.

93. Geoffrey Clarke, *The Post Office of India and its Story* (John Lane, 1921), p. 80.

94. 'Post Office Innovations: Originality and Vigor in India Shame the Conservatism of the English Home Department', *New York Times*, 27 March 1898.

95. Rajnarayan Chandavarkar, *The Origins of Industrial Capitalism in India* (Cambridge University Press, 1994), p. 163.

96. Adam McKeown, 'Global Migration, 1846–1940,' *Journal of World History*, 15 (2) (2004), 155–89, makes a similar point about Eurocentric approaches to migration history.

97. This differs from the insightful rice-based argument of agricultural involution offered by Latika Chakravarty, 'Emergence of an industrial labour force in a dual economy: British India, 1880–1920', *IESHR* 15(3) (1978): 249–328, because large tracts of rice-growing regions did not participate in the Great Indian Migration Wave.

98. Tumbe, *Migration and Remittances in India: Historical, Regional, Social and Economic Dimensions*, p. 125.

99. Tumbe, 'Missing Men, Migration and Labour Markets', 245–67.

100. Philippe Fargues, 'International Migration and the Demographic Transition: A Two-Way Interaction', *International Migration Review* 45 (3) (2011): 588–614.

Chapter 3: Merchants and Capital

1. M.K. Gandhi, *The Collected Works of Mahatma Gandhi*, vol. 6 (New Delhi: e-book, Publications Division Government of India, 1999), p. 424.
2. Chinmay Tumbe, 'Transnational Indian Business in the Twentieth Century', *Business History Review,* 91 (4) (2017): 651–679; Census of India (1901).
3. D.F. Karaka, *History of the Parsis-Volume 1* (London: Macmillan and Co., 1884), Chapter 1.
4. Bakhtiar K. Dadabhoy, *Sugar in Milk: Lives of Eminent Parsis* (New Delhi: Rupa, 2008), p. xiii.
5. Karaka, *History of the Parsis*, p. 34.
6. Ibid., p. 40.
7. Ibid., p. 51.
8. K.N. Chaudhuri, *Trade and Civilization in the Indian Ocean: An Economic History from the Rise of Islam to 1750* (Cambridge: Cambridge University Press, 1985), p. 86.
9. Ruttonjee Ardeshir Wadia, *The Bombay Dockyard and the Wadia Master Builders* (Bombay: Godrej Memorial Printing Press, 1955), p. 106.
10. Ashok V. Desai, 'The Origins of Parsi Enterprise', *IESHR* 5 (4) (1968): 307–17.
11. Amalendu Guha, 'More about the Parsi Sheths: Their Roots, Entrepreneurship and Comprador Role, 1650–1918', in *Business Communities of India: A Historical Perspective*, ed. Dwijendra Tripathi (New Delhi, Manohar Books, 1984), p. 120.
12. Dadabhoy, *Sugar in Milk,* pp. 5–9.
13. On Tata's direct connection with the opium trade, see the petition of Tata & Co. and other opium traders in the Hong Kong Legislative Council No. 21, 25 March 1887.

14. Karaka, *History of the Parsis*, p. 92 and p. 98, using Census data (1881).

15. David West Rudner, *Caste and Capitalism in Colonial India: The Nattukottai Chettiars* (Berkeley: University of California Press, 1994), p. 2.

16. Ibid., p. 3.

17. Raman Mahadevan, 'Pattern of Enterprise of Immigrant Entrepreneurs: A Study of Chettiars in Malaya, 1880–1930', *Economic & Political Weekly* 13 (4–5) 1978: p. 146.

18. Ibid., p. 147.

19. Shoji Ito, 'A Note on the "Business Combine" in India with special reference to the Nattukottai Chettiars', *Developing Economies* (4) (1966), p. 371.

20. Medha Kudaisya, 'Trading networks in Southeast Asia', p. 61, in Lal (2006).

21. Ito, 'A Note on the "Business Combine in India"', p. 370.

22. T.E. Narasimhan, 'To Burma, For Our Properties', *Business Standard,* 3 January 2014.

23. Hardip Singh Syan, 'The Merchant Gurus: Sikhism and the Development of the Medieval Khatri Merchant Family,' *IESHR* 51 (3) (2014): 303–30.

24. Scott C. Levi, *Caravans: Punjabi Khatri Merchants on the Silk Road* (Penguin, 2015), p. 135. It provides a figure of 35,000, of whom most are considered to be Khatri merchants. See also: Stephen Dale, *Indian Merchants and Eurasian Trade, 1600-1750* (Cambridge: Cambridge University Press, 1994); Surendra Gopal, *Born to Trade: Indian Business Communities in Medieval and Early Modern Eurasia* (New Delhi: Manohar Books, 2016).

25. Levi, *Caravans*, p. 46.

26. Ibid., p. 58.

27. Ibid., p. 59 (as cited).

28. Ibid., p. 66.

29. Ibid., p. 70.

30. Ibid., p. 69, 78 and 134.

31. Ibid., p. 153.

32. Ibid., p. 156.

33. Sukhpal Singh, 'Refugees as Entrepreneurs: The Case of the Indian Bicycle Industry', *Journal of Entrepreneurship* 3 (1) (1994): 81–96.

34. Gurpreet Bal, 'Entrepreneurship among Diasporic Communities: A Comparative Examination of Patidars of Gujarat and Jats of Punjab', *The Journal of Entrepreneurship* 15 (2) (2006): 192–94.

35. *Interpreting the Sindhi World*, ed. Michel Boivin and Matthew A. Cook (Oxford University Press, 2010), p. ix and xv.

36. Matthew Cook, 'Getting Ahead or Keeping Your Head? The "Sindhi" Migration of Eighteenth Century India', *Interpreting the Sindhi World*, Boivin and Cook (Oxford University Press, 2010), pp. 133–49.

37. Mark-Anthony Falzon, *Cosmopolitan Connections: The Sindhi Diaspora, 1860–2000* (Oxford University Press, 2005), p. 31.

38. Claude Markovits, *The Global World of Indian Merchants, 1750-1947: Traders of Sind from Bukhara to Panama* (Cambridge University Press, 2000).

39. Devika Kerkar and Chinmay Tumbe, forthcoming research on the House of Motwane.

40. Harish Damodaran, *India's New Capitalists* (New Delhi: Permanent Black, 2008), pp. 26-27.

41. Mark-Anthony Falzon, *Cosmopolitan Connections*, p. 45.

42. Tumbe, 'Transnational Indian Business in the Twentieth Century', Table 3.

43. Census (2001), C-16 Language Table, reports 1.7 million people with Sindhi as their mother tongue, distinct from Kachchhi, placing a lower bound estimate on the size of the community. Regional shares are based on this data. The figure for Rajasthan includes population living near the border and speaking Sindhi, and not necessarily recent migrants.

44. 'Beware of the Marwaries', *Times of India*, 17 January 1844, p. 4, trans. from the *Prabhakar*, 10 December 1843.

45. Thomas Timberg, *The Marwaris* (Delhi: Vikas Publishing House, 1978), p. 11, based on data from Census (1921).

46. Ibid., p. 107.

47. G.D. Sharma, 'The Marwaris: Economic Foundations of an Indian Capitalist Class', *Business Communities of India* (1984), p. 186.

48. N.K. Sinha, 'Introduction', p. vi, J.H. Little, *House of Jagatseth* (Calcutta Historical Society, 1967).

49. Ibid., pp. x–xiii, and Anne Hardgrove, *Community and Public Culture: The Marwaris in Calcutta* (Oxford University Press), pp. 1–2.

50. Timberg, *The Marwaris,* pp. 181–86.

51. Medha Kudaisya, *The Life and Times of G.D. Birla* (Oxford University Press, 2003), pp. 7–8.

52. This section on Marwari network expansion in the 20th century is based on ongoing research with Vegard Iversen.

53. David Hardiman, *Feeding the Baniya: Peasants and Usurers in Western India* (Oxford University Press, 1996), pp. 200–20.

54. As cited in Hardgrove, *Community and Public Culture*, p. 11.

55. Ibid., p. xiii, quote of Jean Law; and Kudaisya, *The Life and Times of G. D. Birla.*

56. Hardgrove, *Community and Public Culture*, p. 13.

57. Timberg, *The Marwaris,* p. 10.

58. Tumbe, 'Transnational Indian Business in the Twentieth Century', Table 3.

59. As cited by Dwijendra Tripathi and Makrand Mehta, 'Class Character of the Gujarati Business Community,' *Business Communities of India*, p. 154.

60. Dwijendra Tripathi and Jyoti Jumani, *The Oxford History of Business in India* (Oxford University Press, 2007), p. 53.

61. Makrand Mehta, 'Gujarati Business Communities in East African Diaspora: Major Historical Trends', *Economic & Political Weekly* 36 (20) (2001): p. 1739.

62. Ibid., p. 1740.

63. 'A city of shops', *Times of India*, 2 March 1936.

64. Mehta, 'Gujarati Business Communities', p. 1744.

65. Ibid., p. 1744.

66. Ibid., pp. 1740–41.

67. Tripathi and Mehta, 'Class Character', p. 159.

68. Chhaya Goswami, *Globalisation before Its Time: The Gujarati Merchants from Kachchh* (Penguin, 2016).

69. Ibid., p. 47 and 51.

70. Mehta, 'Gujarati Business Communities', p. 1745.

71. Bal, 'Entrepreneurship among Diasporic Communities', p. 191.

72. 'English Cricket Match Has 22 Patels', Cricinfo, 20 July 2001, http://www.espncricinfo.com/page2/content/story/101796.html.

73. Bal, 'Entrepreneurship among Diasporic Communities', p. 195.

74. Tumbe, 'Transnational Indian Business in the Twentieth Century', Table 3.

75. Damodaran, *India's New Capitalists*, pp. 305–06.

76. Ibid, p. 298.

77. Sunil Amrith, *Crossing the Bay of Bengal*, pp. 38–40, 60–1 and 134.

78. Damodaran, *India's New Capitalists*, p. 297.

79. Ibid., p. 298.

80. Claude Markovits, *Merchants, Traders and Entrepreneurs: Indian Business in the Colonial Era*, pp. 111–16.

81. Ashin Dasgupta, *Merchants of Maritime India, 1500–1800* (Great Britain: Variorum, 1994), p. 700.

82. Markovits, *Merchants, Traders and Entrepreneurs*, p. 113.

83. As cited in Damodaran, *India's New Capitalists*, p. 297.

84. One of the first references to this phrase is attributed to Adam Smith in *The Wealth of Nations* (1776), Chapter 7, Part III.

85. Sarah Stein, 'Protected Persons? The Baghdadi Jewish Diaspora, the British State and the Persistence of Empire', *American Historical Review,* 116 (1) (2011): 80–93.

86. Ibid., p. 91.

87. Claude Markovits, 'Merchant Circulation in South Asia (Eighteenth to Twentieth Centuries): The Rise of Pan-Indian Merchant Networks', *Society and Circulation* (2003), pp. 131–162.

88. *Kautilya: The Arthashastra*, ed. L.N. Rangarajan (Penguin, 1987), p. 86.

89. Tirthankar Roy, *The Company of Kinsmen: Enterprise and Community in South Asian Business History, 1700-1940* (New Delhi: Oxford University Press, 2009), Chapter 3 on 'Merchants'.

90. This section is based on Tumbe, 'Transnational Indian Business in the Twentieth Century'.

91. Sanam Roohi, 'Historicising Mobility Trajectories of High Skilled Migrants from Coastal Andhra to the US', *Journal of Interdisciplinary Economics*, forthcoming.

92. D. Ajit, Han Donker and Ravi Saxena, 'Corporate Boards in India: Blocked by Caste?', *Economic & Political Weekly* 47 (31) (2012): p. 41; and Census of India (1901).

Chapter 4: Diasporas and Dreams

1. Sunil Amrith, *Crossing the Bay of Bengal: The Furies of Nature and Fortunes of Migrants* (Harvard University Press, 2013), p. 7.

2. I have estimated the size of the Indian diaspora to be 21 million in 2010. The figure for 2018 is based on an extrapolation. The Government of India figures have consistently been on the higher side due to incorrect figures for Myanmar and Sri Lanka by about three million and rounding-off effects.

3. See Chapter 3 for Scott Levi's estimate of over 20,000 Indians in central Asia.

4. Niall Ferguson, *Empire: How Britain Made the Modern World* (Penguin, 2003), pp. 12–13.

5. Marina Carter, 'Mauritius', in Lal (2006), pp. 263–72.

6. Marina Carter, 'The Mascarenes, Seychelles and Chagos Islands', in Lal (2006), pp. 273–75.

7. J. Geoghegan, *Note on Emigration from India* (Calcutta, 1873), p. 26, 31 and 57.

8. Clem Seecharan, 'Guyana', in Lal (2006), pp. 287–96.

9. Gaiutra Bahadur, *Coolie Woman: The Odyssey of Indenture* (Hachette India, 2013).

10. Seecharan, 'Guyana', 287–96.

11. Ravindra K. Jain, *Nation, Diaspora, Trans-Nation: Reflections from India* (Routledge, 2010), p. 9.

12. Patrick French, *The World is What It is: The Authorized Biography of V.S. Naipaul* (Alfred Knopf, 2008), pp. 6–9.

13. Kusha Haraksingh, 'Trinidad and Tobago', in Lal (2006), pp. 278–86.

14. Jain, *Nation, Diaspora, Trans-Nation: Reflections from India*, p. 3.

15. Rosemarijn Hoefte, 'Surinam', in Lal (2006), pp. 297–305.

16. Brij V. Lal, 'Fiji', in Lal (2006), pp. 370–82.

17. Gyanesh Kudaisya, 'Indian Leadership and the Diaspora', in Lal (2006), p. 85.

18. Amarjit Kaur, 'Malaysia', in Lal (2006), pp. 156–67.

19. Jain, *Nation, Diaspora, Trans-Nation: Reflections from India*, p. 6.

20. Rajesh Rai, 'Singapore', in Lal (2006), pp. 176–88.

21. Medha Kudaisya, 'Trading Networks in Southeast Asia', in Lal (2006), p. 63.

22. Gijsbert Oonk, 'East Africa,' in Lal (2006), pp. 254–61.

23. Parminder Bhachu, *Twice Migrants: East African Sikh Settlers in Britain* (Routledge Kegan & Paul, 1986).

24. Surendra Bhana and Goolam Vahed, 'South Africa', in Lal (2006), pp. 242–53.

25. Rozina Visram, *Ayahs, Lascars and Princes: Indians in Britain (1700-1947)* (Pluto Press, 1986).

26. Sumanta Banerjee, 'The Mysterious Alien: Indian Street Jugglers in Victorian London', *Economic and Political Weekly* 46 (14) (2011).

27. Virinder Kalra, 'United Kingdom', in Lal (2006), pp. 336–45.

28. Rupa Chanda and Sriparna Ghosh, 'Goans in Portugal: Role of History and Identity in Shaping Diaspora Linkages', CARIM-India Working Paper RR2012/19 (2012).

29. Kathryn Lum, 'The Ravidassia Community Identity (ies) in Catalonia, Spain', *Sikh Formations: Religion, Culture, Theory* 6 (1) (2010), 31–49.

30. Meenakshi Thapan, 'Isolation, Uncertainty and Change: Indian Immigrant Women and the Family in Northern Italy' CARIM-India Working Paper RR2013/09 (2013).

31. Kathryn Lum, 'Indian Diversities in Italy: Italian Case Study', CARIM-India Working Paper RR2012/02 (2012).

32. Deirdre Pirro, 'A Bridge to India', *The Florentine*, Florence, October 7 2010.

33. Sanjoy Chakravorty, Devesh Kapur, and Nirvikar Singh, *The Other One Percent: Indians in America* (Oxford University Press, 2017).

34. Vivek Bald, *Bengali Harlem and the Lost Histories of South Asian America* (Harvard University Press, 2015).

35. As cited by Chakravorty, Kapur, Singh, *The Other One Percent*, p. 7.

36. Chakravorty, Kapur, Singh, *The Other One Percent*, pp. 29–31.

37. Ibid., p. xix.

38. Josephine C. Naidoo and James D. Leslie, 'Canada', in Lal (2006), pp. 327–35.

39. D. Almond, L. Edlund and K. Milligan, 'Son Preference and the Persistence of Culture: Evidence from South and East Asian Immigrants to Canada', *Population and Development Review* 39 (1) (2013), 75–95.

40. Kundan Kumar, 'Indian Labour in the Gulf: Issues of Migration and the British Empire,' in *South Asian Migration to Gulf Countries*, ed. Prakash C. Jain and Ginu Z. Oommen (Routledge, 2016), p. 73.

41. Tumbe, 'Transnational Indian Business in the Twentieth Century', p. 657.

42. Stefan Tetzlaff, 'The Turn of the Gulf Tide: Empire, Nationalism, and the South Asian Labor Migration to Iraq, c. 1900-1935', *International Labor and Working-Class History* 79 (Spring) (2011), 7-27.

43. I. J. Seccombe and R. I. Lawless, 'Foreign Worker Dependence in the Gulf, and the International Oil Companies, 1910–50', *International Migration Review* 20 (3) (1986): 548–74.

44. Ibid., p. 558.

45. Ibid., p. 564.

46. K.C. Zachariah, *Migrants in Greater Bombay*, p. 347, observed that over half the Keralite workforce in Bombay worked in the service sector.

47. Kumar, 'Indian Labour in the Gulf', p. 82.

48. Chinmay Tumbe, 'Asian Migration to the Gulf States,' *The Handbook of Immigration and Refugee Studies,* ed.by Anna Triandafyllidou (Routledge, 2015).

49. Irudaya S. Rajan and P.R. Gopinathan Nair, 'Saudi Arabia, Oman and the Gulf States', in Lal (2006), pp. 222–33.

50. Philippe Fargues, 'Immigration Without Inclusion: Non-nationals in Nation-building in the Gulf States', *Asian and Pacific Migration Journal* 20(3–4) (2011), 273–92.

51. S. Krishna Kumar and S. Irudaya Rajan, *Emigration in 21st Century India: Governance, Legislation, Institutions* (Routledge, 2014).

52. Sushma Raj, 'Australia', in Lal (2006), pp. 383–85.

53. Carmen Voigt-Graf and Siew-Ean Khoo, 'Indian Student Migration to Australia', *Asian and Pacific Migration Journal* 13 (4) (2004), 423–41.

54. Jacqueline Leckie, 'New Zealand', in Lal (2006), pp. 389–95.

55. Caroline Pluss, 'Hong Kong', in Lal (2006), p. 206.

56. B.R. Deepak, 'Revolutionary Activities of the Ghadar Party in China', *China Report* 35 (4) (1999), 439–56.

57. Cao Yin, 'Kill Buddha Singh: Indian Nationalist Movement in Shanghai, 1914-27', *Indian Historical Review* 43 (2) (2016), 270–88.

58. Swarn Singh Kahlon, *Sikhs in Latin America: Travels among the Sikh Diaspora,* Manohar (2012), p. 13.

59. Ibid., p. 89.

60. Chinmay Tumbe, 'The Internal and International Diasporas of India', forthcoming research paper. The method uses Census 2001 data on languages to estimate the number of language-speakers outside the home state or region, excluding bordering districts. Figures for 2001 are then extrapolated to 2018 using India's overall population growth rate. For the international diaspora, various sources are used to allocate aggregate figures over the ten languages, for the major countries that host Indians.

61. Madhav Sadashiv Gore, *Immigrants and Neighbourhoods: Two Aspects of Life in a Metropolitan City,* Tata Institute of Social

Sciences, Bombay, 1970, p. 51. This book was conceived after discussions with Tarlok Singh, introduced in Chapter 5 as a star of the Partition-related rehabilitation effort.

62. Ibid., p. 98.
63. Claire Alexander, Joya Chatterji and Annu Jalais, *The Bengal Diaspora: Rethinking Muslim Migration* (Routledge, 2015)
64. Devesh Kapur, *Diaspora, Development and Democracy* (Oxford University Press, 2010), p. 124.
65. Table 1 from Tumbe, 'Transnational Indian Business in the Twentieth Century', p. 653.

Chapter 5: Partitions and Displacements

1. Prashant Bharadwaj and Kevin Quirolo, 'The Partition and its Aftermath: Empirical Investigations', *A New Economic History of Colonial India*, ed. Latika Chaudhary, Bishnupriya Gupta, Tirthankar Roy and Anand Swamy (2016, Routledge), p. 233, 240.
2. Navine Murshid, *The Politics of Refugees in South Asia: Identity, Resistance, Manipulation* (Routledge, 2014), p. 11.
3. This is a conservative estimate based on various sources. The upper estimate of sixty million is given by Hari Mohan Mathur, *Displacement and Resettlement in India: The Human Cost of Development* (Routledge, 2013), p. 1.
4. Nalini Ranjan Chakravarti, *The Indian Minority in Burma: The Rise and Decline of an Immigrant Community* (Oxford University Press, 1971).
5. Michael Leigh, *The Evacuation of Civilians from Burma* (Bloomsbury, 2014), pp. 1–10.
6. Hugh Tinker, 'A Forgotten Long March: The Indian Exodus from Burma, 1942', *Journal of Southeast Asian Studies,* 6 (1) (1975): 1–15.
7. 'Refugees from Burma', *Times of India*, 29 April 1942.
8. Leigh, *The Evacuation of Civilians from Burma*, p. 12.
9. Ibid., p. 12.

10. Subir Bhaumik, 'The Returnees and the Refugees: Migration from Burma', in Samaddar (2003), p. 189.

11. Ibid., p. 192.

12. Renaud Egreteau, 'India's Vanishing "Burma Colonies": Repatriation, Urban Citizenship, and (De) Mobilization of Indian Returnees from Burma (Myanmar) since the 1960s', *Moussons* (22) (2013), 11–34.

13. Kavitha Rao, 'Don't Prepone It: Do the Needful. 10 Indianisms We Should All be Using', *Guardian*, 4 January 2016. The word first appears in the *Times of India*'s historical database in 1983.

14. 'Britain Means to Quit, Declares Lord Mountbatten', *Times of India*, 5 June 1947.

15. 'Border Award Condemned', *Times of India*, 18 August 1947.

16. Prashant Bharadwaj and Kevin Quirolo, 'The Partition and its Aftermath', pp. 236–41.

17. Saumitra Jha and Steven Wilkinson, 'Does Combat Experience Foster Organizational Skill? Evidence from Ethnic Cleansing during the Partition of South Asia', *American Political Science Review*, 106 (4) (2012): 883–907.

18. Amitav Ghosh, *The Shadow Lines* (Ravi Dayal and Permanent Black, 1998), p. 204. The book itself revolves around violence on India's eastern front.

19. Ravinder Kaur, 'The Last Journey: Exploring Social Class in the 1947 Partition Migration', *Economic & Political Weekly* 41 (22) (2006), 2221–28. The words 'refugee camp' are used commonly in the Partition literature even though arguably it reflected a camp for the displaced.

20. Ibid., p. 2223. See also, Chinmay Tumbe, '"Happy Birthday Even If Nobody Cares": Partition Fables,' forthcoming.

21. Murshid, *The Politics of Refugees in South Asia,* p. 26.

22. Ritu Menon, 'Birth of Social Security Commitments: What Happened in the West', in Samaddar (2003), p. 176.

23. Ibid., pp. 161–64; Tarlok Singh, *Towards an Integrated Society: Reflections on Planning, Social Policy, and Rural Institutions*, (Orient Longmans, 1969).

24. A.P. Jain, 'History's Biggest Refugee Crisis', *Indian Journal of Social Work* 13 (1) (1952), 49–52.

25. Ibid, p. 51.

26. Ravinder Kaur, 'Narrative Absence: An "Untouchable" Account of Partition Migration', *Contributions to Indian Sociology* 42 (2) (2008), 281–306.

27. Ibid, pp. 281–82.

28. Urvashi Butalia, *The Other Side of Silence: Voices from the Partition of India* (Duke University Press, 2000), p. 139.

29. On Rajasthan: Ian Copland, 'The Further Shores of Partition: Ethnic Cleansing in Rajasthan 1947', *Past and Present* 160 (August) (1998), pp. 203–39; Zafar Choudhary, *Kashmir Conflict and Muslims of Jammu* (Gulshan Books, 2015).

30. C.N. Vakil, *The Economic Consequences of Divided India* (Vora & Co., 1950), p. 80.

31. Jain, 'History's Biggest Refugee Crisis', p. 49; Bharadwaj and Quirolo, 'The Partition and its Aftermath', p. 238.

32. Abhijit Dasgupta, *Displacement and Exile: The State–Refugee Relations in India* (Oxford University Press, 2016), p. 208.

33. Bharadwaj and Quirolo, 'The Partition and its Aftermath', p. 241.

34. Samir Kumar Das, 'State Response to the Refugee Crisis: Relief and Rehabilitation in the East', in Samaddar (2003), pp. 108–120.

35. Jain, 'History's Biggest Refugee Crisis', p. 51.

36. Ghosh, *The Shadow Lines,* p. 215.

37. Jain, 'History's Biggest Refugee Crisis,' p. 51.

38. Ibid., p. 52.

39. As cited in Das, 'State Response to the Refugee Crisis', p. 119.

40. Ibid., p.137.

41. Murshid, *The Politics of Refugees in South Asia*, p. 32.

42. Jain, 'History's Biggest Refugee Crisis', p. 49.

43. Ibid. and Bharadwaj and Quirolo, 'The Partition and its Aftermath', p. 238.

44. Ibid., p. 52.

45. Bharadwaj and Quirolo, 'The Partition and its Aftermath', pp. 236–41.

46. Rita Kothari, *The Burden of Refuge: The Sindhi Hindus of Gujarat* (Orient Longman, 2007).

47. World Bank World Development Indicators 2017: Average Annual GDP Growth Rates for the Period 1961–70 for Pakistan and India were 7 per cent and 4 per cent respectively.

48. K.C. Saha, 'The Genocide of 1971 and the Refugee Influx in the East', in Samaddar (2003), pp. 211–48.

49. Salil Tripathi, *The Colonel Who Would Not Repent: The Bangladeshi War and its Unquiet Legacy* (Aleph Books, 2014), p. 83, pp. 107–08.

50. Saha, 'The Genocide of 1971 and the Refugee Influx in the East', pp. 242–43.

51. Ibid., pp. 214–41, for the rest of this section.

52. I.G. Patel, *Glimpses of Indian Economic Policy: An Insider's View*, p. 146.

53. 'Refugees from Tibet', *Times of India*, 12 April 1961.

54. Rajesh Kharat, 'Gainers of a Stalemate: The Tibetans in India', in Samaddar (2003), p. 287.

55. Website of the Central Tibetan Administration; UNHCR, *The State of the World's Refugees 2000: Fifty Years of Humanitarian Action*, Geneva (2000), p. 63.

56. Bibhu Prasad Routray, 'Tibetan Refugees in India: Religious Identity and the Forces of Modernity', *Refugee Survey Quarterly* 26 (2) (2007), p. 80; Anne-Sophie Bentz, 'Being a Tibetan Refugee in India', *Refugee Survey Quarterly*, 31 (1) (2012), 82–87.

57. Timm Lau, 'The Hindi Film's Romance and Tibetan Notions of Harmony', *Journal of Ethnic and Migration Studies* 36 (6) (2010), 967–87.

58. Ibid., p. 969.

59. Census of Sri Lanka, *The Population of Sri Lanka*, CICRED Series (1974), pp. 45–46.

60. Urmila Phadnis, 'The Indo-Ceylon Pact and the "Stateless" Indians in Ceylon', *Asian Survey* 7 (4) (1967), 226–36.

61. C. Valatheeswaran and S. Irudaya Rajan, 'Sri Lankan Tamil Refugees in India: Rehabilitation Mechanisms, Livelihood Strategies, and Lasting Solutions', *Refugee Survey Quarterly* 30 (2) (2011), 24–44.

62. Mohammad Ishaq Khan, 'The Impact of Islam on Kashmir in the Sultanate Period (1320–1586), *IESHR* 23 (2) (1986), 187.

63. Jagmohan, the Governor of Jammu and Kashmir at the time of the exodus, placed the estimate at 2,00,000–3,00,000 in 1997 ('Migration of Kashmiri Pandits: Ignoring the Realities', *Times of India*, 23 April 1997). Rahul Pandita places the number at 3,50,000 Kashmiri Pandits (Rahul Pandita, *Our Moon has Blood Clots: The Exodus of the Kashmiri Pandits*, Random House, 2013).

64. Jagmohan, 'Migration of Kashmiri Pandits', *Times of India*, 23 April 1997.

65. Vendanan Mandlekar, 'Kashmiri Muslims on the Run Too', *Sunday Times of India*, 10 March 1991.

66. Pandita, *Our Moon has Blood Clots*, p. 82.

67. Census of India: 1981 and 2001, for the districts in Kashmir and 1961 and 2001 for overall Jammu & Kashmir. The Census of 1991 was not conducted in J&K due to disturbed conditions.

68. The Hindu population in Kashmir in 2001 was around 1,00,000 and predicted to be 2,17,000 if the share was 4 per cent as in 1981.

69. Pandita, *Our Moon has Blood Clots*, p. 95.

70. Mallika Kaur Sarkaria, 'Powerful Pawns of the Kashmir Conflict: Kashmiri Pandit Migrants', *Asian and Pacific Migration Journal* 18 (2) (2009), 207.

71. Ibid., p. 211.

72. Charu Malhotra, 'Internally Displaced People from Kashmir: Some Observations', *Indian Anthropologist* 37 (2) (2007), p. 75.

73. Sombala Ningthoujam, Anupama Raina and U. A. Mir, 'Meaning of Quality of Life Satisfaction: Perceptions of Kashmiri Pandits and Buddhist Tibetan Refugees', *Abhigyan* 27 (3) (2009), 47–59.

74. Sanjib Baruah, 'Citizens and Denizens: Ethnicity, Homelands, and the Crisis of Displacement in Northeast India', *Journal of Refugee Studies* 16 (1) (2003), 44–66.

75. Estimate of the Internal Displacement Monitoring Centre for April 2015, http://www.internal-displacement.org/south-and-south-east-asia/india/figures-analysis.

76. Smritikumar Sarkar, 'Land Acquisition for the Railways in Bengal, 1850-62: Probing a Contemporary Problem', *Studies in History* 26 (2) (2010), 103–42.

77. Ibid., p. 113.

78. Prasad, *Tracks of Change,* pp. 103–04.

79. Mathur, *Displacement and Resettlement in India*, p. 100.

80. Michael Cernea, 'Introduction', in S. Parasuraman, *The Development Dilemma: Displacement in India* (Macmillan Press, 1999), p. 18.

81. Mathur, *Displacement and Resettlement in India*, p. 98, cites an official report in the 1980s.

82. S. Dutta, 'Chakma-Hajong Refugee Problem in Arunachal Pradesh: Historical Background', *IASSI Quarterly* 15 (1) (1996), 111–16.

83. Ashish Bose, 'Afghan Refugees in India', *Economic & Political Weekly* 39 (43) (2004), 4698–701.

84. C. Valatheeswaran and S. Irudaya Rajan, 'Sri Lankan Tamil Refugees in India', p. 25, cite a figure over 4,00,000 in 2008.

Chapter 6: Migration and Development

1. Bhimrao Ramji Ambedkar, *Annihilation of Caste* (Government Central Press of Bombay [1979], 1936), Section 14.

2. Ambedkar's speech in the Constituent Assembly Debates, 4 November 1948, Vol. 7, http://parliamentofindia.nic.in/ls/debates/vol7p1b.htm.

3. M.K. Gandhi, *The Collected Works of Mahatma Gandhi*, vol. 91 (Delhi, 1999), p.56.

4. Wilbur Zelinsky, 'The Hypothesis of the Mobility Transition', *Geographical Review* 61 (2) (1971), 219–49.

5. Jan Lucassen and Leo Lucassen, 'Measuring and Quantifying Cross-Cultural Migrations: An Introduction', in Lucassen and Lucassen (2014), pp. 3–54.

6. *Economic Survey of India 2016–17*, Government of India, p. 269, describes this relationship for the current era.

7. Chinmay Tumbe, 'Urbanization, Demographic Transition and the Growth of Cities in India, 1870-2010', International Growth Centre Working Paper C-35205-INC-1 (2016).

8. Based on Census and Sample Registration System (SRS) data. Between 2001 and 2011 actual annual population growth rate was 1.64 per cent and annual natural growth rate was 1.61 per cent.

9. *Economic Survey of India 2016–17*, p. 277, and RBI data on international remittances for 2017.

10. Tumbe, 'Remittances in India: Facts and Issues', p. 479.

11. Sagarika Dey, 'Impact of Remittances on Poverty at Origin', *Migration and Development* 4 (2) (2015), 185–99.

12. Amitabh Kundu and Niranjan Sarangi, 'Migration, Employment Status and Poverty', *Economic & Political Weekly* 42 (4) (2007), 299.

13. David Atkin, 'The Caloric Costs of Culture: Evidence from Indian Migrants', *American Economic Review* 106 (4) (2016), 1144–81.

14. Divya Ravindranath, 'Maternal Health and Child Malnutrition among Households Engaged in Construction Work', doctoral dissertation, Washington University in St. Louis, 2018.

15. Jan Breman, *Footloose Labour: Working in India's Informal Economy* (Cambridge University Press, 1996); P. Sainath, 'Global recession penetrates rural Orissa as migrant workers go home', *The Hindu,* 9 July 2009.

16. Author's analysis of data in the National Family Health Survey-3, 2005–06.

17. *Circular Migration and Multilocational Livelihood Strategies in Rural India*, ed. Priya Deshingkar and John Farrington (Oxford University Press, 2009).

18. Tumbe, 'Remittances in India: Facts and Issues', p. 492.
19. Vegard Iversen, Kunal Sen, Arjan Verschoor and Amaresh Dubey, 'Job Recruitment Networks and Migration to Cities in India', *Journal of Development Studies* 45 (4) (2009), 522–43; Biswajit Banerjee, *Rural to Urban Migration and the Urban Labour Market: A Case Study of Delhi* (Himalaya Publishing, 1986).
20. Dharma Kumar, *Land and Caste in South India,* p. 142.
21. Census of India 1931, Vol. 14, Part I, pp. 93–4.
22. Narendra Jadhav, *Untouchables: My Family's Triumphant Journey out of the Caste System in Modern India* (Simon and Schuster, 2005); Daya Pawar, *Baluta* trans. Jerry Pinto (Speaking Tiger, 2015); Sujatha Gidla, *Ants among Elephants: An Untouchable Family and the Making of Modern India* (Farrar, Straus and Giroux, 2017).
23. Devesh Kapur, D. Shyam Babu and Chandra Bhan Prasad, *Defying the Odds: The Rise of Dalit Entrepreneurs,* (Random House India, 2014), p. xii.
24. Kaivan Munshi and Mark Rosenzweig, 'Networks and Misallocation: Insurance, Migration and the Rural–Urban Wage Gap',' *American Economic Review* 106 (1) (2016), 46–98.
25. Isabel Wilkerson, *The Warmth of Other Suns: The Epic Story of America's Great Migration* (Vintage Books, 2010).
26. Pronab Sen, 'Puzzle of Indian Urbanisation,' *Economic and Political Weekly,* 53 (19) (2018): 37.
27. Gandhi, *The Collected Works,* vol. 68 (Delhi, 1999), pp.108–09.
28. Gandhi, *The Collected Works,* vol. 1 (Delhi, 1999), p.1.
29. Gandhi, *The Collected Works,* vol. 91 (Delhi, 1999), p. 58.
30. Binod Khadria, *The Migration of Knowledge Workers* (Sage, 1999).
31. Jagdish Bhagwati, 'Taxing the Brain Drain', *Challenge* 19 (3) (1976), 34–8.
32. Chinmay Tumbe, 'EU–India Bilateral Remittances', IIMB working paper no. 360 (2012), documents that nearly half of all international remittances are sourced from North America and Europe.
33. Devesh Kapur, *Diaspora, Development and Democracy* (Oxford University Press, 2010), p. 121. Figures normalized by population.
34. Credited to Abid Hussain in an article by S. Murlidharan, *The Hindu BusinessLine,* 23 October 2012.

35. Divya Ravindranath, 'Visa Regulations and Labour Market Restrictions: Implications for Indian Immigrant Women in the United States', *Indian Journal of Labour Economics* 60 (2) (2017), 217–32.

36. Indrani Mazumdar, N. Neetha and Indu Agnihotri, 'Migration and Gender in India', *Economic and Political Weekly,* 48 (10) (2013), 54–64; *Economic Survey of India 2016–17,* Government of India, p. 266.

37. On sex trafficking in colonial India: Nilanjana Ray, 'Speaking of the Unspeakable: The Debate on Sex Trafficking in Colonial India', Conference Paper, Berkshire Conference on the Histories of Women, Genders and Sexualities, Hofstra University, Hempstead, New York (2017).

38. Brij V. Lal, 'Fiji', in Lal (2006), p. 374.

39. Nita Bhalla, 'Almost 20,000 Women and Children Trafficked in India in 2016', Reuters, 9 March 2017.

40. U. Vindhya and V. Swathi Dev, 'Survivors of Sex Trafficking in Andhra Pradesh: Evidence and Testimony', *Indian Journal of Gender Studies* 18 (2) (2011), 129–65.

41. *Glasgow Herald*, 6 July 1954, as cited by Suparna Gooptu, *Cornelia Sorabji: India's Pioneer Woman Lawyer: A Biography* (Oxford University Press, 2011), p. 1.

42. N. Neetha, 'Making of Female Breadwinners: Migration and Social Networking of Women Domestics in Delhi', *Economic and Political Weekly* 39 (17) (2004), 1681–88.

43. Ellen Barry, 'Young Rural Women in India Chase Big-City Dreams', *New York Times*, 24 September 2016.

44. Meenakshi Thapan, Anshu Singh and Nidhitha Sreekumar, 'Women's Mobility and Migration: Muslim Women Migrants in Jamia Nagar, Delhi', *Economic and Political Weekly* 49 (23) (2014), 96–104.

45. Ravinder Kaur, 'Migrating for Work: Rewriting Gender Relations', *Poverty, Gender and Migration*, ed. Sadhna Arya and Anupama Roy (Sage, 2006), p. 195.

46. On nurse migration, Marie Percot and Sreelekha Nair, 'Transcending Boundaries: Indian Nurses in Internal and

International Migration,' *Dynamics of Indian Migration: Historical and Contemporary Perspectives*, ed. S. Irudaya Rajan and Marie Percot (Routledge, 2011).

47. On Mulkis: K.V. Narayana Rao, *Internal Migration Policies in an Indian State: A Case Study of the Mulki Rules in Hyderabad and Andhra* (MIT Cambridge, 1977).

48. Letter to the Editor, *Times of India*, 6 October 1967.

49. Myron Weiner, *Sons of the Soil: Migration and Ethnic Conflict in India* (Oxford University Press, 1978).

50. Weiner, 'The Political Demography of Assam's Anti-Immigrant Movement', *Population and Development Review* 9 (2) (1983), 279–92.

51. Walter Fernandes, 'IMDT Act and Immigration in North-Eastern India', *Economic and Political Weekly* 40 (30) (2005), 3237–40.

52. Sanjukta Das Gupta, *Adivasis and the Raj: Socio-Economic Transition of the Hos, 1820-1932* (Orient BlackSwan, 2011) p. 263.

53. Weiner, *Sons of the Soil*, p. 273.

54. From S. Pushparaman, Tiruchirapalli, Letter to *Times of India*, 28 January 1973, as cited in Weiner, *Sons of the Soil*, p. vii.

55. Duncan McDuie-Ra, *Northeast Migrants in Delhi: Race, Refuge and Retail* (Amsterdam University Press, 2012).

56. Anupama Roy, 'Between Encompassment and Closure: The "Migrant" and the "Citizen" in India', *Contributions to Indian Sociology* 42 (2) (2008), 219–48.

57. Based on an analysis of fifty personalities in Indian history described by Sunil Khilnani, *Incarnations: India in Fifty Lives* (Allen Lane, 2016).

Index